KT-872-622

John Naisbitt
Patricia Aburdene

MEGATRENDS 2000

The next ten years . . .
major changes in your life and world

PAN BOOKS
in association with Sidgwick & Jackson

First published in Great Britain 1990 by
Sidgwick & Jackson Ltd
in an edition adapted for the British market
This edition published 1991 by Pan Books Ltd,
Cavaye Place, London SW10 9PG
in association with Sidgwick & Jackson
9 8 7 6 5 4 3 2 1
© John Naisbitt and Patricia Aburdene 1990
ISBN 0 330 32139 0

Printed in England by Clays Ltd, St Ives plc

For Rory, Lily and Abraham

Contents

Acknowledgements

Thanks must begin with the person owed the greatest debt—our researcher, Joy Van Elderen. She summarized awesome amounts of data, tracked down the critical example in print or by phone and verified and reverified thousands of pieces of data. Through it all Joy remained scrupulously organized, ever graceful and always eager for the next assignment.

Adrian Zackheim at William Morrow could not have done a finer job as our editor. He clarified and polished our ideas and enthusiastically represented our project to his colleagues. We are fortunate to have worked with Larry Hughes and to have been privy to his insights and suggestions.

Thanks go to the Megatrends inner circle: our assistant Linda McLean Harned and our agents Rafe Sagalyn and Bill Leigh. All three devoted themselves to this book from start to finish.

Jerry Kline helped us sort through a wealth of information about biotechnology. We also want to thank The Naisbitt Group for its co-operation.

The most fun we had 'writing' this book was not spent in front of the computer. It was the week in February 1989 when we assembled a group of friends at our home in Telluride, Colorado. From Brazil came Oscar and Leiko Motomuro. From Sweden came Eva and Gustaf Delin, Eva and Lennart Boksjo, Sven and Solveig Atterhed, Klas Mellander and Margareta Barchen. The American contingent were Claire Ryle Garrison and Jim Garrison, Kathy and Steve Rhinesmith and Linda McLean Harned. Steve and Jim also read and annotated the manuscript. Each morning we, the authors, presented two chapters and we all discussed the ideas. In the afternoons our guests hit the ski slopes while we collapsed in exhaustion, heads spinning from trying to absorb all their wonderful insights.

We had the benefit of a gifted set of additional readers: historian David MacMichael, direct mail whiz and politico Tom Mathews, and Norman Macrae, long-time deputy editor of the *Economist*, now retired.

Final thanks go to all the friends and loved ones on whose support and love we depend and to whose warm and lively companionship we happily return now that *Megatrends 2000* is complete.

Introduction

We stand at the dawn of a new era.

Before us is the most important decade in the history of civilization, a period of stunning technological innovation, unprecedented economic opportunity, surprising political reform, and great cultural rebirth. It will be a decade like none that has come before because it will culminate in the millennium, the year 2000.

For centuries that monumental, symbolic date has stood for the future and what we shall make of it. In a few short years that future will be here.

Already we have fallen under its dominion. The year 2000 is operating like a powerful magnet on humanity, reaching down into the 1990s and intensifying the decade. It is amplifying emotions, accelerating change, heightening awareness, and compelling us to re-examine ourselves, our values, and our institutions.

The purpose of this book is to identify and describe the most important trends of the 1990s. Conceived under the influence of the next millennium, these new megatrends are the gateways to the 21st century.

UNCOVERING THE MEGATRENDS FOR A NEW MILLENNIUM

Megatrends do not come and go readily. These large social, economic, political, and technological changes are slow to form, and once in place they influence us for some time—between seven and ten years, or longer. They have the scope and feel of a decade's worth of change.

In 1982, in the book *Megatrends*, we described the trends that were shaping the 1980s. They were the shifts from:

1. Industrial Society → to Information Society
2. Forced Technology → to High Tech/High Touch
3. National Economy → to World Economy
4. Short Term → to Long Term
5. Centralization → to Decentralization
6. Institutional Help → to Self-Help
7. Representative Democracy → to Participatory Democracy
8. Hierarchies → to Networking
9. North → to South
10. Either/Or → to Multiple Option

These shifts continue pretty much on schedule. But they are now only part of the picture as we enter the 1990s and a new set of forces come into play.

The practice of dividing the world up into a list of megatrends might at first seem a little too arbitrary. Its purpose, however, is not to render life simplistic or superficial, but to establish a categorical foundation on which a greater depth of knowledge can be built.

'We are drowning in information and starved for knowledge', we wrote in *Megatrends*. In fewer than ten years, the growth of information has only quickened. This book presents ten new structural megatrends against which to relate the accelerating information of the 1990s.

The millennium trends of the nineties will influence the important elements of your life—your career and job decisions, your travel, business, and investment choices, your place of residence, and your children's education. Americans have long been able to form such choices across a continent. After 1992, West Europeans will be able to do so too, and opportunities for people who live in the Pacific Rim will be even more remarkable. To make the most of this extraordinary decade, you must be aware of the changes that surround you.

And indeed, there have never been more media—new television networks and channels, video and film, record numbers of new magazines, newsletters, journals, and newspapers—dedicated to delivering you the changing news of the day. But what is the news really telling you? How much information are you absorbing?

Without a structure, a frame of reference, the vast amount of data that comes your way each day will probably whizz right by you.

Events do not happen in a vacuum, but in a social, political, cultural, and economic context. This book describes for you that context. You need not agree with or accept every element of this world view. But do use this structure as a context within which to measure the news of the day, opposing viewpoints, and new information. The important thing is to craft your own world view, your own personal set of megatrends to guide your work, ideals, relationships, and contributions to society.

THE MILLENNIAL MEGATRENDS: GATEWAYS TO THE 21st CENTURY

As we enter this new decade, our candidates for the most important, the overarching trends influencing our lives are:

1. The Booming Global Economy of the 1990s
2. A Renaissance in the Arts
3. The Emergence of Free-Market Socialism
4. Global Lifestyles and Cultural Nationalism
5. The Privatization of the Welfare State
6. The Rise of the Pacific Rim
7. The Decade of Women in Leadership
8. The Age of Biology
9. The Religious Revival of the New Millennium
10. The Triumph of the Individual

TOWARDS THE MILLENNIUM

We cannot understand the megatrends of the 1990s without acknowledging the metaphorical and spiritual significance of the millennium. We must recognize its power to evoke our most positive, powerful visions alongside our most terrifying nightmares. In the 1990s apocalyptic themes will emerge and re-emerge with stunning regularity. Disaster, it seems, will always be just around the corner; the superpowers having just signed a nuclear arms agreement, we come face-to-face with the 'greenhouse effect'.

The word 'millennium' is abridged from the Latin for '1000 years'. In 1987 the Soviet Union celebrated the millennium of the introduction of Christianity into Russia in AD 987. The biblical millennium refers to the 1000-year period after Christ's Second Coming and, after an apocalyptic battle when the kingdom of God is established on earth. On a secular level the millennium has come to mean a golden age in human history, a time to close the door on the past and embark upon a new era.

As we move toward this extraordinary date, the mythology of the millennium, consciously or not, is reengaging us. Some Christian fundamentalists have warned their flocks to prepare for the literal Second Coming of Christ. On the opposite end of the religious spectrum, a wide assortment of metaphysical and occult groups, today's populist religions, are predicting the earth will undergo some sort of cataclysmic shift around the year 2000. Headlines about global warming and holes in the ozone layer convince many that the time is at hand.

There is more than one way to interpret the millennium. As the date draws nearer, we shall encounter many. The year 2000 is not just a new century but a religious experience related to the religious-revival megatrend.

A NEW WORLD VIEW

The 1990s present a new world view. The cold war ended in the last years of the 1980s. The postwar period of nationalism and ideological cold war is over, and a new era of globalization has begun.

The arts are flourishing worldwide. There is an international call to environmentalism. Communist countries experiment with democracy and market mechanisms. Among nations, the desire for economic cooperation is stronger than the urge for military adventure with its huge human and financial costs.

West Europe will be seeking to establish a 'single economy', just as the idea that any region can have a single economy disappears. Asia has rewritten the rule book on economic development, many of its inhabitants having achieved the standard of living of Europeans. There will be a strong movement toward increasing free trade. Even in the poorest nations of Africa, privatization and models of self-reliance are on the ascendancy. There is a new respect for the human spirit.

This is an increasingly interconnected world. The authors of this book are Americans, and we will cite most of our examples from our own country which we know best. But more than in *Megatrends*, we will be describing trends also influencing all of Europe and all of the Pacific Rim. It is easier to do so today because the common technologies of information, service, and electronics unify these regions. A society's occupations, what its members do for a living, colour every aspect of its cultural and political institutions. So, in a global economy, the people of the developed world grow similar to their neighbours and we will reach for examples from around the world to illustrate the megatrends.

We are often asked why our books seem so positive and why we do not describe more of the problems facing humankind.

Headlines about crime, drugs, the Brazilian rain forest, AIDS, chemical warfare, corruption, and double-digit deficits assault us daily, causing us to wonder whether any good can exist side by side with so much of the bad? If the evil, ignorance, and negativity we all read about are true, how can any positive trends be valid?

The people reporting the bad news are doing their job. We respect them for it. And we admire the activists whose life's work is to right the world's wrongs. Our mission is a different one. Because the problems of the world get so much attention, we, for the most part, point out information and circumstances that describe the world trends leading to opportunities.

On a practical level, one has to be a diehard generalist (and perhaps a bit mad) to attempt to describe the trends of an entire decade. It requires sifting through a staggering amount of information, a task made a little easier with a point of view. Our perspective, our market niche in the vast world of information, is to highlight some of the positive, without ignoring the barriers to achieving positive results.

MILLENNIUM AS METAPHOR FOR THE FUTURE

As we approach the year 2000, the millennium is re-emerging as a metaphor for the future. In the biblical millennium the establishment of a heavenly kingdom on earth could occur only after the final battle between Christ and the Antichrist—the clash of complete opposites. Like the ancient drama, the modern millennium ignites our vision for a better world—alongside our nightmares of the world's end.

The dichotomy is ever-present. Perhaps that is why arms control cannot eliminate our fear of nuclear weapons, why declining unemployment figures, record-breaking new business starts, and new job creation fail to calm fears of a depression in the 1990s.

Beneath the spectre of nuclear weapons is a growing sense of hope that, if we can just 'make it to the year 2000', we will have proved ourselves capable of solving our problems and living harmoniously on this fragile planet.

THE MILLENNIAL FUTURE

When we think of the 21st century, we think technology: space travel, biotechnology, robots. But the face of the future is more complex than the technology we use to envision it.

The most exciting breakthroughs of the 21st century will occur not because of technology but because of an expanding concept of what it means to be human.

Today we are emerging from a 20th-century version of Dark Ages—the combined impact of industrialization, totalitarianism, and intrusion of technology into our lives. With most of the century behind us and the millennium ahead, we are entering a renaissance in the arts and spirituality. The magnet year 2000 is pulling forth bold experiments in market socialism, a spiritual revival, and a burst of economic growth around the Pacific Rim.

The wider our horizons and the more powerful our technology, the greater we have come to value the individual. Because of George Orwell's book, *1984*, that year has for decades symbolized the supposed coming dehumanization of modern society. Now the year 1984 has come and gone—and the importance of the individual has massively increased, even in Communist bloc countries.

Notice how many groups set their goals with reference to the year 2000, goals for ending hunger, a drug-free society, a cure for cancer. The milestone of the millennium acts like a deadline, encouraging us to confront and resolve our problems so we can meet it with a clean slate. Those problems we do not willingly confront, it seems, are being thrust upon us. The 1990s will force us to make choices about planetary concerns from nuclear accidents to chemical and environmental pollution.

Humanity will probably not be rescued *deux ex machina* either in the form of a literal Second Coming (the fundamentalist expectation) or by friendly spaceships (the New Age version). Though we will be guided by a revived spirituality, the answers will have to come from us.

Apocalypse or Golden Age? The choice is ours. As we approach the beginning of the 3rd millennium, the way we address that question will define what it means to be human.

1

The Global Economic Boom of the 1990s

In the decade of the 1990s the world is entering a period of economic prosperity.

There is no single factor behind the economic boom, but instead an extraordinary confluence of factors. We are in an unprecedented period of accelerated change, perhaps the most breathtaking of which is the swiftness of our rush to all the world becoming a single economy. Already it may be said that there is no such thing as a US economy, so enmeshed is it in all the other economies of the world. There won't be any such thing as a European economy or Japanese economy or Soviet bloc economy or Third World economy either.

Each year US companies create and sell over $80 billion in goods and services in Japan. Is that part of the US economy or the Japanese economy? Are Korean stocks and shares purchased in London by an Australian part of the Korean, British, or Australian economy? To which economy belong the Swiss components put into Nissans made in Britain for sale in the Austrian Alps, but with a view to the establishment of a Japanese joint venture in Czechoslovakia or possibly the Andes or China later? Of course, they all are part of one economy, the new global economy, and that economy is on a booming course as it races towards the year 2000.

It is as if America's fifty states were economically self-sufficient with little trade among them and then were suddenly integrated into a single economy. Imagine the economic explosion.

This is going to happen everywhere, not just in post-1992 Europe. The economic forces of the world are surging across national borders, resulting in more democracy, more freedom, more trade, more opportunity, and greater prosperity.

This chapter is in three sections. The first section deals with the forces behind the creation of the coming worldwide economic boom. The second section ('High-Wage Economy') is about the affluent character of an information economy, using the United States as the prototype. The last section ('1992') is about the historic coming together of the twelve countries of the European Community and the implications for the rest of the world.

THE GLOBAL BOOM

The Doomsayers

The doomsayers in our midst hate to hear that economic good times are just around the corner, so sure are they that the world is going to hell in a handbasket. Starting with the Club of Rome's *The Limits to Growth* (1972), doomsday books have become a growth industry. Forecasters of world famine surface every couple of years or so to warn of the end of the world, apparently unembarrassed as farmers build mountains of unsaleable food up to the sky. President Jimmy Carter's 'Report on the Year 2000' was proved wrong before the ink was dry. An energy crisis was seen around every corner. During seven years of uninterrupted economic growth in the United States, there were predictions of certain recession or depression every other month. Many economists have foreseen impending global economic collapse for a decade.

Their dismal record notwithstanding, the doomsayers still get a lot of help from the media. Bad news or the prediction of bad news is news. Good news is more often ignored. Professor Ted Smith of Virginia Commonwealth University conducted a study for the Media Institute in Washington, DC, called 'The Vanishing Economy: Television Coverage of Economic Affairs 1982–1987'. He examined how the three national television networks in the United States treated America's unprecedented years of economic expansion beginning at the end of 1982. He reviewed the tapes and transcripts from the three nightly news shows on ABC, NBC, and CBS.

He found that 'as the economy progressively improved the amount of economic coverage on network television news progressively declined' and turned 'progressively more negative in tone'. For every year he studied, 'the number of negative economic stories exceeded the number of positive stories by a ration of 4.9 to 1 or more. As the performance of the economy improved . . . the ratio of negative to positive stories increased steadily from 4.9 to 1 in 1982–1984 to 7.0 to 1 in 1986–87'.

Mrs Thatcher complains that the 'moaning minnies' of British television and British academic economists have consistently misreported her years in office. As all the statistics showed the prosperity of the British people to be growing better and better, the BBC and other 'chattering classes' managed to give the impression that the plight of the British people was growing worse and worse. When the TV channels and the dons were told that the figures did not support this impression, they said that any economic advances achieved under Mrs Thatcher had been at the expense of bitterly alienating the working class, compared with the 'one-nation' Conservatism of Harold Macmillan's day.

The voting figures show the reverse. In Macmillan's 1959 the Conservatives won a parliamentary majority of almost exactly 100, and so they did in Thatcher's 1987. Between Macmillan's 1959 and Thatcher's 1987 there was a net swing among the British manual working class of 10.5 per cent away from Labour to Margaret Thatcher, while the net two-party swing among non-manual workers was 4.75 per cent away from Margaret Thatcher to Labour. This was mainly because in the middle classes more Tories than Labour swung to the middle-of-the-road Alliance. Most of these people said Mrs Thatcher was becoming hated by working classes, precisely while the working classes were voting they liked her better. 'Quite simply,' reports Essex University's Professor Ivor Crewe when reporting statistically on Mrs Thatcher's years, 'the Conservative advance over both the long and the short term has been wholly within the working class.'

There will be some bad news in the decade ahead. It will be amplified by the media; it will be fanned by the doomsayers; it will be misinterpreted by many of the best educated. The booming 1990s will continue along their prosperous path.

Economic Considerations More Important Than Political

The new global economy cannot be understood if it is thought to be merely more and more trade among 160 countries; it must be viewed as the world moving from trade among countries to a single economy. One economy. One marketplace.

This is the next natural level in the economic history of civilization. In the beginning we had economically self-sufficient villages. The self-sufficient city-states that followed traded very little. For hundreds of years we then had a collection of individual nation-states, largely economically self-sufficient. *Within* the nation-states the economic tasks over the years were divided up. Now we are well into the process of re-sorting economic tasks *among* nations and moving toward the economic interdependence that implies.

In the global economy, economic considerations almost always transcend political considerations.

Over the centuries heads of state were all-important because the relationships among states were primarily political relationships. With economic relations on the ascent, a country's CEOs (Chief Executive Officers) are now often more important than their political figures. Take Sweden, for example. Who is more important and known, Jan Carlzon, head of SAS, and Pehr Gyllenhammar, head of Volvo, or the top political figures whose names are not even known outside Sweden? Who has the most effect on your lifestyle, on your home, your wardrobe, your enjoyment—the business innovators of Japan, the designers of Italy, the opera singers like Kiri te Kanawa of New Zealand, or whatever obscure politicians happen to be prime ministers of Japan, Italy and New Zealand this week?

In the global economy, presidents, prime ministers, and parliaments are less and less important.

Their main international task is becoming the realignment of political structures to facilitate the globalization of all economies.

Free Trade Among All Nations

For a global economy—one marketplace—to work, we must eventually have *completely free trade* among nations, just as we do within the nation-states themselves. No one knows what the imbalance of trade is between Birmingham and Manchester, between Melbourne and Sydney, between Tokyo and Osaka, between Denver and Dallas; nor will we—in time—between the United States and Japan.

This is already beginning to happen.

- The year 1992 will bring down all trade barriers among the twelve nations of the European Economic Community.

- Australia and New Zealand's free-trade agreement went into effect December 1988.

- Brazil and Argentina are working on a free-trade agreement. This could lead to the beginnings of a South American common market.

- The 1988 accord between the United States and Canada to drop all trade barriers was a giant's step. Similar agreements with Mexico will be worked out in time, making North America a huge free-trade zone.

- Beginning in the Autumn of 1988 there was suddenly a lot of talk about a US-Japan free-trade accord, something unthinkable just a few months earlier.

Some misinterpret these developments as trends toward regional agreements that will close off trade from without. They are, rather, steps toward worldwide free trade.

As we turn to the next century, we will witness the linkup of North America, all Europe, and Japan to form a golden triangle of free trade.

The big, powerful, overarching megatrend is toward worldwide free trade, underneath which we witness the much weaker counter-trends of protectionism. We are moving toward a world where trade among countries will be as free as trade and traffic between California and Colorado, between England and Scotland, between Queensland and New South Wales.

Telecommunications and Economics

The movement to global free trade is being driven by an alliance between telecommunications and economics that permits you to deal with a business associate in a Tokyo office from a mountain perch in Colorado as if you were across a table—sharing conversation and documents. On 14 December 1988, the first fibre-optic telephone cable across the Atlantic went into service. This new cable can carry 40,000 calls simultaneously, tripling the volume of the three existing copper cables plus satellites, which together can carry a total of 20,000 calls.

A fibre-optic cable across the Pacific went into service in late 1989, linking the United States and Japan. North America, Europe, Asia, and Australia are being strung with fibre-optic cable. By 1992 more than 16 million miles of fibre-optic cable will be in place.

The technological leap is extraordinary. A single fibre-optic cable can carry more than 8000 conversations, compared with 48 for a copper wire.

Fibre-optic cable calls are faster and much clearer than copper wire. Not surprisingly, demand is exploding. People in the United States made 4.7 billion minutes of overseas calls in 1987, up from 580 million in 1977, more than an eightfold increase in a decade. A second transatlantic fibre-optic cable that will carry 80,000 simultaneous telephone calls is scheduled to go into service in 1991.

Telecommunications—and computers—will continue to drive change, just as manufacturing did during the industrial period.

We are laying the foundations for an international information highway system. In telecommunications we are moving to a single worldwide information network, just as economically we are becoming one global marketplace. We are moving toward the capability to communicate anything to anyone anywhere, by any form—voice, data, text, or image—at the speed of light.

No Limits to Growth

The global boom of the 1990s will be free of the limits on growth we have known in the past. In fact, there will be virtually no limits to growth. There will be an abundance of natural resources throughout the 1990s, from agricultural products and raw materials to oil. Everything that comes out of the ground will be in oversupply for the balance of this century and probably much longer.

Since the mid-1980s there has been more than enough food to feed the world's population; hunger persists because of political and distribution problems. Population growth has slowed almost everywhere, except Africa, and in many areas has slowed dramatically. Furthermore, we are poised on the edge of another green revolution through biotechnology.

We need fewer raw materials, as we have been moving away from material-intensive products for decades—for example, the widespread substitution of plastics for steel. Miniaturization is another factor lessening demand for materials. In recent years the prices of raw material have been the lowest in recorded history in relation to manufactured goods and services. In general, they will continue to fall.

A prototypical example of the shift away from the material-intensive is fibre-optic cable. Just seventy pounds of fibre-optic cable can transmit as many messages as one ton of copper wire. Equally important, those seventy pounds of fibre-optic cable require less than 5 per cent of the energy needed to produce one ton of copper wire.

In both materials and energy, that is an analogue for the new economy. And before the year 2000 a single optic fibre will be able to transmit 10 million conversations at the same time, compared with 3000 in 1988.

No Energy Crisis

There will be no energy crisis to impede the 1990s global boom. Quite simply, the world is using less energy while producing more. There is almost no chance of another shock like the 1974 OPEC oil crisis. Since then the twenty-four countries of the Organization for Economic Cooperation and Development (OECD), including the United States, Japan, and Western Europe have—through conservation and efficiencies—reduced their energy consumption by 20 per cent, equal to a billion tons of oil a year, the current combined production of the United States and Western Europe.

About a decade ago the history of energy consumption in the

United States reached a turning point. For the first 200 years of its history the United States consumed more energy each year than the year before. But each year since 1979 the United States has used less energy than the year before. That's the new trend. As the post-industrial economy succeeds the industrial one, rich country after rich country will be following it.

In the meantime, the world is producing much more oil. In the decade until 1988 many new areas became significant oil producers: India, Egypt, Brazil, Colombia, Syria, Oman, China, the North Sea, Alaska. In 1989 South Yemen joined the fold. In 1979 proven world oil reserves were 611 billion barrels and doomsayers said they were falling fast. Today they are 887 billion, and growing.

New producers have cut deeply into OPEC's market share and kept oil prices low. From 1979 to 1989 non-OPEC production increased more than 7 million barrels a day (from 22 million to more than 29 million).

During the same period OPEC output fell from 31 million to 17 million barrels a day. The new oil club has dramatically reduced the West's dependency on OPEC.

Although there is strong opposition in some quarters, there is no question that nuclear energy has reduced the West's dependence on oil. More than 35 per cent of the electricity in OECD countries now comes from nuclear plants, the energy equivalent of 6 million barrels of oil a day.

Little noticed has been the progress in photovoltaic energy. During the 1990s the cost of photovoltaic cells, which convert sunlight directly into electricity, will drop to a point where they will be used commercially to generate electricity on a large scale. The average price could go down to US $1.50 per watt by the year 2000. If that happens—and many experts think it will—the total production could increase more than a hundredfold, and world sales would soar to US $7.5 billion a year. Direct solar power could become the world's main energy source in the 21st century.

Producing a lot more energy and using a lot less: the combination of these two global trends will increase the availability of oil and keep the price down. Thus the world's most extensively traded commodity and longtime bogeyman for the doomsayers will accelerate rather than limit the booming global economy of the 1990s.

The Tax Reform Revolution

The growing worldwide thrust to lower taxes, which London's *Financial Times* calls a 'tax reform revolution', will also help expand the global economy of the 1990s.

Driven by the need to be competitive in a global economy, country after country has dramatically reduced taxes on individual incomes. It started with Ronald Reagan's tax reform measures of 1981. At that time the US government could take as much as 75 per cent of a citizen's income. By 1989 the highest tax bracket was down to 28 per cent.

In Mrs Thatcher's Britain reductions in tax rates have been a centrepiece of the nation's economic recovery. The Labour government of the 1970s reached a top tax rate of an astounding 98 per cent on investment income; Mrs Thatcher's top rate is 40 per cent.

In the 1980s, the Labour governments of Australia and New Zealand have cut income taxes more sharply even than Conservative governments elsewhere. Beginning in 1989, Japan's new tax law dropped the highest income tax rates to 50 per cent from 60 per cent. Brazil dropped the top rate from 60 per cent to 25 per cent. Since 1984, 55 countries have dropped their top tax rates.

Even Sweden, notorious for sky-high rates on personal incomes, has discovered tax reform. Prodded by the challenges of 1992 and the effort to become more competitive, Sweden is in the process of reducing the top tax rates from 75 per cent to 60 per cent. It may seem like a modest shift, but for nine out of ten working Swedes with incomes below $26,000 tax rates will fall from as high as 60 per cent to 30 per cent. 'It never would have happened without US tax reform,' says Sven-Olof Lodin, a tax economist with Sweden's Federation of Industry.

In a very competitive world, lower income taxes encourage people to work harder and to be more forthcoming in their income declarations. In the long run they result in more, not less, tax collected by governments. The tax cuts in previously overtaxed Britain have sent it into budget surplus. Taxes in the United States are so low (although the government is taking in 89 per cent more revenue than before reduction) that it has become something of a tax shelter, attracting energetic, entrepreneurial talent from other countries, which in turn helps advance the US economy.

Downsizing

Alan Greenspan, the chairman of the Federal Reserve Board, draws attention to another trend down the road to a global economy. What he calls the 'downsizing of economic output' makes it easier and more efficient to trade.

Fifty years ago, Greenspan notes, radios were quite bulky. Now they fit into a pocket. Most modern products, including building materials, are smaller and lighter, yet more efficient and more effective. We wear fabrics that are warmer yet lighter. Computers are shrinking with the miracle of the chip. In global financial transactions, electronic impulses have replaced paper. Airplanes can carry a lot more people relative to the materials needed to build and fuel them.

Add to this the continuing growth of information as the main economic commodity entering into trade. Instead of selling tractors, selling ideas (most of which are lighter). The smaller the bulk and weight, the easier to move among nations. This should be added to the list of factors rushing us toward a fully realized global economy.

Inflation and Interest

Inflation will be contained because there is now worldwide competition for price and quality, a new phenomenon.

Interest rates will be contained because there is plenty of capital in the world today, and there is worldwide competition in the renting of money. This competition will grow. If a British bank raises your mortgage rates, borrow after 1992 from a German bank.

Asian Consumer Boom

The economies of Asian countries are exploding, creating more competition for Europe and North America but also creating more customers for everybody, one of the major themes of Chapter 6, 'The Rise of the Pacific Rim'.

Japan is moving from an export-driven economy to a consumer-driven economy, a bellwether shift that other Asian countries will follow in the 1990s.

As the Asian economic miracle spreads throughout the Pacific, wage increases everywhere are creating millions of consumers. Pushed by an expanding domestic market, South Korea posted a growth rate above 10 per cent in 1988 for the third straight year. Per capita gross national product (GNP) jumped from $3098 in 1987 to $4040 in 1988. Korean income per head is now above $4000 a year. A 10 per cent growth rate doubles incomes in seven years, quadruples them in fourteen, octuples in twenty-one. Growth will not continue at that rate, but the upvaluation of the currency (the Korean won) will increase purchasing power against the dollar. All the dragons' currencies will upvalue like the yen. Taiwan's per capita GNP already exceeds $6000.

There will be similar gains in Thailand, Malaysia, Indonesia, and Singapore.

Asians will be *the* consumers of the 1990s. During the decade 80 million more will be added to the wealthiest Asian countries (versus about 10 million in Europe). That means great opportunities for North Americans and Europeans, as well as for Asian producers.

The Advancement of Democracy and the Spread of Free Enterprise

The global shift from authoritarian regimes to democracy lays the political groundwork for economic growth.

Communist dictatorships have failed everywhere, and the talk of 'democratizing' government is reverberating throughout the Soviet Union and Eastern Europe. In his December 1988 speech to the United Nations, Mikhail Gorbachev spoke of democracy many times and never once mentioned the word 'communism'. 'The ideal of democratizing the world order,' he said, 'has become a powerful socio-political force.'

Democracy in the Third World advanced dramatically in the 1980s. Led by Brazil and Argentina, much of South America, including Chile in its plebiscite of 1988, has gone from dictatorships to democracies. Also on the 1980s growth of democracy list were Pakistan, Philippines, South Korea, Taiwan, and Mexico.

The democratization of Spain and Portugal has meant that for the first time all Western Europe is governed by democracies.

In 1988 the percentage of the world's population classified by Freedom House as living in 'free' countries reached 38.3 per cent

19

and for the first time became the largest category. This was nearly double the 1975 figure of under 20 per cent. In the 1990s, the figures may double again.

Democracy is by far the most successful context in which to nourish the individual entrepreneur, the most important force for economic growth.

Peace, Not War

By 1988, Europe had been at peace for forty-three years—longer than any time in its history. The relative absence of war in the world, along with the détente between NATO and what will soon be the ex-communist countries, speaks well for the development and full realization of a single global economy.

The year 1988 was an impressive one for peace: the cessation of the Iran-Iraq War; the beginning of the withdrawal of Soviet troops from Afghanistan; peace in Angola. In a stunning speech before the UN in December 1988, Mikhail Gorbachev denounced war as a way of settling things.

It has begun to dawn on people everywhere that war is now an obsolete way of solving problems, certainly among developed countries.

Among the world's forty-four richest countries there has been no war since 1945.

Regional conflicts in the 1990s will not involve the superpowers very much. Vietnam and Afghanistan taught the United States and the USSR the excessive cost of attempting to resolve differences through military power.

Of all countries, the United States and the Soviet Union are now among the least likely to go to war. The USSR has shifted its foreign policy away from one based on 'class struggle' to one based on 'world humanity' and 'human survival'. The Soviets are less likely to pursue expansionism because foreign policy will be decided not only by the Politburo but with much wider participation.

The United States seems to be shifting its national security position from battling communism to responding to economic competition in the global marketplace.

It is now clear that the 1980s was the decade when economies became more important than ideologies.

This new world view frees the financial and human resources that have been going into the arms race—in the Soviet Union, in the United States, and elsewhere—for positive purposes. Our preoccupation with the horror of nuclear war is slowly dissolving, and beneath it stand the grand opportunities of a global economy.

Environment

The world, of course, will not be without problems and enormous challenges.

But population is pretty much under control, except in Africa, although the population doomsayers continue to make their dire predictions. In 1989, for example, Brazil announced that in one generation the country's fertility rate had been cut almost in half. The fertility rate was 5.75 children per woman in 1970. Today it is 3.2.

Environmental considerations continue to be troubling: the ozone layer; acid rain; the greenhouse effect; the destruction of the rain forests. But there is also a growing global consensus that we all must work on the environment together. There is even competition among nations for leadership in attending to the environment.

George Bush ran as an environmentalist in his campaign for the presidency, pledging to convene a world environmental conference that would include the Soviet Union and China.

Mikhail Gorbachev mentioned his concern for the environment at least twenty times during his 7 December 1988 speech to the United Nations.

Margaret Thatcher, following an extraordinary conversion, is sounding like a green. As the *Economist* said, 'Having at first seen her role as that of saving Britain from socialism and the western world from communism, she now believes that her leadership will be needed to solve the environmental problems of the planet'.

When the Group of Seven (the United States, Japan, West Germany, Britain, France, Canada, and Italy) held its fifteenth annual economic summit in Paris in July 1989, environmental issues got major attention for the first time. Some even called it the 'environmental summit'. The group pledged to work together to preserve the global environment, saying in its communiqué: 'Decisive action is urgently needed to understand and protect the earth's ecological balance. We will work together to achieve the common goals of preserving a healthy and balanced global environment in order to meet shared economic and social objectives.'

This is part of the growing sense that a new era of cooperation among all countries is required to deal with our common global environment.

The world's preoccupation with defence and the cold war, which is receding, is being replaced by concern about the destruction of our natural environment, now our most important common problem.

The Extraordinary Decade of the 1990s

Consider all these trends:

- Economic considerations transcending political considerations
- The movement to worldwide free trade
- The powerful drive of telecommunications
- The relative abundance of natural resources
- Competition for reduced taxes
- The downsizing of economic output
- Inflation and interest containment
- The Asian consumer boom
- The advancement of democracy and the spread of free enterprise
- The obsolescence of war
- Our new attentiveness to the environment

These are not just random forces; they all relate to and reinforce each other, a confluence of forces shaping a new globalized world.

Gorbachev says that the world economy is becoming a single organism, and no state, whatever its social system or economic status, can develop normally outside it.

The Myth of America's Decline

In the late 1980s it became fashionable among a growing number of intellectuals to assert that the United States was in decline—as in the decline (and fall) of the Roman Empire.

The best-articulated version of this intellectual spasm was Paul Kennedy's 1988 book, *The Rise and Fall of the Great Powers*. Kennedy's message was that the United States, like other great powers before it, rose to global dominance largely through economic achievement. To maintain its global position, the United States needed to devote increasingly large proportions of wealth to its military as others have done. As the US economy matured, the US commitment to the military became disproportional to its wealth-creating capacities, and the US thereby engaged in Kennedy's oft-quoted 'imperial overstretch'. When economic power declines, Kennedy's history tells us, a decline in military and political power soon follows.

The alarm of Kennedy's book was fuelled by the widespread hysteria over America's twin domestic and trade deficits and its 'loss of competitiveness'.

It was all too easy to embrace the conclusion that America was in decline. Many did. Indeed, it seemed the news was received in some academic circles with ill-disguised glee.

Actual facts in the 1980s were moving in the direction opposite to what Kennedy said.

To begin with, the United States is not increasing military commitments to protect economic interests. The percentage of America's GNP committed to defence is declining. Currently the United States is spending 6 per cent of GNP for defence, down from 10 per cent during the Eisenhower and Kennedy administrations.

Compare this with the Soviet Union, which has been spending up to 25 per cent of its GNP for the military, but intends to start cutting this sharply. Both nations have learned lessons about 'imperial overstretch' in their experiences with Vietnam and Afghanistan. The percentage of GNP the United States spends on defence in the 1990s will decline further as the cold war recedes and as Europe and Japan contribute more to their mutual defence.

Funding the Competition

Much is made of the fact that America's share of world industrial production has dropped from 50 per cent in the 1950s to 25 per cent today. Following World War II and the devastation of Europe and Japan, the United States was the only major nation with its industrial base intact. The US economy was without rival. Not only was it inevitable that the United States would lose some of that 50 per cent share of world production, it was US policy that this should happen. The US went ahead and funded the competition with the Marshall Plan in Europe and aid to Japan in the Pacific. The 1950s were abnormal years in global competition.

If you take more appropriate years like 1913, just before World War I, and 1938, just before World War II, or the years of the mid-1960s, the US share of world manufacturing output was almost exactly what it is today. And that is not counting non-manufacturing output in which the United States has been winning an increasingly larger share of the market.

Says Charles Wolf, director of RAND Corporation research on international economic policy, 'Since the mid-1970s, the economies of Japan and the Pacific Rim countries, including China, have grown more rapidly [from their smaller base] than the US economy. On the other hand, the US GNP has grown more rapidly than that of Western and Eastern Europe, the Soviet Union and much of the so-called developing world, leaving the overall US share of the global product unchanged'.

The United States today produces 25 per cent of the world's industrial production and still has only 5 per cent of the world's population.

America's Supposed Twin Deficits

In the late 1980s politicians, Wall Streeters, and most of the media became hysterical about America's budget and trade deficits. It was said that these twin monsters would surely bring the most powerful economy to its knees, perhaps even lower, if something were not done. President Bush was not even sworn into office when the conventional wisdom pronounced that if he did not do something about the deficits, his presidency would be a disaster. These deficits were time bombs about to go off.

In reality the domestic budget deficit is not out of line with what it has been for the last forty years, is declining, and as a percentage is not greater than other Western countries. In 1989 the budget deficit was less than 3 per cent of national income, less than half what it was in 1982 just before a six-year economic growth period during the Reagan years. If the surplus at state and local levels is taken into account (as it is in other tallyings) the combined result would be a government deficit much lower than those of Japan, France, and West Germany, all of which harbour earnest critics of America's government deficit.

In constant dollars, the total US government deficit has fallen by 57 per cent since 1986. As a share of the GNP, it is one of the lowest in the world.

As for the 'debt burden' being piled up, Milton Friedman, the Nobel prizewinner in economics, points out that the federal debt at the end of 1988 was a smaller percentage of national income than in any year from the end of World War II to 1960, and that 1945–60 was a great boom period for the United States.

Perversely, the hysteria over the budget deficit has served a good purpose: it has scared lawmakers out of spending more. To balance the budget, there have been many calls from all quarters to raise taxes. But the history of raising taxes in the United States is that for every new $1 raised, $1.50 is spent by the Congress. America's democracy is not the sort where tax hikes really cut deficits at all.

The Deficits and the Stock Market

The US stock market went up both when the budget deficit was rising and when it was falling. The budget deficit had fallen substantially in the year just before 19 October 1987. The Wall Streeters overheated their markets, and when the crash came, they blamed it on the budget deficit.

Overnight capitalists became socialists beseeching the central government to fix things.

In the twelve months following the crash, the US economy produced 3.7 million new jobs (56 per cent of them 'managerial and professional', the highest pay and skill category), and real disposable income rose more than 4 per cent.

The 1987 crash was a great gift. It demonstrated for all to see that the casino economy of the stock market is not connected to the real economy.

The So-called US Trade Deficit

Although the anguish about the 'enormous' US trade deficit abounds, it is by no means clear that the United States actually *has* a deficit with Japan or with the rest of the world. One has the uneasy feeling that much of the alarm is being whipped up for one dangerous reason alone: to invoke protectionism, the real threat to the global economy.

In calculating the so-called trade deficits, the only things that are counted are what customs officials check off on their clipboards at ports of entry, the goods and tangibles of the industrial period.

The book you are reading was published in Japan by Nihon Keizai Shimbun. Suppose it had been translated into Japanese and printed in the United States, packed in boxes, and shipped to Japan: that would be counted on custom officials' clipboards as an export for the United States; an import for Japan. Of course, that was not done. Rights were purchased in Japan, and the book was printed there. The authors were paid a purchase price and will receive royalties, but not a penny of it counted in trade. This kind of transaction is duplicated millions of times a year by US citizens dealing with the rest of the world.

US architecture, engineering, and consulting firms collect billions of dollars in fees from around the world each year, yet none of them counts in the so-called trade deficit.

In Japan in 1986 US companies like IBM, Texas Instruments, and Coca-Cola sold goods and services created in Japan to Japanese citizens to the tune of $81 billion. Not a penny counted in the trade figures. That same year Japanese companies created goods and services within the United States to sell to Americans that totalled only $13 billion (none of it counted either). In 1986 foreign branches of American companies sold $720 billion worth of goods overseas, seven times the so-called trade deficit for that year. Almost 20 per cent of the merchandise imported into the United States is manufactured by foreign branches of American companies.

The United States' biggest import item by far is money. Its largest exports by far are bonds, stocks, and other financial instruments. How are we to interpret today's financial figures when for the first time the world is functioning as a single economy? With all the financial interplay in the world, there is now no such thing as a US economy.

The texture of the global economy is far more complex than the layer that passes through customs and gets counted in the trade statistics. Yet we permit commentators in the media and elsewhere to assess the health of the overall US economy by examining a single incomplete statistic. We base decisions about our personal finances on conventional wisdom about a growing trade deficit that does not in reality even exist.

There is a need for new concepts and new data if we are to understand the new global economy. Because they are using old concepts (e.g., a collection of nation-states trading concrete goods) and old data, alarmists shout about perceived trade deficits and yell for protectionist measures borrowed from the old era.

Much is made of the United States now being 'the world's largest debtor nation'.

To begin with, half that so-called debt is in stock in US companies. In a truly global economy, does it really matter that ten shares of AT&T stock are now owned by an Englishman in Manchester rather than a banker in Wichita?

America and Britain Buy Up the World

Another supposed economic trend that has people in the United States inflamed is that foreigners, especially the Japanese, are 'buying up America'. Not true. Certainly not true of the Japanese.

Foreigners own less than 5 per cent of the assets of the US economy, which turns out more than $4.5 trillion worth of goods and services a year.

Japan is not the biggest foreign stakeholder in America. Not by a long shot.

Perhaps because of the exaggerated presence of Japanese ownership in Manhattan, Los Angeles, and Honolulu, Japan has become the target of concern. Perhaps it is because Japan was the enemy of the United States not so many years ago.

Of the total direct foreign investment in the United States ($250 billion at the end of 1987), the British held the biggest share with 28 per cent, followed by the Dutch with 21 per cent, and the Japanese with only 12 per cent. Even in 1987, when Japanese direct investment reached a record $7.4 billion, it was still less than half of British investment. (How is it that Americans are not exercised about the British invasion?) Today, Europeans have five times the stake in US plant and equipment that the Japanese have.

The British are the most prolific acquirers of US businesses, buying almost seven times more US companies than the Japanese in the recent decade.

Here are the top buyers and the number of companies they bought from 1978 to 1987:

Britain	640	Switzerland	86
Canada	435	Netherlands	81
West Germany	150	Australia	68
France	113	Sweden	63
Japan	94	Italy	31

While Britain has been successfully expanding its foreign investments, its alarmists also have been wailing that it has run into a grave crisis in its balance of payments. Its overseas deficit on current account amounted to £15 billion (around US $24 billion) in 1988. Presumably, Britain's foreign assets should therefore have declined by £15 billion. Actually, they increased by £4 billion instead.

One reason is that Britain got a capital gain of around £16 billion on its foreign investments, and an income of £6 billion from them. This £22 billion exceeded the £6 billion which foreigners earned in 1988 from their financial assets in Britain (£2 billion capital gain, £4 billion income). There was an efficient explanation of why Britain was able to have a current overseas deficit of £15 billion, and yet see its overseas financial assets expand.

The right course for a sophisticated country is to invest the money it earns in the most profitable way. That is what 'deficit-ridden' American and 'deficit-ridden' Britain have both done.

British and Japanese investments in the United States jumped markedly in 1988: Britain from $15.1 billion in 1987 to $21.5 billion in 1988; Japan from $7.0 billion in 1987 to $14.2 billion in 1988. A big increase, but still a tiny percentage of the huge US economy. In Colorado, Australia is the largest foreign employer, with ownership of forty companies.

The United States is buying more businesses overseas—$309 billion worth by 1987—than all other countries together are buying in the United States. Furthermore, US assets abroad are grossly understated because Americans have been on the buying side for a long time, and the worth of those assets is carried at the original cost rather than current market value. In the words of the *Economist*, 'America still buys the world. Since the mid-1980s, America's foreign investment has risen faster than either Japan's or Britain's.'

So what if foreigners own 5 per cent of America's assets? Many of the purchasing corporations are owned by American and other people from all over the world. What's foreign? What's domestic? In a global economy we should expect outsiders to throng to buy a larger percentage of any profitable country's assets. Isn't that what partly defines a global economy? How much of California is owned by citizens of the other forty-nine states? Twenty per cent? Thirty-five per cent? We don't know because the United States has been a single, integrated economy. Economic nationalism is dead. We are all part of one economy now.

In the 19th century foreign investment was crucial in financing America's economic growth. By 1890, at the top of America's initial economic development, the United States was a net debtor of $2.9 billion, nearly 4 per cent of its total national wealth at the time. Today, according to US Commerce Department data, the US net 'debt' represents less than 1.4 per cent of its total wealth.

Far from an indicator of 'decline', foreign investment is a fuel source for the thriving US economy. Foreign investments raise the productive capacity, efficiency, and size of the US economy. That the small slice going to foreigners is increasing somewhat should trouble no one.

Foreigners will continue to invest in America. 'It is a mystery to me,' says Milton Friedman, 'why it is regarded as a sign of Japanese strength and US weakness that the Japanese find it more attractive to invest in the US than in Japan. Surely it is precisely the reverse—a sign of US strength and Japanese weakness.'

The Best-positioned Country

In relation to the Soviet Union, the power of the United States in the world has greatly increased in the last decade. The United States produce one quarter of the world's gross national product—more than Japan and the Soviet Union (number two and number three) *combined*. It is astonishing that so many

29

Americans think that Japan has a larger economy than the United States has.

A nation in decline is not a nation that for the last eight years has created far more jobs than *all of Europe and Japan combined.*

A nation in decline is not a nation that has become the economic model for others, a nation whose form of capitalism is being copied around the world.

The United States, of course, owes Japan a rather large debt for shaking US business out of its smugness in the 1970s. As it moves into the 1990s, America is about to return the favour.

Much of the talk of US decline is in a context that sees the world economy as a zero-sum game: if Japan gains, someone has to lose. Not true. The global economy is expanding as it has never expanded before. All economies can grow. Everyone can win.

The power balance in the world is not likely to change very much in the 1990s. Single-market Europe will have a great presence, but so will North America. The United States will continue throughout the 1990s to be the world's biggest economy—by far.

The postwar era ended in the 1980s. The whole world is shifting from national security to economic venture. In the 1990s globalization is the game, and economic power is more important than military power in determining a nation's influence.

The cold war era is over; it has given way to the age of globalization.

In the global economic boom of the 1990s, human resources are the competitive edge for both companies and countries. In the global economic competition of the information economy, the quality and innovativeness of human resources will spell the difference.

In this regard, no country in the world is better positioned than the United States. It certainly has it all over Japan. Japan is a society that has one culture, one history, one race. Superb as the Japanese are, that is limiting. The United States, on the other hand, has the richest mix—including Japanese—of ethnic groups, racial groups, and global experience that the world has ever known, and it is the *richness* of this mix that yields America's incredible creativity and innovation.

It is not by chance that the United States has 188 Nobel prize-winners and Japan has 5.

The United States is constantly replenishing and enhancing its rich mix of talent. In 1988 it admitted 643,000 legal immigrants, more than all other countries put together. Indeed, since 1970 the United States has allowed more legal immigration than the rest of the world combined.

Who are these immigrants? Currently, most are Asian and Hispanic. More important, they are the most aggressive, most entrepreneurial, most assertive people, who fight fiercely to get to the United States.

It is the habit of Americans to brag about previous immigrants and to complain about the current ones.

These immigrants are adding immeasurably to America's talent pool and at a time when birthrates in the United States are down. Contrast this with immigration policies in European countries whose birthrates are even lower. West Germany is the oldest country in the world (average age), followed by the Netherlands and then the Scandinavian countries. These ageing countries with their low birthrates have some of the toughest immigration laws in the world. They won't let anybody in. Japan, also growing older faster, won't let anybody in either.

In the 1990s the United States will have a younger population than either of its major competitors—Europe and Japan.

America's great import is people. Yet Americans have not even begun to experience the real potential of their fantastic human resource mix, which will be their competitive edge in the global economy as we move toward the next millennium.

HIGH-WAGE ECONOMY: AMERICAN PROTOTYPE

During the 1990s well-educated, skilled information workers will earn the highest wages in history, further reinforcing the decade's affluence.

Ironically, a lot of people think today's economy is creating mostly low-wage menial jobs that can't support families. Abroad in the land is a bizarre stereotype that would have the United States shift from an industrial economy, in which everyone was a highly paid autoworker, to a service society, in which all those autoworkers are now working only in fast-food parlours.

Where do people get this low-wage idea? It is a bit of misinformation circulated by those who would artificially prop up old industrial jobs, interests like organized labour. Labour's scenario goes something like this: If people can be convinced that the only well-paying jobs are industrial jobs, they will support legislation that 'protects' those industrial jobs from global competition. That is, they will accept laws that prohibit the United States from importing competitively priced goods. A terrible idea, which others must not copy. Free trade is essential to the global economy of the 1990s. What sense does it make to protect jobs that were so 'well-paying' they became inflationary, uneconomic, and uncompetitive in a world economy?

The Low Wage Thesis: Sources of Mythology

In late 1986 Barry Bluestone and Bennett Harrison, who are generally considered pro-labour economists, published a study for the Joint Economic Committee of Congress (JEC) claiming that six out of ten new jobs created between 1979 and 1984 paid around US $7000 a year or less. The economy, they concluded, was generating low-paying service jobs, a finding inconsistent with that of the non-partisan Bureau of Labour Statistics, which had repeatedly found an increase in jobs paying high wages and said so. The authors later altered their figures; 40 per cent of jobs, they now said, paid US $11,000 or less.

Nonetheless, their original conclusions seem to have passed into the collective consciousness as true. 'Six out of ten new jobs pay under seven thousand dollars a year' is regularly repeated by the media and echoed in speeches of Democratic candidates who feel compelled to adopt the albatross of Big Labour's protectionism.

Fortunately the real salaries people earn in America's information economy are more uplifting. From March 1985 to March 1989 an extraordinary 73 per cent of the new jobs created fell into the top three upper-paying Department of Labour categories: professional administrative, sales and technical, and precision crafts. From March 1988 to March 1989 alone, 53.4 per cent of the new jobs created fell under the category termed 'professional and managerial'. Certainly not low-wage jobs.

The further the information economy evolves, the better the jobs, and the more they pay.

Had Bluestone and Harrison studied 1988, they would have come up with very different figures. However, even the Labour Department agrees that between 1977 and 1981, there *was* a low-wage trend. Study those years, or a chunk of them, as the authors of the low-wage theory did, and you miss the opposite trend beginning in 1982: millions of well-paying new jobs that only increased as the 1980s progressed.

More than 70 per cent of new job growth has been in occupations which average US $20,000 per year, says former Secretary of Labour Anne McLaughlin.

The evidence is overwhelming. The information economy is producing an extraordinary number of well-paying, challenging jobs. However, you must possess the required skill to do those jobs. Tragically, the unskilled, the undereducated will command salaries that match their economic value in an information society—not very high. The information economy jobs require such a high degree of competence that the United States does not presently have the human resources to fill them. Nor will it for the rest of the 1990s. That demographic reality at least provides some incentive for corporations to train the unskilled.

Other Indexes

Other economic indexes, such as retail sales, provide more evidence of the high-wage economy. In 1987 America's eighteen largest retail chains showed sales up a stunning 13.8 per cent.

The US Chamber of Commerce constructed a 'Prosperity Index' (employment minus inflation) that shows Americans are better off than ever. The chamber's index sat at 53.2 in 1968, hit bottom at 46.7 in 1975, and rose to 59.3 in the first quarter of 1989. Admittedly, the chamber is a fairly conservative group.

But the nonpartisan consumer magazine *Changing Times* reached about the same conclusion. Its 'Prosperity Index' (consumer spending plus net worth) figures that the average American enjoys the highest prosperity level in US history. Meanwhile, the 'Misery Index' (unemployment plus inflation) looks less and less miserable. First devised by Democrats, it stood at 20 when Carter lost the presidency to Reagan in 1980. In 1988 it was less than 10.

Some interesting evidence for the high-wage economy comes from Massachusetts. Between 1985 and 1987 the state lost nearly 75,000 manufacturing jobs, five times as big a percentage loss as the national rate. Yet state per capita income *increased* 40 per cent faster than the national average in that same period. Why? Because Massachusetts also created so many high-skilled, well-paying information jobs. Ironically, its governor in running for President embraced the low-wage job myth even though some of the best evidence against it came out of his information-rich state.

Whither the Middle Class?

The corollary to the low-wage jobs myth is the notion that the rich are getting richer, the poor poorer, and the middle class is shrinking. It is the sort of viewpoint espoused by David Gordon, who, in the *Washington Post*'s Outlook section, writes, 'The most important story about the US economy in the eighties is the economic warfare that the wealthy and powerful have been waging against the vast majority of Americans'.

Barbara Ehrenreich, in the *New York Times Magazine*, asks, 'Is the Middle Class Doomed?' She writes: 'Some economists have even predicted that the middle class . . . will disappear altogether, leaving the country torn, like many third-world societies, between an affluent minority and a horde of the desperately poor.'

Authors like Ehrenreich and Gordon support their contentions with studies by the Joint Economic Committee (the same group that got the low-wage job myth going). In July 1986 the JEC released a study stating that the wealth of the top 0.5 per cent had increased from 25.4 to 35.1 per cent between 1963 and 1983.

A week later the JEC authors admitted they were just plain wrong. Wealth at the top had actually increased only from 25.4 per cent to 26.9 per cent, even if you use their rather misleading way of measuring wealth. Although the authors have conceded their mistake, the data gets recycled again and again by people like Gordon and Ehrenreich.

The slight shift of wealth toward the top is 'marginally statistically significant,' says Robert Avery, an economist at the Federal Reserve. But he adds, 'if you include employees' accumulated pension rights (which are normally not counted as wealth), that tilt becomes a slight decline.' Pension funds are making the middle class wealthier. So are several other factors.

The Middle Class Is Disappearing Upward

Reports of the death of America's middle class, it appears, are greatly exaggerated. If the middle class has died, it has definitely gone to heaven—that is to say, it has graduated to the 'upper' classes. That is the conclusion of two Bureau of Labour Statistics economists writing in the Labour Department's *Monthly Labour Review*.

In 1969, 58.8 per cent of American families could be called middle class (defined as earning between $20,000 and $55,999 in today's dollars). In 1986 the percentage had shrunk to 53 per cent. Where did it go? Not to the 'lower' class, which itself shrunk from 33.7 per cent to 31.7 per cent, but to the 'upper' classes. The percentage of families earning US $56,000 or more doubled from 7.5 per cent in 1969 to 15.3 per cent in 1986.

Both black and white families are moving to the upper-middle-income group. Between 1981 and 1987 white families with incomes of more than $50,000 increased from 18.2 per cent to 24.4 per cent. Black families registered greater change; the percentage earning incomes over $50,000 grew from 6 per cent to 9.5 per cent.

The Incomes of Working Women

If the rich are getting richer, it is not by collecting interest cheques, playing the futures market, or investing in tax shelters. It is because millions of women get up and go to the office in the morning. Two incomes—sometimes two good incomes—are better than one.

In 1967 only 6.7 million families earned more than $50,000 a year (in 1987 dollars). By 1987 that figure had grown to 16.9 million households. These households usually consist of two-income well-educated professional married couples, over thirty-five. 'The working woman is lifting millions of families out of the middle class', concludes the *Wall Street Journal*.

The Inheritance Factor

A huge new factor will make those high incomes go even further. Today's baby boomers, in their thirties and forties, are the children of the first large-scale middle class in history. Their parents will bequeath the children substantial inheritance, often in the form of real estate. And not just in the United States. 'The generation of Britons now reaching retirement age was the first to put a big proportion of its savings into home ownership,' writes the *Economist*. 'Only when they die, bequeathing their property to their children, can this most popular form of British investment be cashed in.'

Blacks are Benefitting

By some measures America's information economy is certainly benefitting blacks as much as whites.

From 1982 to 1987 black family income grew 13 per cent, compared with 11.4 per cent for white families. But more dramatic gains have come in employment. The proportion of people employed increased 23.1 per cent for blacks and only 11.2 per cent for whites. Black male teens gained 36.3 per cent. But black female teens gained the most: 38 percentage points.

Most black families headed by married couples have joined the middle class. More than three-quarters of employed black family men earn middle-class incomes or better, according to James Smith, senior economist at the Rand Corporation. By the very nature of the information economy, the well educated benefit most. The black elite—upper middle class and wealthy —has grown faster than the black middle class.

More Elderly Are Joining the Middle Class

Once a substantial proportion of the poor population, the elderly now have a per capita income *higher* than that of the average American. The median per capita income of elderly people has doubled since 1960. Although they constitute one-sixth of the population, the elderly own one-third of all household net worth and 40 per cent of financial assets.

Are the Poor Getting Poorer?

By every measure, the United States as a whole is better off financially than it was twenty years ago, which is not to say it has succeeded in eliminating poverty. Nor is poverty 'worse than ever', as some charge. In 1959, 22.4 per cent of Americans lived in poverty. In 1973 it hit its lowest—11.1 per cent. By 1983 it had increased to 15.2 per cent; then it began to drop off again. Since 1986 it has hovered around 13.5 per cent. Incomes of the poorest one-fifth, including female-headed families, are not decreasing. For the most part they have stayed the same. Not 'worse than ever', but nothing to be proud of either.

The contrast between poverty and prosperity is overdrawn, reasons economist Robert Samuelson, who nonetheless concludes: 'The American dream is passing by a big part of the population'.

There is a growing consensus that the root of poverty is failure to create families. More than one-third of the 10.4 million female-headed families in America are poor. When couples marry, they overwhelmingly escape poverty; about 94 per cent of married couples are *not* poor. In the early seventies 1 family in 9 was headed by a woman, but beginning in the early 1980s there were huge increases in the number of unwed mothers. Today 1 family in 6 is headed by a single mother. There are 5.5 million poor families with children, contrasted with 4.1 million in 1979. That means the poor are overwhelmingly children.

Virtually all the experts agree that the welfare policy has not worked. Economic growth so far has not helped the hard-core poor. Samuelson, an objective voice in an otherwise ideological debate, writes of 'a general prosperity sitting atop a stubborn poverty'.

'Economic growth,' he says, 'powerful as it is, won't cure everything. It won't turn low-skilled workers into engineers or technicians . . . mend broken families or eradicate crime.'

The challenge is how to absorb the poor into the mainstream society. As Great Society veterans can attest, that is a difficult task. It will be made easier, however, by the labour shortages of the 1990s and the trend from welfare to workers described in Chapter 5.

Wage Trends Are in Step with Information Economy

A study of wages during the past fifteen years tracks America's shift from an industrial to an information economy. In 1973 the median income for males aged thirty-five to forty-four was US $26,026 in today's dollars. Those between forty-five and fifty-four earned $25,718.

That year was a benchmark year—just before the OPEC oil crisis and the subsequent rise in inflation, just before the emergence of Japan as the leading industrial power. In effect, 1973 was the last hurrah of America's industrial period, when union bargaining power arguably reached its height.

After that fateful year, real male incomes declined. But by 1985 they had regained the 1973 level. Males between thirty-five and forty-four earned US $25,886, just under the 1973 figure; and those between forty-five and fifty-four earned $26,702 about $1000 above it. Wages have increased ever since.

When we compare the incomes of men and women, an interesting trend emerges. Women's wages did not suffer the same dip as men. Women have moved steadily upward. In 1973 women from thirty-five to forty-four earned US $13,673. By 1985 their earnings had increased to $16,114. Still a lot lower than male wages but moving steadily upward. That is because women were never a big part of the union-based high-wage phase of the industrial economy. And women have taken two-thirds of all the new jobs of the information economy.

Getting Ahead in a High-Wage Economy

There is no doubt about it: wages are down for unskilled, uneducated male workers. In 1987 college grads averaged US $31,371, high school grads $20,314. In the benchmark year of 1973 the unemployment rate for uneducated males was three times that of college graduates, but both had reason to be worried. Before the information economy really took off, stories about college grads driving cabs were legend.

In today's information society, it is the unskilled who are standing in the unemployment line. The unemployment rate for college graduates (one in four US workers) is 1.7 per cent; for people with one to three years of college, it is 3.7 per cent. High school graduates have unemployment rates of 5.4 per cent, but among high school dropouts unemployment is 9.4 per cent —nearly six times that of college grads.

Today half of all American adults get at least some college, compared with one-quarter in the 1950s. Among those households earning US $75,000 or more per year, two-thirds of the heads of households are college graduates.

Did the unskilled, uneducated white male have it made in industrial America? You bet. Those days are gone forever.

The Challenge of the High-Wage Economy

If the industrial society was 'a man's world', the information society is wide open to the well-educated and technically trained, be they male or female. The system also favours ambitious, intelligent immigrants and other go-getters who can start off in 'service' jobs that pay not US $7000 a year but $7 an hour. With experience—$10 an hour. How much better off are they than the last wave of immigrants who sweated it out in the factory jobs of industrial America?

The issue is not poor-quality jobs or low wages. It is not 'death of the middle class' but the real potential for everyone to do well. The problem is how to educate and train people to qualify for an abundance of good jobs.

There are not nearly enough Americans with college degrees or advanced vocational and technical training to fill the more than 2 million new managerial, administrative, and technical jobs coming on-line annually. Without mass immigration from Western Europe (unlikely since it is entering its own boom years) or mass liberalization of immigration laws, there is no way the United States will have the optimum work force needed for the information economy.

Finally, the 120 million people in the US work force today must constantly upgrade their skills over the course of the 1990s. It will require a tremendous human resource effort to transform corporate America into the decentralized, customer-oriented model of the information society. Yet that is what is needed for the United States to participate fully in the booming global economy. With new markets, with a single-market Europe, and with new competitors from Asian countries, corporations need people who can think critically, plan strategically, and adapt to change.

That is the challenge of the information age. Let us address it and its opportunities, recognizing that the information economy is a high-wage economy.

1992

It has been said that Europe discovered America, and now, 500 years later in 1992, Europe will discover Europe.

The end of 1992 is the target date for a Europe without frontiers, for the twelve-country members* of the European Community (EC) to knock down the trade barriers that Europeans have put up to protect themselves from each other: a frontier-free Europe, the removal of all barriers to the flow of people, goods, services, and money among the twelve nations.

What Does 1992 Mean?

- 1992 means that a Greek lawyer will be able to set up a practice in Copenhagen and that a Spanish shoe company could open a shop unhindered in Dublin.
- 1992 means that a Japanese or American businessman can fly into one European Community country, pass through customs once, and then visit the other eleven without seeing another customs or immigration official.
- 1992 means that a Portuguese bank can be the partner of a new venture in the Paris fashion industry.
- 1992 means cross-border corporate mergers and take-overs that may be as frequent and bizarre as they are in the United States.
- 1992 means creating an EC-wide job market for professionals, technical personnel, and skilled workers.
- 1992 means opening up competition across borders in bidding for government contracts for telecommunications and other public purchased goods.
- 1992 means that the outrageously high inter-European airplane tickets should come down—more in line with the fare between, say, New York and Chicago.
- 1992 means that a truck travelling from Denmark to Italy, whose average speed for the trip is now twenty miles an hour because of border checkpoints, will be able to travel

*United Kingdom, Ireland, France, Portugal, Spain, Denmark, West Germany, Italy, Netherlands, Greece, Belgium, and Luxembourg.

from point to point uninterrupted, cutting delivery time and costs in half.

- 1992 means more Pan-European Telecommunications, Inc., and fewer Irish National Widgets.
- 1992 means goods and people moving as easily from France to Germany as they can from California to Oregon.
- 1992 means it will no longer be possible for Ford to sell the same car for £10,000 in Britain and £8000 in Belgium.
- 1992 means that companies will be able to compete as freely throughout the Community as at home.
- 1992 means an end to duty-free sales on trips inside the European Community because they would not be considered international.
- 1992 means that a single administrative document will replace seventy separate customs forms across the community.
- 1992 means a zone without passport controls, and Euro-passports bearing the name of the country below that of the European Community.
- 1992 means that students will be able to study at universities of their choice knowing that their degrees and diplomas will be recognized in all twelve countries.
- 1992 means that people should be able to retire in whichever European country they choose.
- 1992 means that a watch, refrigerator, or car would be repaired under a common European Community warranty system in one member country even if it has been purchased in another.
- 1992 means that there will be more competition at all levels of the single market, bringing greater choice of attractively priced goods and services.

In short, 1992 for the EC means something like the United States, without the political unity. It could mean a few new European headaches as well.

The three most important things about 1992 are:

1. It is a response to the growing competition from the North American economic pairing of the United States and Canada, and the Japanese-led Pacific Rim. Separately none of the 12 European countries is a massive

international business force; together they are the largest economic power in the world.

2. It is part of a global trend toward worldwide free trade, the larger long-term trend to which protectionism is the small, short-term countertrend.

3. All this is happening at a time when Poland, Hungary, Czechoslovakia, the Baltic states and other Eastern European countries are seeking to be part of free Europe again, and when the re-unification of West Germany and East Germany has become a probability. It will be astonishing if East European countries do not become EC members in the years ahead.

Legislature and the Courts

In 1985 the European Commission proposed the Single European Act, which consisted of three hundred legislative directives intended to remove all physical, fiscal, and technical barriers to trade in goods and services among the twelve present members. About one-third of the directives have been passed by the Council of Ministers. Some of the directives will take effect before 1992; others may not until later. What it amounts to is a form of mass deregulation, the economic phenomenon of our age, 'a fashionable medicine which European countries know they should swallow like good patients, even if they dislike the taste'.

Much of the development of the integrated Europe will be accomplished through the courts. In fact, that process began a decade ago, in the celebrated case of Reive Zentral, a little-known West German company that wanted to import crème de cassis, a liqueur made from blackcurrants. The government of West Germany refused it import status because the product didn't contain enough alcohol to be called a liquor by West German standards. The company took legal action and ended up in the European Court of Justice in Luxembourg, a court that is becoming more and more a part of the story of 1992. The court ruled that West Germany could not block the import of a drink that was on sale in France, unless it was threatening harm to consumers—which crème de cassis clearly wasn't. The body of law being built on this decision was incorporated in the Single European Act. When in Europe, we always order a Kir.

Comparisons with US Market

The United States, where goods and people flow freely among the states, has been a model for the EC. It is certainly less than a perfect model. For example:

- The United States did not deregulate interstate trucking until 1980, and in forty-three states the right to be in the trucking business is still restricted.
- Interstate branch banking is largely prohibited.
- Sales taxes among the states range from zero to nine per cent.
- Twenty states have local preference laws for public procurement.

Such less-than-free-market anomalies do not prevent the United States from being one great market.

The advantages of the US market include one language and one currency—matters that are part of the 1992 discussion in Europe.

Financial Services Are the Cutting Edge

By 1992 all capital and exchange controls will be removed. Financial services, including banking, securities, and insurance, will compete freely across the Continent. The campaign to open up financial services will permit the free flow of all sorts of capital, the right to sell financial services across borders, and the right of financial firms to become established in other EC countries.

The Council of Ministers is now considering creating a single banking licence valid throughout the European Community. Indeed, universal banking is to become the EC norm, far freer than banking in the United States—both geographically and in the range of services offered. That will significantly reduce bankers' fees for various services. Price Waterhouse has estimated that prices in Italy could come down by 14 per cent, France by 12 per cent, West Germany by 10 per cent, and Britain by 7 per cent.

What about the entry of non-EC banks? Could a South Korean bank get itself established in Luxembourg and then radiate freely across the European Community? Unlikely. As it stands now, each EC country decides whom to let in. That will probably continue.

Today, if you are Italian or French, you cannot legally open a bank account outside your country. But by the end of 1990 you will be free to do so in eight of the twelve countries. The other four countries—Spain, Portugal, Ireland, and Greece—will prohibit such external accounts until 1992. As a generality, commercial banking will become Europeanized; consumer banking will remain nationally centred.

How about stock markets? While London is overwhelmingly Europe's most important exchange, most European companies do business at their local exchanges. This could change. Local exchanges could become irrelevant, especially to the big players. Look for a European over-the-counter discount market.

Uncertainty is the only certainty. Whatever happens, 1992 will continue to preoccupy the strategic thinking of Europe's financial services.

Japanese are striving to become good Europeans—before 1992.

Japanese companies are now scrambling to upgrade their operations and images in Europe. They are increasing their research and development and moving more decision-making power to Europe. These efforts are partly driven by a conviction that the EC is going to become ultraprotectionist, and the Japanese want to be inside.

Furthermore, the European Commission's antidumping actions for the past two years have really focussed Japanese attention. It is clear to the Japanese that if they want access to the huge European market, their products must not read 'Made in Japan'.

The goal of the Japanese camera company Canon is nothing less than to make its products from components supplied in Europe. 'We plan to be able to supply everything we need for our European operations in Europe,' says Canon's president, Ryuzaburo Kaku.

Kaku is devoted to the idea that Canon has to contribute to the regions in which it does business. 'For example, we are not going to take the profits from our French plant back to Japan,' he says in a blush of European good citizenship. 'We want that to be a French company, to pay taxes in France and re-invest in France. If we are going to work internationally, that is the philosophy that has to follow.'

The coming of 1992 has created a new political climate within which Europe's economic integration is being accelerated by a surge of cross-frontier mergers and take-overs that governments would have blocked just a few years ago.

The 1987 merger of Sweden's Asea and the Swiss group Brown Boveri was a groundbreaker and an important example of a company's worming its way into the EC. The new company, ABB, has a strong EC presence through a German subsidiary (Sweden and Switzerland are not members of the EC). Asea moved its headquarters to Switzerland, and the merged ABB conducts research at three centres: Vaesteraas, Sweden, Asea's former homebase; Heidelberg, West Germany; and Basel, Switzerland.

'FORTRESS EUROPE'?

Many Americans, Japanese, and Soviets fear that the European Community will turn in on itself and become 'Fortress Europe', blocking outsiders' goods. Community officials are right when they say that as the world's largest trading entity it would be 'mad' to turn protectionist.

France, Italy, and Spain, countries with old protectionist habits, probably expect the EC to become protectionist. But West Germany, Britain, and other northern countries, with their free-trading histories, certainly expect the single European market to be open to the world.

France and Italy limit the number of Japanese cars imported each year by 'voluntary restraint agreements'. There are quotas in all EC countries on US-made jeans and Asia-made T-shirts. And the cheap lamb Britain imports from New Zealand cannot in turn be sold in other countries.

Free-trading Mrs Thatcher feels very strongly about it. 'It would be betrayal,' she says, 'if while breaking down constraints on trade to create the single market, the Community were to erect greater external protection.'

Political Implications

The change of 1992 is economically driven, as a response to global competition especially from Japan and the United States.

While some European governments—notably the French—are waxing romantic about the political prospects for a frontier-free Europe, politics are not driving the change, but being pulled by it. Sovereign power is being overwhelmed by money-market power. Most governments are scrambling to keep up with the economic charge that is off and running.

The Brussels-based European Commission is not likely to win a much larger role than competition and merger policy. But Jacques Delors, president of the European Commission, thinks that by the late 1990s some form of European government will be needed. (Mrs Thatcher begs to differ.)

Brussels now has power over trade policy and customs duties, agriculture, and competition policy. Delors says that 'in 10 years time 80 per cent of economic, perhaps even social and tax, legislation will be of Community origin'.

To the question, Is the European Community a step toward political union, a step toward a United States of Europe? the answer is no. Certainly not in the foreseeable future. There is some sentiment for it in France and Germany, but for most Europeans 1992 is seen only as a good way to make themselves richer.

And 1992 is an insurance policy for stable democracies. Any Community government that installed a Communist or fascist government would lose because, in the words of the *Economist*, 'half of its national wealth would be telecommunicated abroad in its first hour'.

Problems and Complications

Certainly 1992 is not a smooth turn of the wheel. Here are a few complications:

- France, Britain, and Holland worry that abolishing border controls diminishes the capacity to counter terrorism and drug trafficking.

- Denmark insists on keeping its passport-free arrangements with the other Nordic countries. This means that a Finn or Swede could go to Copenhagen and then have free access to all the other eleven Community countries.

- Politically not everyone is for a single market. The Green party in West Germany predicts it will hurt the environment: 'The strong will gain and the weak will suffer'.

- Nor can language barriers be voted away. None of the nine main tongues spoken in the community will stop wagging after 1992.

- There is an absence of a common currency. Will there be one after 1992? Most EC governments (except Mrs Thatcher's) want it, but it seems unlikely this century.

Industrial and technical standards are a sticky wicket. Italy has a so-called purity law which says pasta must be made of durum wheat rather than of cheaper kinds of wheat. Italians must eat 'real pasta'. In other words, no one else can sell cheaper pasta in Italy.

Because of the lack of common standards, some telephone equipment is twice as expensive in West Germany as in France. The price per installed telephone line ranges from $225 to $500 in Europe. In the United States—where there is standardization —it is only about $100. Europe will have to get its act together on standards to be economically competitive with the United States, Canada, and Japan.

But the most difficult problem of all is clearly taxes. Countries don't like to have their tax policies dictated by someone else. It's a sovereignty issue. A single market in Europe will probably require drastic cuts in the disparities among value-added tax (VAT) rates in different EC countries. That means some European governments will have to accept heavy tax revenue losses as their taxes become more harmonized with those of their neighbours. (The US experience shows that adjacent states can maintain differences in sales taxes of up to about 5 percentage points without the 'tax leakage' really hurting them.) The European Commission wants countries to impose VAT and excise taxes on a uniform basis and align their tax rates. Britain is screaming the loudest, and saying 'let competition decide'.

One growth industry will certainly be lawyers and consultants—trying to make sense of it all after 1992.

PROSPECTS FOR INDIVIDUAL COUNTRIES

Denmark

Denmark should find it easy to adjust to an open market. Possibly the least protectionist of all European countries, Denmark has no basic industries to protect. More than 40 per cent of its gross national product is based on foreign trade, three times the US percentage. Companies in Nordic countries are buying heavily into Danish businesses. About 80 Norwegian, 284 Swedish, and 60 Finnish companies operate in Denmark. Corporations from other countries, including the United States' Motorola, have also bought into Danish firms to get a gateway to the EC countries.

The influential Social Democratic party had long campaigned for maintaining the nation's Scandinavian identity rather than merge into Europe to the south. But in a watershed referendum in 1986 Danes approved the single market's charter by 56 per cent.

Italy

Italy's big business has moved ahead of its government. Carlo de Benedetti, the head of Olivetti and master of the take-over, says that Italy no longer exports masons and waiters to northern Europe. It now sends captains of industry eager to create pan-European business empires. Of the sixty-eight European take-overs and mergers completed in the two years to February 1988, twenty-eight involved Italian firms.

The Netherlands

After years of sluggish growth the Dutch economy is expanding as fast as the EC average. It should continue to do so well into the 1990s. International trade, the backbone of the Netherlands, will benefit from the $1 billion in infrastructural improvements planned for Rotterdam's port—the world's largest—in the next four years. By the century's end, capital improvements in Rotterdam could total an additional $7 billion.

Spain

Relaxed foreign-investment restrictions, plus relatively cheap labour whose productivity has been rising fast, make Spain one of Europe's most commercially attractive nations for incoming business. The economy will get a shot in the arm with the 1992 staging of both the Summer Olympics in Barcelona, and a world's fair in Seville to celebrate the 500-year anniversary of Columbus's discovery of America.

Juan Luis Cebrián, editor of *El País* (Madrid), says, 'People here are beginning to feel that Spain is an important country—a thing that we never imagined before—and this is because of Europe.' Spain is getting used to feeling like a European country again.

France

France is the most excited about the new European Community. Opinion polls show a very high level of awareness of, and enthusiasm for, 1992. That's partly because of a massive publicity and information campaign by the French government, which wants French industry to restructure and become internationally more competitive. As of June 1988, more than 87 per cent of all French companies said they were taking active measures to prepare for 1992.

France's technological base, already one of the most impressive in Europe, is expanding. The French lead the way in home-automation technology, a market that could swell to $12 billion by 1995. Completion of the $11 billion Eurotunnel linking France to Britain, combined with the massive privatization movement, which is being continued by France's Socialist government, also promises to advance France's standing in the global economy.

Great Britain

Britain seems the most wary. It has always regarded the Continent with some suspicion. Some British doubters of the Channel Tunnel see it as a conduit for rabies, terrorism, and other blights from Europe. So 1992 has gone somewhat unheralded in Britain. This is ironic because a Briton, Lord Cockfield, has been its chief architect. He was the EC commissioner responsible for proposing to turn Europe into a single market, according to the grand design he drew up in 1985. In much of the British government he was looked at askance, a man gone overboard on enthusiasm for Europe. When his reappointment came up for renewal in mid-1988, Mrs Thatcher replaced him with someone else.

But things are shifting. The British Labour party originally showed outright opposition to the removal of trade barriers.

Now it chastises Mrs Thatcher for not having a 'cohesive industrial policy' toward 1992.

Ireland

Despite 19 per cent unemployment and widespread emigration, the Irish Republic isn't about to roll over and play dead. An increasing number of foreign businesses are finding it hard to resist Ireland's generous tax breaks, cash grants, and R&D subsidy programmes.

Portugal

Politically stable Portugal, with its increasingly productive but still quite low-wage work force, is buzzing with enterprise. Foreign investments reached $445 million in 1987, triple the total in 1986. Particularly active areas include construction, glass manufacturing, and real estate.

Since 1983 the Bank of Portugal's holdings of foreign exchange have skyrocketed from $200 million to $3 billion. Unemployment, at less than 5.9 per cent in 1989, is among the lowest in the EC.

West Germany

West Germany, the strongest of the EC team, has a methodical, workmanlike approach to 1992. And, more than ever, West Germany is focussing attention on small business, a sector that accounts for half the country's gross national product, two-thirds of its jobs, and most of its industrial training.

Belgium

Brussels is not yet the Washington, DC of Europe, but it is moving in that direction. To this capital of the European Economic Committee has come an invasion of bureaucrats, lobbyists, trade associations, and politicians. The country is enjoying a period of sustained economic growth, and Belgians are aggressively working out new forms of cooperation and partnership with their domestic and foreign competitors. Belgium has the most open economy in Europe: exports and imports account for 70 per cent of the GNP. In preparation for 1992, Belgium has reformed its stock market and begun to reform the country's complex tax structure.

Greece

Its backward administrative structure and not well-developed economy are expected to make it difficult for Greeks to adjust to a post-1992 world. But Greece could benefit the most because the wealthy north EC members have agreed to provide tens of billions of dollars to the poorest EC countries to help stimulate and restructure their economies. It's like California and Connecticut pledging economic aid to Mississippi and Arkansas, an effort to strengthen the whole of the Common Market by assisting the weakest parts.

Luxembourg

Tiny Luxembourg has only 400,000 inhabitants in the heart of a trading market with more than 320 million people. It is an important reinsurance centre (the Bermuda of Europe) and business is booming. It is now becoming a centre for pension fund administration. Its standing as an offshore banking haven (tax advantages, low banking costs, and strict banking secrecy) is probably not in jeopardy. Luxembourg's central location in the European Community, its social and political stability, and the strong back-up support of the banking community, make it well positioned to enlarge its financial services.

Who Else Might Join? All Those Easterners?

To qualify for membership in the EC, a country must be European and democratic. Several European countries not members of the EC look as if they want to jump on the bandwagon. Austria will apply in 1990. Norway, Sweden, Finland, and even Switzerland have shown interest. But Switzerland may never join; the Swiss recently voted against joining the UN.

As 1992 approaches, more will push for membership so as not to miss out on the economic benefits. Even if ex-communist countries do not join, there will probably be fourteen countries in the EC by the mid-1990s, and possibly eighteen by the year 2000.

The most awkward of the 'old candidacies' is that of Turkey, which applied in 1989. It is larger geographically than any of the EC twelve and has a population the same size as Great Britain. It also has low wages, which are regarded as a competitive advantage, and a tremendous number of underemployed, who could freely flood membership countries. Turkey wants in partly as a means of attracting private foreign investment. Prime Minister Turgut Ozal argues that investment would keep more Turks at home. Some view Turkey as 'not Westernized enough'. Naturally EC member Greece doesn't like Turkey at all. Islamic Turkey does have a European code of law, a mostly free press, and Western-style theatre and music, including opera, but it is problematical for the near future.

The newest candidates are the countries of Eastern Europe. They are struggling to become democracies. Nobody can tell what will have happened to them by the year 2000. There might by then be a united Germany, half a dozen EC candidates from former communist Europe (Hungary, Poland, Czechoslovakia, Romania, Bulgaria, divided parts from Yugoslavia) plus a number of successor states to a fissiparious Soviet Union. These two events—1992 and the death of European communism—may be happening together in this next decade.

1992 as Strategic Vision

Even if Eastern Europe does not produce EC members quickly, Western Europe's 1992 is an extraordinary phenomenon. Nothing like it has ever before been tried in history. The most ambitious attempt ever to remove trade barriers, it is an awesomely massive deregulation project.

The excitement in Western European government and business circles is almost euphoric. The process is now irreversible. It is also generational. Some older Europeans see European economic integration as a threat to their security; most younger ones see it as an opportunity.

It is consonant with global economic trends, and companies are talking and planning for 1992 as if it were already here.

'A single-market Europe by the end of 1992'. It is a strategic vision like John F. Kennedy's strategic vision: 'We are going to put a man on the moon by the end of the decade'.

Like all powerful strategic visions, it is specific and has a time frame. It could later lead to a free-trading bloc from Bordeaux to Vladivostok.

2

Renaissance in the Arts

In the final years before the millennium there will be a fundamental and revolutionary shift in leisure time and spending priorities. During the 1990s the arts will gradually replace sport as society's primary leisure activity. This extraordinary megatrend is visible in an explosion in the visual and performing arts that is already well under way. It has exploded most dramatically in the country that least expected it in the US.

There have been many headlines during the 1980s about the precarious financial situation of the arts in America. The Reagan administration cut federal funding of the arts, to what was alleged to be the bone.

Today the US-government (federal and other) spends only an annual $2 per capita on the arts, versus about $9 of government expenditure in Mrs Thatcher's Britain, around $27 in West Germany and the Netherlands, $30–32 in France and Canada, and $35 in Sweden. It was said that this niggardliness would cause the US to drop into barbarism.

Instead, during a period when America has been rejecting a welfare-state approach to the arts, the most significant figures are:

- Since 1965 American museum attendance has increased from 200 million to 500 million annually.
- The 1988–89 season on Broadway broke every record in history.
- Membership in the leading US chamber music association grew from 20 ensembles in 1979 to 578 in 1989.
- Since 1970 US opera audiences have nearly tripled.

DARK AGE OVER

In a sense, the 20th century has known its own Dark Ages; high technology and industrialization replaced human beings with machines. Totalitarianism and war devastated people, museums, and cathedrals.

Today, as we move toward the millennium, we leave behind the devastating wars of this century. Even the cold war is over. Much of humanity is freer to ponder, to explore what it means to be human.

It is a spiritual quest, but its economic implications are staggering.

The affluent information society has laid the economic ground-work for the renaissance, creating new patrons whose wealth would make the Borgias green with envy. It has spawned an educated, professional, and increasingly female work force. For people committed to personal fitness programmes, particularly middle-class women, spectator sports hold less allure; they prefer to spend Sunday afternoon at a museum rather than watching football on TV.

Arts lovers tend to be educated; baby boomers are the most schooled generation in history. Today's consumer is sophisti-cated enough to appreciate the arts and can pay the price of admission.

The 1990s will bring forth a modern renaissance in the visual arts, poetry, dance, theatre and music throughout the de-veloped world. It will be in stark contrast with the recent industrial era, where the military was the model and sport was the metaphor. Now we are shifting from sport to the arts.

In the United States business will fund the start of that historic shift. Already the leading US arts patron (corporations) are beginning to abandon sports and turn to the arts to define their image, to help market products. Opera has replaced rock music in automobile ads. Among sophisticated consumers, corpora-tions can win more prestige by supporting the arts than by hawking products with down-market TV jingles which today's sophisticated consumers resent.

This renaissance is not confined to kingdoms like New York, Paris, and Tokyo; it is flourishing in small and medium-size cities, suburbs, and rural areas. Attendance at the Alabama

Shakespeare Festival in Montgomery, Alabama, for example, has grown from 3000 in 1972 to more than 300,000 in 1989. So widespread is America's arts boom that business and job opportunities in artistic fields are expanding dramatically—from arts telemarketing to corporate art consulting.

Even cuts in federal arts funding, painful by most accounts, have had a paradoxically strengthening effect, pressing corporations into service and forcing arts organizations to become more sophisticated about marketing and generating new revenue sources. The result: a stronger arts community, freer to set its own agenda, more independent of government or even foundation funding.

TODAY'S ARTS REVIVAL

From the Great White Way to Anytown, USA

The American-led arts renaissance has started just as America's sports crazes of yesterday reach the TV screens of the world. Try this statistic on your favourite American sports fan, or favourite British disparager of American culture (who likes to forget about British football hooligans):

New York's Broadway Theatre at Broadway and Fifty-Third Street sells more tickets than either the Giants or the Jets combined.

Broadway's total 1988–89 season was the biggest in history. Eight million theatre goers paid out $262 million, a 25.4 per cent increase over the 1986–87 season, according to George Wachtel of the League of American Theatres and Producers. This is enormously good news to those who write plays in English, such as Britons and Australians. It is good for all foreign, as well as American, composers.

Typically half of all ticket sales are for one of the big British musicals—*Phantom of the Opera*, *Les Misérables*, *Cats*, *Starlight Express*, or *Me and My Girl*—says the trade paper *Variety*. Each new hit outsold the previous record holder. *Phantom* opened with $19 million in advance sales, replacing *Les Misérables* with $11 million. *Cats*, the previous record holder, is staged by fourteen companies worldwide and grosses $2 million a week—just in the United States.

And the brightest new lights are not on Broadway; 90 per cent of American theatre is outside New York, according to a special report on regional theatre in *Town & Country* magazine. Two hundred professional theatres operate in 155 cities across the country. In Minneapolis and St Paul alone there are twenty-four legitimate theatres. From Portland, Maine, to Ashland, Oregon, Sarasota, Florida, and Anchorage, Alaska, local theatre is prospering. In 1988 attendance and box-office income broke records at forty-five theatres studied by the Theatre Communications Group.

'American theatre is more thrilling, stronger, greater than ever,' says Gary Sinise, of Chicago's Steppenwolf Company. 'New York was where theatre was 40 years ago. Now it's everywhere.'

South California's San Diego is a big theatre town. Its Old Globe Theatre has 50,000 season subscribers—nearly double the members of any other theatre in the United States. Production costs in San Diego are 30 to 40 per cent those of Broadway. The Globe's huge hit *Into the Woods* cost only 10 to 15 per cent of what a Broadway première would cost.

The *Marriage of Figaro* Syndrome

In the US, over half a million new opera buffs—seduced by music, history, drama, glorious costumes, and imaginative sets —are being born each season. And audiences have tripled in just over a decade and a half: The 1987–88 season reached an astounding 17.7 million, compared with 6 million in 1970–71, says the Central Opera Service. Opera's success is remarkable when you consider that its cost must cover not just an orchestra but singers, costumes, and expensive sets.

Three-quarters of the 113 professional opera companies in North, Central, and South America were founded after 1965, many in the 1980s. Opera is shedding its old-fashioned image and becoming accessible to a wider audience. Thanks go in part to 'surtitles', which appear above the stage offering a running translation of foreign-language operas. John Adams's *Nixon in China* demonstrates how the centuries-old format can be revitalized for audiences of the 21st century. In the 1987–88 US season, there were 141 premières, compared with only 16 during the 1974–1975 season.

It is no longer necessary to trudge to a major city for a night at the opera. Regional operas appear in veterans' and civic auditoriums, at performing arts centres and arts festivals. Some 654 companies have budgets under $100,000.

The Springfield (Missouri) Regional Opera performs in Fantastic Caverns. 'Opera in a Cave', as it was billed, seated 712 opera lovers.

Symphony Orchestras

Most arts lovers believe that US symphony orchestras are in desperate financial straits. Two-thirds of the top orchestras ended the 1986 season with deficits.

The next year, with better management and marketing, the picture was brighter. The 1986 and 1987 seasons were the biggest in history. More than 25 million symphony goers, attended performances at the top 280 orchestras. Many more attended performances by more than 500 smaller symphonies. Although attendance at the biggest orchestras dropped off somewhat during the 1987–1988 season, local and regional groups are thriving.

Regional orchestras grew from sixteen in 1975 to 57 in 1989. Chamber music is undergoing the biggest boom of all: from 393 groups in 1985 to 578 in 1989.

Many of the most striking performances are in the open air:

- The Hollywood Bowl sold 761,000 tickets in 1988, up more than 100,000 since 1982. Profit offset the Los Angeles Philharmonic's season deficit.
- The Chicago Symphony draws 20,000 for a single concert at the Ravinia Festival in the suburb of Highland Park.
- The Boston Symphony's Tanglewood Music Festival in the Berkshire Mountains has over the years attracted more than 10 million music lovers.
- Caribana, Toronto's Caribbean festival, attracts 600,000 spectators a year.

Single-composer festivals attract a huge following: from the OK Mozart International Festival in Oklahoma and New York's

Mostly Mozart Festival to the Carmel, California, Bach Festival and Anchorage, Alaska, Basically Bach Festival.

Dance: In Search of a New Partner

Professional dance in the United States has grown 700 per cent since 1972, according to Donald A. Moore, executive director of Dance/USA.

Dance companies and host cities are pioneering an exciting new way for communities to bring fine arts to their people. Cities that cannot afford a full-time ballet or dance company are sharing sponsorship with another city. The Cincinnati Ballet became the Cincinnati/New Orleans Ballet. New York's Joffrey Ballet created a second home in Los Angeles. Dancers from the Tampa Ballet and Denver's Colorado Ballet divide their time between the two cities. The Cleveland–San Jose Ballet was born when Cleveland was seeking a partner city to increase its ballet audience and income. San Jose chose to import a quality developed company rather than undertake the long, costly process of growing a dance troupe. Business helped a lot: E. F. Hutton gave $250,000, and Apple Computer founder Steven Wozniak contributed $250,000.

These new arrangements could also work for theatre troupes, chamber orchestras, even opera companies.

All totalled, twelve cities are now building sister-city arrangements for dance companies.

Publish or Perish

·In 1988, 55,483 new book titles and editions were published in the United States, according to *Publishers Weekly*, compared with about 41,000 in 1977. In 1988 US publishers sold $15 billion worth of books, compared with $13 billion in 1987.

Not all of this is literature, but book readers are increasing fastest among the young.

One in five American adults buys at least 1 book a week. People eighteen to thirty-four years old buy 2.6 books a week.

Bookstores in shopping malls make it is easier to buy a book today than it was twenty years ago. The market for commercial best-sellers—where the chains make their money—is expanding all the time.

'We are going into the suburbs that have never had a bookstore and giving people an opportunity to buy,' says Dara Tyson, manager of public relations for Waldenbooks, whose more than 1100 US stores are mostly in suburban malls.

'Smaller publishers—with sales under $15 million a year —experienced their fastest sales growth of the decade in 1987 . . . an increase of 14.5 per cent over 1986,' reported *Publishers Weekly*.

Publishers have little trouble finding would-be authors today and will have even less tomorrow. More than 200 American institutions offer Master of Fine Arts degrees or doctorates, compared with a dozen twelve years ago. And this is a market that everybody writing in English will be trying to sell to— because authorship itself is fun.

THE ART BOOM

Van Gogh's 'Sunflowers' fetched $39.9 million at auction, three times the previous record. It was soon upstaged by his 'Irises', which brought $53.9 million.

These icons of today's renaissance are only one facet of the US art boom of the 1980s. The boom also bolstered a burgeoning market for quality prints and lesser-known artists.

'We've been a beneficiary of the trickle-down theory,' says Don Austin, founder of Chicago area-based Austin Galleries, a group of thirteen stores selling signed and numbered limited-edition prints. 'As art in the auction houses has expanded, we have felt the growing market. Twenty-three years ago there was no market for limited edition prints. Now they make up eighty per cent of our sales.'

'There are more people collecting art today as a percentage of the population than ever before, even during the Renaissance,' says economist and art historian Leslie Singer.

Blockbuster Museum Shows

Most of us cannot afford the great masters. But in record numbers we are moved by the beauty of their masterpieces. In

59

just twenty years attendance at US museums doubled from 200 million in 1965 to 391 million in 1984. By 1987 it reached 500 million, says Edward Able, executive director of the American Association of Museums. Attendance continued to grow in 1988 and 1989.

On a typical Saturday, hundreds of thousands of Americans browse in galleries or at art fairs. The Minneapolis-St Paul area has more than 30 art galleries.

'Gallery hopping is my favourite way to spend a Saturday afternoon,' says Los Angeles City Councilman Joel Wachs, who estimates he spends a quarter of his salary on artworks. 'It's more than relaxing; looking at art is one of the things that give me a lot of fulfillment.'

LA Art

Nurtured by the thriving entertainment industry—not to mention aerospace, insurance, banking, and oil—the energy of the Los Angeles art scene now seems well-set to rival New York's. 'Los Angeles is the most promising new art market in the country,' says Arnold Glimcher, president of the Pace Gallery in New York.

Fifteen major museums or galleries have been built in California since 1962. They include architect Arata Isozaki's $23 million Museum of Contemporary Art and the $35 million Robert O. Anderson Building at the County Museum. 'Museums used to be musty places for musing alone. Today we have a better-educated audience that wants something more than backpacking on the weekend,' says the County Museum's Earl Powell.

An impoverished curator's dream, the J. Paul Getty Art Museum Centre, to open in 1992, was required (because of US tax laws) to spend $2.4 million *a week* on acquisitions and programmes in 1986. That's nothing: *Art and Antiques* magazine predicted in December 1986 that by the year 2000 the endowment will have swelled to $10 billion, which would mean that the museum would have to spend close to $2 million *each weekday*.

A Booming Art Market

'Ours is an art-struck age,' writes Thomas Hoving, editor of *Connoisseur* and former director of the Metropolitan Museum of Art. 'Our civilization equates art with immortality.'

Executives at Sotheby's and Christie's must be feeling pretty immortal. In 1987 the two leading art auction houses broke the $1 billion barrier. In the 1988–1989 season the combined sales of the two giants exceeded $4 billion. This is higher than the GNP of Jamaica, and all countries smaller than that.

According to Sotheby's new Art Index, prices of Impressionist art increased 73.6 per cent and of modern paintings (1900 to 1950) 50.3 per cent in 1988. The Standard & Poors 500 stock index rose a mere 17 per cent. How many are investing in art as just another financial instrument?

The Museum Boom

During the 1980s new museums have opened in almost every major US city from Dallas, Atlanta and Miami to San Antonio and Portland. There are new wings in Boston, Baltimore, Akron, Minneapolis, and San Jose.

There was expansion in more than fifty big US museums and this proved to be something that people are willing to pay for. In 1986 the voters of Seattle approved an eight-year property tax to raise $29.6 million for a new museum to open in 1990. Exhibit space will triple.

Europe's Museum Boom

The museum boom is part of the renaissance that is proceeding as fast in other rich countries as well as the US. Since 1960, Japan has built more than 200 new museums. At one stage in the 1980s, Thatcher's Britain was opening a new museum every eighteen days. France has led Europe in building the grandest new museums, but West Germany has built the most—300 new West German museums in the past ten years.

Cologne already has eight museums; it has continued to spend half as much locally on the arts as the federal government spends on the whole country. Frankfurt spends even more.

The French tradition breathes new life into old buildings by turning them into museums. The Louvre was a royal palace; the Picasso Museum, a stately mansion. The City of Science and Industry at La Villette was built on the site of the old Paris slaughterhouse.

Now has come the new Musée d'Orsay which was once a magnificent train station built for the Paris Exhibition of 1900.

The Musée d'Orsay rivals the Centre Pompidou, with its wildly coloured exterior pipes and air vents, as the architectural wonder the locals love to hate (just as they at first detested the Eiffel Tower). But the Musée d'Orsay is popular with foreigners —most American critics and historians loved it—and 4 million people visited it in its first year. This has prospered despite the fact that Paris has so many other attractions.

ECONOMICS OF THE MODERN RENAISSANCE

France has poured public money into its arts and may have concentrated too many of them in Paris and on tourists. In America there have been cuts in federal arts funding during the Reagan years. Many of those Reagan cuts have had a paradoxically invigorating effect. They have pressed big American corporations into helping to increase the artistic attractions of 'our town'. And they have forced arts organizations to become more sophisticated about marketing, and about generating new revenue sources. The result: a stronger arts community, freer to set its own agenda, more independent of government or even foundation funding, and less tied to thinking of the arts as being part of the welfare state.

When insurance company president Les Disharoon took on the monumental volunteer task of helping the Baltimore Symphony build a $40 million endowment in only twenty-two months, he explained to the sixty-seven business groups he addressed that more people in Maryland (350,000) heard the orchestra than had attended Baltimore Colts football games. The Colts have since moved to Indianapolis, a decidedly sports-minded town.

'You've got to dig in and find the facts that make people know a symphony is as critical as an airport or pro baseball team to the whole pattern of lifestyle that makes people want to come and live in a city,' says Disharoon.

Among the 'facts':

- Cleveland's Playhouse Square Centre, home to three theatres, generates an estimated $35 million boost into the downtown economy.

- A Los Angeles Chamber of Commerce study showed the economic impact of the arts on LA totalled more than $5 billion a year.
- In Britain the arts are a $17 billion a year industry, the same size as the British automotive industry. More than a quarter of the total earnings from tourism are directly attributable to the arts.

The advance of telecommunications means that more and more sophisticated people have a freer choice of where to work. To attract them, communities must pay more attention to symphonies, opera, art, and ballet, says David L. Birch, the director of MIT's Programme on Neighbourhood and Regional Changes. In a recent poll in the US, 92 per cent of the respondants said the arts were important to the quality of life in their communities.

The Mobil Oil Corporation, whose advertisements urge corporations to support the arts, believes the arts spark economic development, encourage commercial and residential real estate projects, foster tourism, and attract new business.

Summer Festivals

Blockbuster museum shows and summer festivals increase revenues for restaurants, hotels, retailers, and parking facilities —all direct contributions to the local economy.

The 'Van Gogh in Arles' exhibition at the Metropolitan Museum of Art in New York City attracted 252,604 out-of-towners, who spent $223 million on hotels, restaurants, entertainment, transportation, and shopping. Nobody even counted what 200,000 Van Gogh fans from New York itself spent.

If a big museum show is not scheduled to pass through your town, you might generate as much revenue starting a festival. One hundred thousand visitors spend about $80 million in Edinburgh during the city's annual three-week festival.

An export business has started in festivals. At the Spoleto USA Festival in Charleston, South Carolina, 80,000 music and art lovers have contributed about $300 million to South Carolina's economy over the past ten years. The festival, founded by Gian Carlo Menotti, is the second home of the annual arts celebration of Spoleto, Italy, and has given birth to more than a dozen new arts organizations in Charleston.

The world's biggest museum of contemporary art, 500,000 square feet, will not be in Paris, New York, or Tokyo, but in North Adams, Massachusetts.

In a blue-collar town three hours west of Boston, an abandoned twenty-eight building factory complex will be transformed into a $50 million artistic landmark known as the Massachusetts Museum of Contemporary Art, or Mass MoCA. The state voted a $35 million bond issue, and $15 million must still be raised. The new museum is expected to do wonders for slumping real estate prices.

Philanthropy is a great boost to the local arts scene in the US, especially in places to which rich men retire. But most communities must build arts institutions the old-fashioned way, with human capital, talent, coalition building, and sweat equity.

Sherman County, Kansas, an agricultural community with a population of only 7000 transformed the vacant Carnegie Library in Goodland, Kansas, into the Goodland Carnegie Arts Centre in a mere eight months. The secret—garage sales, bake sales, community auctions, benefit shows, progressive dinners, and voluntarily contributed labour. In the end the Goodland Arts Council raised $75,000 and brought the arts to farm country.

Small-time arts entrepreneurs in big cities know the meaning of sweat equity, too. The dream of two Florida women, Faith Atlass and Helene Pancoast, was realized when Miami's old Flowers Bakery in a noisy inner-city neighbourhood was transformed into a 2.2-acre cluster of seventy artists' studios, galleries, classrooms, and meeting rooms now known as the Bakehouse Art complex. American Bakeries contributed much of the $250,000 facility, while the founders raised $300,000 from the city and county. A Rockefeller Foundation study had projected Dade County would have 18,000 artists by 1990. Now the county is ready.

New Careers and Business Opportunities in the Arts

Time was you prayed your child would not become an artist, a musician, or an actor. But in the US the arts boom has opened up a wealth of new career opportunities. Between regional orchestras and local acting troupes, young people have a better chance to make a living (albeit modest) doing what they love.

- 'The number of painters, authors, and dancers in the US has increased some 80 per cent over the past decade —three times faster than the growth rate for all occupations and well above the growth rate for other professionals,' writes University of Maryland sociologist John P. Robinson in *American Demographics*.
- Between 1960 and 1980 the US work force increased 43 per cent, while the number of artists, writers, and entertainers shot up 144 per cent.
- Even during the 1980s, when the United States created new jobs at an unparalleled pace—16 million between 1983 and 1988—jobs in artistic careers outpaced overall job growth.

There are today 1.5 million Americans in arts occupations, according to the Census Bureau. They work as actors, directors, announcers, architects, authors, dancers, designers, musicians, composers, painters, sculptors, craft artists, artist printmakers, photographers, and higher-education instructors of art, drama, and music. And that doesn't count people in art-related fields: poster and frame shop owners and employees, people in arts management, classical music sales and media people, arts entrepreneurs, public television employees, agents and promoters, curators, art dealers, or art consultants.

'More and more corporations are hiring a person to oversee the corporate art collection,' said Judith A. Jedlicka, president of the US Business Committee for the Arts. Some corporate art consultants are employed directly by companies; other earn commissions acting as middlemen for artists and galleries.

New York's Judith Selkowitz is an art consultant, advising firms on the purchase of everything from 'a few posters for the back office. to paintings and sculpture for fifty-storey skyscrapers'. Tamara Thomas, of Fine Arts Services, of Los Angeles, acquires $3 million of art a year for banks, real estate developers, law firms, and utilities.

Today's arts revival is stimulating new business opportunities in artistic niches.

With all those paintings bought for record prices at Sotheby's and even at your local gallery, someone has to transport the precious stuff. Boston-based Fine Art Express places art in custom-designed boxes, insures it, and sends it on its way in temperature-controlled trucks with burglar alarms.

Dansource, a Dallas-based placement service founded by Tauna Hunter and Michael Gleason, links dancers and companies nation-wide. Dancers pay a $100 fee to have the firm forward their curriculum vitae and videos to interested dance companies.

Have you ever seen a painting that would be perfect above your sofa, only to learn the museum shop didn't stock a reproduction? Print Finders, a New York-based mail order service, will locate the reproduction, frame it, and ship it out. Says founder Diane Moore: 'If it exists, we'll find it'.

As the arts become more important in society, individuals, corporations, cities, and towns will increasingly make their decisions under the influence of the images, personalities, and lifestyles of the arts.

Whether you are a student, an account executive, a real estate developer, or a small business owner, this millennial megatrend will change the way you plan your career, craft your advertising campaign, and build your next project.

SELF-RELIANCE: GROUNDING THE RENAISSANCE

The American arts boom of the 1980s surged forth just as every arts-lover said that the 'Reagan cuts' would cause it to collapse.

The US federal government allocated $167.7 million to the arts in 1988. In 1988 the US government spent $1143 per person on defence, $74 on education and 70 cents on the arts. Most of the rescue has come from the biggest art patrons in history— American business. Though some arts lovers find it appalling, they have to admit American government parsimony has roused American corporations to contribute $1 billion a year to the arts—compared with only $22 million in the Great Society year of 1967, a forty-five-fold increase.

In general, American arts organizations generate $20 in additional funding for every $3 of government subsidy. The

European art organizations will boom hugely when they learn how to imitate this. Major opera companies in France, West Germany, Austria, and Scandinavia still receive 70 to 85 per cent of income from their governments. Britain's Royal Opera receives about 46 per cent. New York's Metropolitan Opera gets a mere 3 per cent from the federal government.

The Arts Entrepreneur

In the United States the arts have had to become more businesslike, more innovative in how they attract and generate income. They have learned to market 'products', and dicovered new 'products' to sell. Examples:

- Membership schemes: through more sophisticated membership campaigns, the San Francisco Museum of Modern Art increased membership from 3500 in 1974 to some 20,000 today. Public service television is financing more of itself by similar membership campaigns plugged on screen. There are 'friends of the symphony' groups everywhere in the US.
- Rent a museum: museums play an expanded role as places of public gathering: 'In the past, religious buildings had a strong role in the society. Now art is coming to take over the position where the gods are no more,' says Arata Isozaki, architect of the Museum of Contemporary Art in Los Angeles. 'Art is something like the religious act. Even the activity of raising funds and collecting art for the museum is like the religious activity of the past.'

What is a more beautiful setting for your organization's next gala affair than an art museum with high ceilings and $1 billion worth of paintings on the wall? For that matter, what about a class reunion or wedding reception?

- Use your space: The Kennedy Centre in Washington, DC, rents parking spaces to tourists by the day and commuters by the month. The California Museum of Science and Industry in Los Angeles is one of the few museums to offer space to a McDonald's restaurant in exchange for a cut of profits.
- Museum shops: New York's Metropolitan Museum of

Art's museum store sold $53 million worth of goods in 1988, up from about $7 million in 1975. Net 1988 profit was $9.2 million, a huge chunk of the museum's operating revenue. More than half the sales were from mail-order business. In addition to the general catalogue, there is a 'poster and presents' catalogue and one just for children.

The Smithsonian museums in Washington, DC, earned $46 million in 1988 retail revenue, making them one of the city's leading retailers. The museum shops generated $1000 per square foot compared with only $200 for most department stores.

Traditional taxpaying retailers might begrudge museum shops their tax-exempt status. But if the government chooses not to fund the arts directly, it seems fair to give them a little boost by guaranteeing that tax exemption.

During the Renoir show at the Boston Museum of Fine Arts, the museum shop sold $8.3 million worth of T-shirts, sweat shirts, exhibition catalogues, posters, and appointment calendars. At $2 apiece Renoir shopping bags grossed $100,000.

Orchestras Join in the Tune

Encouraged by the museums' success, orchestras are trying every marketing tactic in the book—parties, street fairs, free concerts, auctions, and T-shirts. The Buffalo Philharmonic went after the business audience by sending a string quartet to play in offices. Others go for younger audiences with popular music programmes. On 'Jeans Night' at the St Louis and the Phoenix Symphony, the 'no tie' dress code is strictly enforced.

'We're doing the kind of things sports teams did ten years ago,' said Louis G. Spisto, when he was director of marketing at the Pittsburgh Symphony. 'Nothing is sacred to me. We've gotten away from traditional orchestra marketing. It's like soap.'

In the nothing-is-sacred department the Pittsburgh Symphony presents 'The Smart Set', the orchestra's version of a singles gathering for young professionals. The underlying objective: to generate new audiences and revenues.

'Telemarketing is the technique for the 80s,' claims Robert Schlosser, audience development director at the Mark Taper Forum in Los Angeles. 'Last year, we doubled new subscribers, and our telemarketing response is five times greater than our direct-mail efforts. The savings in both time and money are extraordinary.'

When the Arena Stage in Washington, DC, realized it was not attracting young people to its subscriber lists, it revamped its sales procedures to allow young people (who dislike buying advance tickets by mail) to phone in for seats, often at the last minute. The plan worked. Now 90 per cent of Arena's single tickets are sold by phone.

Lincoln Centre thanked major contributors in full-page advertisement in The *New York Times Magazine* and other publications. Sixteen corporate donors gave $100,000 or more, eleven between $50,000 and $100,000, and scores gave $1000 to $49,000.

FROM BASEBALL TO BALLET

Sometime in the millennial 1990s the arts will replace sports as society's dominant leisure activity.

In the US, by one measure they already have: A landmark 1988 report by the National Endowment for the Arts calculated Americans now spend $3.7 billion a year attending arts events, compared with $2.8 billion for sports events. Between 1983 and 1987 arts spending increased 21 per cent, while sports expenditures decreased 2 per cent. Just twenty years ago people spent twice as much on sports as on the arts.

In less than a generation Americans have reversed their leisure spending habits.

It seems clear that free-market spending on arts will eventually be double that on spectator sports.

This dramatic change will be reflected around the world, because it parallels the shift from an industrial to an information society. It has been accelerated by the coming of age of the baby boomers (a well-educated and consequently arts-loving generation) and by the fact that women now make and spend more of the family's leisure-time money.

The arts and sports will engage in an increasingly competitive battle for people's leisure time and dollars.

Earlier we noted that a New York theatre sells more tickets than the Giants or the Jets combined. The same trend is reflected across the nation.

In once sports-mad Boston—home of the Celtics, Red Sox, and Bruins—*twice* as many people now go to the theatre, museums, or art shows as attend sports events. In the Washington, DC, area the number one leisure activity is visiting museums or galleries, which attracted 55.3 per cent of the population last year. The four major professional sports teams —the Redskins, Bullets, Capitals, and Orioles—each brought in between 13 and 16.4 per cent of the population. Sports hoopla notwithstanding, people in Washington were *three to four times* as likely to have looked at some art instead.

When sports and the arts are compared, arts attendance is now winning—and by a huge margin. But society is only beginning to acknowledge this revolutionary megatrend and its implications. In particular:

Corporations are bound to switch their sponsorship and advertising from sports events to the arts.

So greatly has corporate arts support increased in the US in the 1980s that it was once predicted it would reach $1 billion by 1990. Instead, it passed the $1 billion benchmark in 1988.

This still pales in comparison with corporate spending on sports. Although figures are almost impossible to come by (sports get so much money it is hard to count), no one would be surprised if business spent $5 billion a year on sports sponsorships, endorsements, advertising. Many would put it a lot higher. This figure leaves museum directors and symphony fund raisers with their mouths wide open.

Although people spend more time and money on the arts, corporations still spend billions more on sports. Why?

Much of it is simply lag time. Most companies have not recognized the *existence* of an arts revival, let alone analysed how it is changing leisure time and spending patterns. They have not done the cost/benefit analysis that demonstrates the arts are a terrific bargain.

The Arts are a Cut-rate Ticket to a Well-to-Do Audience

The arts attract consumers with high disposable incomes. College graduates, professionals, and other high-income group members are far more likely to attend arts events than other Americans, writes sociologist John Robinson. Yet sponsoring the arts is inexpensive advertising, often a best buy for the money, with the largest exposure.

'An art exhibition has longer staying power than a sports event. Exhibits run for six to eight weeks and the corporate name is out there the entire time,' says Carol F. Palm, manager of cultural programmes at United Technologies.

The arts provide entry to a market that puzzles advertisers —women. Advertising executives are struggling to reach today's woman, who makes 80 per cent of health care decisions and buys one half of all new cars, compared with 20 per cent fifteen years ago. She is not the traditional housewife, not superwoman, and certainly not drinking beer with the guys after the game.

Women are arts fans. They attend ballet 100 per cent more than men, musical theatre 25 per cent more, and the symphony 27 per cent more than men, according to a study by the University of Maryland's John Robinson. No wonder the Ford Motor Company is also using opera in its ads for the Scorpion.

Arts and TV

The TV has yet to discover its calling to bring the arts and other spiritualizing fare to people who are starved for quality. Millions of better-off American viewers a week automatically switch past the sitcoms to the offerings on the 189-member stations of public television. Telecasts of *Live from Lincoln Center* and *Live from the Met* reach more than 100 million annually. The Corporation for Public Broadcasting receives $470 million a year in contributions.

Opera radio audiences are growing at an impressive rate. The Metropolitan Opera reaches an estimated audience of 140 million on radio. The 1985–86 season of Chicago's Lyric Opera reached 40 million. Two years later the audience had reached 45 million. Louisville's Kentucky Opera radio audience nearly doubled in two years from 40,000 to 75,000 in the 1987–88 season.

It is no great surprise that there is no opera on US network television. The objective of the mass media, after all, is to appeal to as *large* an audience as possible. Network TV is a product of the industrial society and has built an impressive business transporting sports and comedy to the 'masses'. That was good enough until the early 1980s, when the big three networks began losing their audiences to the increasing options of cable.

By the mid-1980s American advertisers had cut commitments to the three big networks, having discovered that those people who still watch network TV tend to be older, to have lower incomes and less education than cable audiences—who, a Saatchi & Saatchi survey reported, tend to be younger and more upscale and growing the fastest. More than half of all households already have cable. By 1993 cable will reach 60 per cent. Cable advertising revenue increased from $862 million in 1987 to $1.3 billion in 1989 and is projected to reach $2.8 billion in 1995, according to New York's Cable Advertising Bureau.

'We believe that cable television will become the primary source for the distribution of entertainment in the United States,' says Steven J. Ross, chairman of Warner Communications.

US arts lovers know where to find the programming they favour. The Arts & Entertainment (A&E) network offers drama, live performances, and documentaries. It began in 1984 with 800 cable system subscribers, an audience of 9 million, and a single advertiser. In 1988 A&E boasted 350 advertisers, including Ford, Toyota, and AT&T.

'These advertisers come to us because we deliver the demographics they are looking for,' says A&E network CEO Nicholas Davatzes. A&E viewers are older (thirty-five to fifty-five), well educated (half are college grads), and well-to-do. Most have incomes between $30,000 and $75,000 a year. Today the channel reaches 38 million households and more than 3000 cable systems.

You can watch the arts on public and cable television, but will you ever get theatre or the symphony on the network?

'Most Americans believe that commercial television is not carrying enough arts programming,' concluded the Louis Harris poll on *Americans and the Arts V*. 'Commercial television could attract larger audiences by offering more arts presentations.'

From Broadcasting to Narrowcasting

For arts lovers, however, some of the best news is not on television at all. It is in the shift from broadcasting to the ultimates in narrowcasting. Videocassettes, tape decks in automobiles,

Walkman devices, and home CD players put the power of the airwaves in one's own hands. Media analyst Paul Kagan Associates says 62 per cent of households have VCRs and predicts that by the year 2000 the percentage will approach 100.

With so little arts programming in the major media, millions of fans are building sophisticated home libraries and programming their own arts agendas. When CDs first appeared, classical music sales soared to unprecedented levels, according to *Billboard* magazine. Although they have levelled off somewhat, sales continue to grow 5 to 10 per cent annually, according to New York's J&R Music World, the 1988 Retailer of the Year.

In 1988, 3 billion videocassettes were rented in the US, up from 700 million in 1984, according to Paul Kagan Associates.

'Fine arts lovers have kept the cultural video segment growing 15 to 20 per cent a year, as rapidly as the overall market,' says Tom Adams of Kagan Associates.

Kultur Video, in West Long Branch, New Jersey, America's leading supplier of ballet, opera, and classical music videos, grew 1000 per cent between 1983 and 1987, making the firm number 277 on the INC magazine 500 fastest-growing small businesses. Sales doubled between 1987 and 1988. In 1986 Kultur Video offered 60 titles; by 1989 the figure had increased to more than 155, including performances by Maria Callas and Mikhail Baryshnikov and classics such as Giselle and Don Giovanni.

Like any future-oriented company, this video supplier is thinking international. It has just landed an exclusive first rights contract with the Soviet Union for programms in opera and ballet from the Kirov and Bolshoi.

Advertising Images

Corporations are turning toward the images and sounds of the arts and reconsidering the use of sports to promote products. For sixteen years the Miller Brewing Company has used athletes in macho settings to sell Miller Lite, the best-selling light beer in the United States and the number two beer of any type. Miller made headlines in *Advertising Age* when it considered putting all those athletes on the bench. 'Miller Brewing Co will phase out the use of ex-athletes and sports-related celebrities', read a

December 1988 story in *Ad Age*. Miller later backed away from those plans.

Brewers might be the last to consider switching to opera singers to woo customers, but practically everybody else is. Advertising agencies, increasingly filled with and headed by women, are turning to classical themes to sell products.

Opera featured prominently in the hit films Moonstruck and Fatal Attraction. Within a couple of months during 1988, the number of advertisements using opera music on American TV networks rose from nil to ten.

Tott's champagne hired opera star Kiri Te Kanawa to sing Puccini's *Gianni Schicchi*. A highbrow brew like champagne deserves music to match. British Airways and Bolla wine have used opera to attempt to link their products with a quality image.

But—hold your breathe—so has Cheer, one of America's most advertised detergents. Forget 'ring around the collar'. Today's housewife gets Mozart's *Don Giovanni* and *The Magic Flute*. 'There's something deep about the music,' says Gerry Miller of the Leo Burnett USA agency, who created the Cheer campaign. 'Even if you don't listen to opera, it gets you.' That is partly because it sounds so different, whereas the sports themes are so commonplace. TV coverage of sports events seems almost littered with beer commercials.

In consequence, pro athletes 'face a tightening market for national endorsements', according to a story by Brian Moran in *Advertising Age* which fears that the association of athletes with drug use, sexual misconduct, and fierce contract battles has made athletes less desirable to advertisers.

They are turning to something more like the arts instead.

'The arts are a natural, inevitable ally for any successful business,' says Rawleigh Warner, Jr, Mobil Corporation's former chairman of the board and CEO. 'We sense in the arts that same search for an ideal of quality and excellence that imbues many of our business decisions.'

'Art and technology seem to go together,' says United Technologies's Carol Palm. 'Both are expressions of new ideas. Both stand for quality.'

A Turning Point

The 1980s marked an extraordinary turning point for the arts. In 1980 contributions to the arts, culture, and humanities from US corporations, foundations, and individuals totalled $3.15 billion. By 1988 that figure at $6.41 billion had nearly doubled—in less than a decade.

Corporate dollars have flowed into the arts at a pace no one could have anticipated a few years earlier.

In 1985 the National Gallery of Art received $2.7 million from corporations in support of eight exhibitions. Just three years later that figure jumped to $6.3 million for twelve shows. Sponsorship came from companies such as IBM, Ford, Pacific Telesis, AT&T, GTE, Du Pont, and Southwestern Bell.

The 1990s: From Sports to the Arts

In the 1990s, corporate sponsorship of sports will plateau, while arts sponsorship continues to grow dramatically. This will happen in Europe and the richer nations of the Pacific Rim, as well as in the US.

Those who are awaiting this flood of corporate money into the arts had better note, however, that it will be set on a decidedly commercial course—unsettling to some. Traditionally corporations have sponsored the arts as philanthropists, as some will doubtless continue to do. But the new arts funding push of the 1990s will focus mainly on the marketing and public relations value of the arts. Though some purists will find it distasteful, the result is that the arts boom will accelerate in step with big companies' desire to make more money. Among American companies already moving this way:

- American Express's Cause Related Marketing programme rewards customers for using the card by contributing to non-profit groups, often arts-related. American Express gave $3 million to the First New York International Festival in 1988. Cardholders could get tickets, a festival guide, and information through an AmEx 1-800 number.
- When Chase Manhattan underwrote the Guggenheim's 50th Anniversary Show, the bank's Visa, Master Card and cash card customers were admitted free. Chase waived Visa card fees for customers who renewed their membership at the Guggenheim.
- To launch the expensive Allante sports car, General Motors' Cadillac division called on New York's Affiliate

75

Artists to arrange sixteen private concerts at the homes of wealthy prominent people. An Allante was discreetly parked outside.

'We see a move away from the notion of pure philanthropy to a stance where you form an alliance with the arts to help meet your business goals as well as help the arts,' says Judith Jedlicka of the Business Committee for the Arts.

In the 1990s top corporate ranks will fill with more women arts fans and more men under forty-five who are less committed to the time-honoured alliance between business and sports. With these new leaders at the helm, companies will take a good hard look at what an arts dollar will buy. Statistical proof, showing consumers spend more time and money on the arts than sports, will accumulate. The results will be published everywhere from *Advertising Age* to *Working Woman*, from *The Financial Times* to advertising agencies' hand-outs.

Inside companies, people increasingly reach for the metaphors of the creative arts to describe business life. Work is 'creative'. Effective people are 'performers' or real virtuosos. The CEO is like the conductor of a symphony. Outside corporate walls the renaissance that has already brought record audiences to opera, ballet, and theatre will reach a lively pre-millennium pitch.

This new renaissance has started in the United States, during a period when federal government money for the arts was being cut. In the 1990s, it will spread as a megatrend across other rich countries, whether more taxpayers' money is put into the arts or not.

As sponsorship of the arts will look like being successful, politicians may get on the band wagon too.

3

The Emergence of Free-Market
Socialism

The transformation of socialism will become clearer during the 1990s. The century's last decade will be the stage for an extraordinary period of experimentation to salvage socialism, by giving that name to something entirely different.

The two principal players in this global drama are that odd couple Mikhail Gorbachev and Margaret Thatcher: Thatcher dismantling the welfare state; Gorbachev dismantling the command economy of the largest socialist state.

This chapter describes what is happening in Marxist socialist countries, principally the Soviet Union, China, and Eastern Europe. The rest of the story—the decline of the welfare state in Western Europe and the United States—will be considered in Chapter 5.

When we look back from the year 2010 or 2020, it will be plain for all to see that socialism, facing almost certain death, was radically transformed on the doorstep of the 21st century.

There are six main reasons for the demise of classical socialism:

1. **The global economy.** In a global economy no individual country—capitalist or Communist—can sustain a closed, self-sufficient economy. The relative efficiency of capitalist economies has made them better able to accommodate and regroup into a world economy. Any country that attempts to remain economically closed and

apart from the global game will be left hopelessly behind. Certainly President Gorbachev understands this—and is driven by it. It is precisely as if Ohio, let us say, had decided not to participate in the US economy, insisting on self-sufficiency. To be a part of the global economy, a country must be much more competitive than within a protected environment.

2. **Technology.** Telecommunications made the global economy possible in the first place; now that same technology is accelerating its development. Financial services, the most evolved sector of the global economy, have more to do with electronics than with finance or services, which have been with us a long time. What is new is high-tech telecommunications.

3. **The failure of centralization.** The lack of any successful centrally planned economies has finally been acknowledged. The Soviets, under Gorbachev, concede their command economy has been a disaster. The decentralized, entrepreneurial, market-driven model is everywhere more successful.

Socialism, which at one time looked as if it might take over the world, is now faced with a challenge: Change or perish.

4. **The high cost of welfare state-socialist schemes.** The cost of central government-supplied human services has caught up with almost all countries and overwhelmed many. Bankruptcy is on the minds of many social service ministers and prime ministers. The demographics we ignored for so long have now caught up with all of us. The ratio of working people to pensioners has declined dramatically since the end of World War II and will decline even more as the 1946–64 babyboomers pass sixty-five in 2011–29. People everywhere are blowing the whistle on growing public spending. Many of us will spend much of the last decade of this century asking the question: What should government do for those who cannot help themselves and how can government meet such obligations without bankrupting the treasury?

5. **The shift in the work force.** We all know there has been a worldwide decline in the number and importance of

the blue-collar working class, the basis for unions and socialist parties. The labour theory of value gave birth to socialism. But it is only the beginning of the end. The percentage of labour in manufactured goods is headed in the direction of zero. A new theory is needed.

6. **The new importance of the individual.** The very nature of an information economy shifts the focus away from the state to the individual. Unlike a widespread Orwellian-instructed view that computers would tighten the control of the state over individuals, we have learned that computers strengthen the power of individuals and weaken the power of the state.

At once, as we globalize our economies, individuals are becoming more powerful and more important than they were in the industrial era.

It is extraordinary to witness how fashionable it has become in the socialist world to invoke the primacy of the individual over the state, over the collective.

In the late 20th century the confluence and interplay of these six phenomena have forced the Soviet Union and its allies to consider an awesome dilemma: Either reinvent socialism for the 3rd millennium or face discarding it entirely. The great drama of the 1990s will be the struggle between these two options. It is not yet clear whether 2000 will see the disappearance of socialism or the development of a new hybrid form of socialism with market mechanisms.

We are now in a transitional period, when virtually all centrally planned economies are experimenting with a wide range of market mechanisms: privatizing the means of production and distribution; creating stock markets; decentralizing; allowing bankruptcy; letting markets set prices; deregulating.

The Socialist party's prime minister of France, Michel Rocard, calls himself a 'free-market Socialist'. Bob Hawke, the prime minister of Australia, sees himself as a 'market-driven Socialist'. The Labour government of neighbouring New Zealand has been more free market still. Spain's Socialist government of Prime Minister Felipe González has embraced an array of free-market mechanisms resulting in what has been called 'supply-side socialism'. One of Gorbachev's economic advisers, Abel Aganbegyan, says that humankind has created nothing that works better than the marketplace. Thus the changes taking place in the Soviet Union and in Eastern Europe that we all read about are happening all over the world.

Though it at first seems to be a contradiction in terms, an oxymoron, 'free-market socialism' is the transitional phase for socialist countries as they enter the 21st century.

The world is undergoing a profound shift from economies run by governments to economies run by markets.

GORBACHEV'S REVOLUTION

Nowhere is the reconceptualization of socialism more dramatic than in the Soviet Union. Led by Mikhail Gorbachev, it is nevertheless being pushed from behind by extraordinary global change.

Think about Gorbachev's situation when he took over (by a narrow five to four vote of the Politburo) in March 1985.

Looking east, he sees China. Huge Communist China, looking less Communist every day, was accelerating its free-market experimentation. As a former minister of agriculture, Gorbachev is aware that during the previous five years Chinese farmers have shown the greatest productivity gains anywhere in the world. It is clear to him that China's success came by its eliminating the collective farm system and instituting the beginnings of marketplace incentives. As Gorbachev watches, the Chinese have announced their 'cities' policy, moving the market incentives that worked on the farm to the factories of the cities.

What if China follows the path of the economic-booming 'Four Tigers'—South Korea, Singapore, Taiwan, and Hong Kong? What kind of boost will China get when joined by Hong Kong in 1997? And what of the possibility of Taiwan's eventually also joining China, as some young Chinese on both the mainland and Taiwan are now advocating? What would be the impact of a great, powerful Chinese economy on the Soviet Union? Especially if the Soviet Union continues to stagnate?

Looking west, Gorbachev sees Europe, a Europe that just the previous month (February 1985) announced that the twelve countries that make up the European Economic Community will become by the end of 1992 a single barrier-free market, the largest in the world. All in all, he cannot fail to see an accelerating global economy that will be extremely competitive, nor can he ignore an unmistakable future scenario: the Soviet Union falling farther and farther behind.

The Soviet Union is a 'superpower', yet what kind of superpower has a pathetic Third World-looking domestic economy, in which 25 per cent of its GNP is in the military and space sector, where manufactured products are of such poor quality that few are purchased outside its political orbit?

No wonder, when asked what his chances of successful reform were, Gorbachev said: 'It doesn't matter what our chances of success are, we have no choice.'

From the very beginning Gorbachev saw that *perestroika*—the reform and restructuring of the economy—would be impossible without *glasnost*—openness and criticism of the old ways. He has constantly emphasized that *perestroika* will not work without *glasnost*.

Tragic as the June 1989 Tiananmen Square massacre was, it may serve Gorbachev and other reformers in the Soviet Union and in Eastern Europe. It demonstrated for all the world to see what the reformers have been saying: you can't have successful economic reform, which everyone wants, without political reform, which many are resisting.

There can be no *perestroika* without individual liberties. That is the real revolution that has begun in the Soviet Union.

With it comes the balancing act between the need for economic advancement and the rush of political instability. Gorbachev will have to walk that high wire for a long time to come.

Entrepreneurship Welcome

In November 1986 the Supreme Soviet—the parliament— passed a law allowing for the first time in seventy years what was called 'individual enterprise'. For the first time a person could start his own business in three categories: restaurants, dressmaking, and auto repair. During the following year new categories were added. One year after the individual enterprises became legal, there were twenty-nine categories in which you could start your own business and 60,000 individual enterprises in the country. Today there are more than fifty categories, and more than 1.5 million private enterprises. Entrepreneurism is a huge growth industry in the Soviet Union today.

On New Year's Day 1988 state enterprises became subject to some of the same market considerations that apply to 'individual enterprise': profits, job performance, and decentralization. Wages are now based on job performance or an enterprise's profitability. For the first time workers not measuring up can be fired. The Law of State Enterprises, as it is called, is proceeding —slowly.

Bankruptcy

Under the new law successful enterprises are permitted to keep much of their profits, reinvesting them or increasing wages. Unprofitable enterprises will go bankrupt—a fresh idea in the Soviet Union.

The timetable is to free all production throughout the country by 1991. Most likely that schedule will not be met, but the direction is set.

The way industrial planning worked before this new economic accountability is almost incomprehensible to people in Western industrial democracies. Everything was decided in Moscow. Moscow decided on the yearly allotment of equipment and materials for *every* factory in the country and created a work plan for every factory. Moscow also established how many products would be produced each year in each factory. Even the payroll came from central planners in Moscow. No wonder it was often referred to as a command economy.

Threatening the Social Contract

Implicit in many of the changes in Gorbachev's Russia is the breaking of the social contract between the state and its citizens. This is a serious matter. The state guaranteed every citizen a (low-wage) job, subsidized housing, subsidized food, and free medical care. In return the citizen was supposed to keep his mouth shut, accepting the party and the state as absolute authority. Now Gorbachev is saying, 'Open your mouth, criticize, this is the era of *glasnost*. Take responsibility, change societal structures to allow personal initiative, this is the era of *perestroika*. And by the way, if you don't perform on your job, you will be fired.' This breaking of the old contract has been hard for many Soviets to take. Since the 1917 Revolution four generations have had guaranteed jobs for life—regardless of performance. ('We pretend to work, and they pretend to pay us', is the old Russian saying.) Now that is suddenly changing. Gorbachev is insistent on this. In June 1987 he said, 'It is particularly important that the actual pay of every worker be closely linked to his contribution to the end result and that no limit be set on it.'

Agricultural *Perestroika*

In 1988 Gorbachev began a revolutionary process to break up the Stalinist collective farm system. It called for a shift from massive state farms and collectives to small leasehold units. Extraordinarily, he called for the leasehold system to cover *all* of the agriculture sector. 'The idea,' he said, 'is that this path should be taken by the whole of agriculture, the entire agrarian sector.' Across the board, individual enterprise was to be encouraged to make the peasant farmer 'the master of his land'.

In March 1989 the Central Committee passed a resolution permitting groups of workers or families to lease land from the state farms or collectives for life, even to pass the land on to their children The lessees can choose their own crops and keep the profits.

The shift to leasehold farming is the greatest change by far since 1929, when Stalin began driving Russian peasants onto collective farms, liquidating millions by starvation and executions in the process. Peasants were forced to become 'day labourers' and were allowed only tiny plots for personal use. Not surprisingly, these tiny plots—amounting to only 3 per cent of the arable land—were what they really cared about. Nearly 70 per cent of the vegetables consumed in the Soviet Union were grown on this 3 per cent, nearly 40 per cent in value of Soviet food production. Meanwhile, on the collective farms, per acre productivity was about one-ninth of that on a similar American farm.

Leasing

Leasing has become the key idea in rationalizing the shift to market mechanisms.

In the early years under Gorbachev, a large question was how the Soviet Union was going to justify the economic experimentation that looked a lot like capitalism when one of its basic tenets was that the state must own all the means of production. Then Moscow discovered leasing (or perhaps rediscovered it; Lenin experimented with it, but Stalin wiped it all out by 1930), not only for farms but for factories and services as well. The idea is to lease the means of production to individuals or cooperatives for fifty to ninety years; in some cases the leases are to be renegotiated every seven or ten years. Technically the state continues to own the means of production, but those who have leased a factory could feel as if it were theirs. They pay a leasing fee to the state, and they keep their profits.

Many Soviet (presumably Marxist) economists are now asserting that there is no greater incentive than profit. One of Moscow's leading economists and adviser to Gorbachev, Pavel Bunich, also says that, 'the leasing system will become the basic system of socialism.' He projects that the ideal Soviet economy would be 40 per cent privately operated and 60 per cent politically. Some economists go further, calling for outright private ownership instead of leasing.

The workers and individuals who lease the farms and factories will be in charge of the destinies of those enterprises, a breathtaking shift from the centralized Stalinist command economy of the past. The leasing system is being put in place. Only time and nerve will tell how widespread it will become.

The Barriers to Gorbachev's Reforms

Gorbachev and his reforms are not, of course, universally supported. 'Gorbachev and the people around him have the support of most of the intelligentsia, and most of the people,' says Vadim Zagladin, assistant to Gorbachev in Gorbachev's capacity as president, 'but we have twenty million bureaucrats between us and the people who are fighting us tooth and nail.' The bureaucrats are loath to give up their special positions and perks.

Most members of the intelligentsia have been extraordinarily energized by the changes, by the new openness. An almost universal comment is: 'I never thought I would see this happen in my lifetime'. Some intellectuals are unsettled and grousing.

But they are a small minority. Aleksandr Gelman, one of Russia's most famous contemporary playwrights, has this to say, 'Some said they couldn't use their talent because they didn't have freedom. When they got freedom, it came to light that they didn't have talent. Now some of them are arguing against freedom.'

An interesting source of hostility to Gorbachev has been a backlash against *glasnost* about Stalin. Stalin's crimes and 'evilness' (that's the word many Soviets use) are now openly discussed in journals and on television. A whole generation of Russians is now being told that Stalin was not some kind of Marxist god but a genius of evil who committed horrendous crimes and set the country back immeasurably.

Vladislav Starkov, the editor of *Argument & Facts*, which has 20 million readers, says that after running a critical assessment of Stalin, he got thousands of letters, many of which he printed, attacking the series. Many in the Stalin generation naturally identified with Stalin and are now being told what a terrible person Stalin was. One woman wrote, 'You want to throw my whole life away'.

At a dramatic moment in the June 1988 party conference a worker proposed building a monument to Stalin's victims. It was a turning point at the conference. To deal with reforms, it recognized that it must deal with the past. Plans for the monument are going forward. Of the de-Stalinization of the Soviet Union, Aleksandr Gelman says, 'We change our memory as we change our future.' (Communism is the system in which the past cannot be predicted.)

The Role of China

As early as 1987, China watchers in Russia began saying openly that China's economic direction played a central role in determining the policies of *perestroika*.

China, says Sergei Stepanov of the Institute of Economics of the World Socialist System, 'is the only other socialist country where the economy and the task of reform are on a similar scale with ours [the USSR's]. For our purposes, that makes China our main foreign reform laboratory.'

There are several points to be considered in comparing Soviet Union and Chinese market experimentation:

- Part of the Chinese strategy has been to make more resources available for consumer goods by slashing military spending and production. But because the Chinese have more teenagers than the Russians (who have dispiritedly had a low birth rate for years), Deng always feared he might have to repress risings by students, who wanted to go much closer to freedom than he did.

- Both China and the Soviet Union see themselves as models for other socialist countries, albeit along different paths. The Chinese have allowed economic reform while retaining rigid political control, as evidenced in its repression of the 1989 student movement. Gorbachev is reforming economically while democratizing politically. Deng Xiaoping has always felt more frightened, taking 'two steps forward, one step backward'; Gorbachev has been more bold, trying to reform everything simultaneously.

- Despite Deng, China's economic liberalization is far more advanced, especially in agriculture, where Deng first abolished the collectives and returned to a family farm system. Food production and farmers' incomes have soared. China reformed agriculture first, putting food in everyone's stomach before moving on to other reforms. In the cities private food stands are everywhere, along with private restaurants, repair shops, and other businesses. Now factories may keep some of their profits, which can be used to increase salaries or modernize as managers see fit.

- China is not as encumbered with a purity of ideology as the Soviet Union, which as mentor to other socialist countries must ideologically justify every shift. Deng says that 'it doesn't matter whether a cat is black or white as long as it catches mice'. In the Soviet Union what has mattered most is the colour of the cat. Since communism did not take over the government of China until 1949, there are many who remember life before Mao Zedong and can therefore still mix the past with the present. In the Soviet Union no one remembers life before Lenin and Stalin.

- A few Chinese companies have issued shares, and there are the beginnings of a stock market in China, something the Soviets have only begun to think about and will probably adopt eventually.

- Capitalism existed in China before 1949, and for centuries the Chinese have been among the world's great traders. The tradition of enterprise was only partially developed under the Czar's feudal system in Russia and not at all under the Communist ideologies that followed.

- In 1988 China already had 20 million private entrepreneurs; the Soviets have only just made them legal, although they have always flourished in the black market sector.

- China had been involved in economic reform since 1978, when Deng came to power. Gorbachev has been in power since 1985.

'We are much more entrenched in conservatism than the Chinese were when they started to change,' says Fyodor Burlatsky, a former speech writer for Nikita Khrushchev, aide to Yuri Andropov, and now a journalist, playwright, and Gorbachev confidant.

Family farming is being tried in parts of the Soviet Union, and Burlatsky believes the Chinese model 'can be applied broadly in our country'. The great gains in China, he thinks, have been made mainly because 'peasants have a stake in the results of their labour like never before.'

'In Russia, the entrepreneurial spirit has never developed,' says Burlatsky. 'Just last century we were still a nation of serfs, and then the new system [Soviet communism] was set up in a way that smothered all individual initiative.' Those who act entrepreneurially face another obstacle. 'The main problem is social jealousy on the part of bureaucrats,' Burlatsky explains. 'Local officials can't bear the idea of people making several times their salaries. The Soviet press is full of stories about local party or state officials who, instead of facilitating free enterprise, quash every initiative. To cite just one example, officials in Krasnoyarsk shut down a cooperative of taxi drivers on the ground that its members were earning too much money.'

For Gorbachev to say—as he has—that capitalism is doing better than socialism sets him apart from all who came before and is central to his openness.

87

Pluralism

Will a multiparty system, considered by many the only proof of 'true' democracy, come to the USSR? While Gorbachev holds, at least publicly, to a one-party system, his openness alone is reason for optimism. For it is openness that sets the stage for artistic, scientific, and economic creativity.

Note the historical inventiveness of the Chinese. Their greatest periods were when China was without a rigid ideological structure, when several different philosophies, such as Taoism and Confucianism, competed. When rigid Confucianism was permitted during the Ming and Manchu dynasties, Chinese inventiveness slumped.

From China's economic, if not political, advances in the 1980s Russia sees it has some things to learn. If China were to exceed the Soviet Union's standard of living, the USSR would be humiliated.

- China's agricultural output has doubled in less than a decade. The 800 million peasants now work the land as sharecroppers, on contracts of up to fifteen years. Their children may inherit the fields.

- Peasants have been encouraged to expand their private plots, and for good reason. When private plots accounted for less than 4 per cent of farm acreage, they produced a third of the country's meat and dairy products and half of its potatoes.

- The rest of the farmland was in state collectives. Even when they could choose how to sell up to 30 per cent of what they grew, they were nowhere as productive as the private plots. In China the 55,000 communes created under Mao have been done away with.

In China the government has cut back on central planning, emphasized light industry over heavy industry, pushed for competition, and withdrawn subsidies from unprofitable enterprises.

China has really pushed private enterprise. More than 80 per cent of China's new restaurants, repair shops, and service outlets set up since 1976, when Deng took over, are now privately owned.

The Chinese continue their claim to be building socialism with Chinese features. As a mayor of the city of Shenyang explained, when China uses bankruptcy, leasing, and shareholding to promote its socialist economy, 'these sorts of things are no longer capitalist'.

June 1988 Conference of the Communist Party of the USSR

One of the great landmarks of reform in the Soviet Union was the party conference of late June 1988.

Party congresses had been held regularly each five years, but this was the first specially called conference of the party since 1945. Stalin did away with them. The 1945 conference was the eighteenth, so the June 1988 conference is widely referred to as the Nineteenth Party Conference.

A conference of the party is called when there is some special consideration to take up. The Nineteenth Party Conference was called to deal with political reform in the Soviet Union. It marked the beginning of the shift of power from the party to the government.

Anticipation was enormous. Delegates were elected from every part of the country. Many were party war-horses, but there were also many new faces. There had been a growing sentiment in the Soviet Union that the economic changes so much talked about could sucessfully come about only with the democratization of the society. Economic reform and political reform must be parallel.

More than 300 delegates asked to speak, but fewer than 100 were able to during the four-day conference. The others were asked to submit their ideas in writing for the final summation. One delegate called upon Andrei Gromyko, the then president of the country, who was sitting right behind him, to resign, saying he was part of the old leadership.

Delegates were for *perestroika*; delegates were against it. They argued; some almost came to blows. Speakers for *perestroika* and *glasnost* were applauded by half the delegates; conservative responses were applauded by the other half. Gorbachev listened attentively to all speakers, many of whom he did not like one bit. The whole country watched on television—mesmerized. People had never seen anything like it before. A high-ranking official of the Central Committee, Dimitri Lisovolik, said for him the conference was 'a political rebirth'. And so it was for many who attended or watched on television.

The Nineteenth Party Conference was the real beginning of separating party power from government authority, separating central power from local power, and economic reform from politics. The conference has become a symbol of the new political culture in the Soviet Union. During the proceedings there were long delays in voting results because there was no machinery to count the votes of the 5000 delegates. They had to be counted manually. In the past there had been no need for vote-counting mechanisms because, of course, all votes were unanimous.

The Last Meeting of the Old Supreme Soviet

The political reforms debated at the Nineteenth Party Conference were adopted as constitutional changes by the Supreme Soviet (the parliament). After three days of discussions and amendments in late 1988, the Supreme Soviet shifted power from the Communist party to popularly elected legislative bodies. Three very important changes became law:

1. The old ceremonial post of president was made an executive position with broad authority to shape domestic and foreign policy. Gorbachev was elected president in May 1989 and is limited to two five-year terms, as are all government officials. The new law also says that the president can be ousted by the legislature.

2. A two-tier parliament was created. The first and larger body, which was elected in March 1989, is known as the Congress of the People's Deputies, with 2250 members elected from the fifteen republics of the Soviet Union. It is this Congress of Deputies that elects the president by secret ballot, meets as needed during the year to set overall economic and social policy, and elects the new 422-member Supreme Soviet, which will meet on a more permanent basis. Positions on the Supreme Soviet rotate each year so that some time during the five-year term almost all deputies of the congress will have a turn to serve on this more important body. The relationship between the two bodies, however, is not yet clear. The Congress of Deputies was supposed to elect the Su-

preme Soviet and then go away, but has so far refused. What seems to be evolving is an upper and lower house system like the United States Congress and other parliaments. The new Supreme Soviet will be a true deliberative legislative body, replacing the 1500-member old Supreme Soviet, which had been a rubber-stamp parliament for decisions of the Communist party leadership. Indeed, until summer 1988, when a handful of votes were occasionally cast against the majority, all votes of the Supreme Soviet had been unanimous for sixty years.

3. The March 1989 contests for the Congress of the People's Deputies were multi-candidate, secret-ballot elections, the first real national elections in Soviet history. The elections of deputies to hundreds of regional and local legislative bodies also allowed multiple candidates and secret balloting.

In addition, the fifteen republics of the Soviet Union have greater representation in the Congress of Deputies (one-third of all delegates) than they had in the old Supreme Soviet. Now martial law may be decreed only in consultation with the republics, an important consideration in light of the movement toward greater independence in many Soviet republics.

Gorbachev, the first Soviet leader since Lenin to receive a legal education, has been pushing for a 'rule of law'. The old Supreme Soviet effectively voted itself out of existence, but not before approving new laws meant to guarantee the independence of judges. A new commission is completely redrafting the Soviet constitution.

Gorbachev sees these political changes as essential to reshaping the country and reviving the economy. His aphorism 'Political reform is a kind of oxygen needed by the public organism' is widely quoted. Gorbachev has said his aim is to create a system of 'socialist checks and balances', with a powerful central executive counter-balanced by a strong legislature and strong republics.

Gorbachev labelled *perestroika* 'a time for offbeat, unusual solutions'. Always looking at the big picture, he said it had been impossible to achieve 'ideal documents' at 'the first try'.

It may take many tries. As the 1990s begin, the indications are that *perestroika* is slowing down, the economy is getting worse, and ethnic unrest is increasing. Gorbachev's role, in the end, may be presiding over the beginning of a genuine social revolution that will get very messy and chaotic before the new order emerges. A large irony in the making is that the countries of Eastern Europe, who could never have started their revolutions without Gorbachev, may have straighter paths to the free market.

EASTERN EUROPE

The year 1989 has seen the end of old-style communism in Eastern Europe as dramatically as 1789 saw the end of French absolute monarchy. The Berlin Wall crumbled in November, and Czechoslovakia and Bulgaria dashed down the road towards freedom a few days later. Hungary and Poland had preceded them some time earlier; those two are, in some way, the bellwether countries. As Hungary and Poland lead, the other ex-communist countries (East Germany, Czechoslovakia, Bulgaria and eventually Romania) will follow quite shortly behind.

Hungary

Since 1968 Hungary has been far and away Eastern Europe's leader in reforming Stalinist socialism. Today it is the most prosperous of the Eastern bloc countries but is not yet competitive with the West.

Even before 1989 Hungary's 'liberal-communist' economy permitted personal profit-making, bankruptcies, bond trading, shareholding, private prosperity, and local branches of Citibank and McDonald's. Private businesses include retail shops, supermarkets, home construction, consumer goods, nightclubs, elegant restaurants, plumbing, and taxi service. A chain of privately run supermarket-department stores called Skala is now bigger than the old state-run monopoly.

Despite this impressive list, Hungary must take even more radical economic steps to enliven its stagnant economy. If it does so, it will no longer be a socialist system. There is to be a free election in early 1990, and communism is being abandoned in name as well as in fact. At what point does 'free-market socialism' cease to be socialism? This is an important question because many of the people and countries going through this process may want to continue to think of themselves as socialist. Hungary confronted the question earlier than any other socialist country.

On the one hand, 30 per cent of Hungary's production comes from the private sector; the country even has millionaires. On the other hand, it is in the process of deciding if it has to guarantee employment. That would mean pressing against the ideological bars of the cage. Hungary is stretching socialism to new limits.

Hungary's farms, which previously could not raise enough food to feed the population, now do so handsomely and have a big surplus for export. Farmer cooperatives lease more than 80 per cent of agricultural land from the state. So successful have these cooperatives become that they are now branching into new businesses like farm equipment repair and even computer software.

At the same time big state-run industries—steel, coal, manufacturing—are bleeding the economy with huge losses.

In one year Erno Rubik, the Hungarian inventor of the Rubik's Cube puzzle, brought in more profit and hard currency than all of Hungarian heavy industry combined. Mr Rubik is a millionaire. Hungarian heavy industry is a mess.

One interesting experiment started in 1987, when the 10,000 employees of the big Taurus rubber works could choose to buy 'profit tickets' in the company. These stakes provided a designated share of Taurus' annual earnings and could be held indefinitely, even passed on to family members. They certainly look an awful lot like common shares, as in capitalism. If all or most state-owned industries were to permit this sort of arrangement, at what point would socialism cease to exist?

According to Peter Lorincze, secretary-general of the Hungarian Chamber of Commerce, a personal income tax is one key, because it will alleviate the tax burden on the business sector: 'This measure is probably the most important reform step since the new economic mechanism was introduced in 1968, and is a natural successor to the earlier one.'

The economic liberalization programme Hungary began in 1968 reduced central planning, enhanced the decision-making powers of enterprise managements, and created an important sphere of individual activity free of state central planning. Small-scale commerce and craftsmen's shops sprang up, and workers were allowed, after putting in normal factory hours, to organize themselves into teams and sell their services to the factory at premium rates.

The new Hungarian constitution, adopted for 1990, will provide for multi-party government, freedom of association, free press, free elections, and expansive privatization.

The March 1990 election will be fought and probably won by opposition parties (called movements until 1990). With that extraordinary change, Hungary begins a new era in Eastern European politics. The multi-party parliamentary elections are scheduled under a system that may leave the opposition very split. Four of the political parties dissolved by the Communists forty years ago have come back to life, and new parties are being created. In a preview of the 1990 multi-party elections, in Godollo, twenty miles northeast of Budapest, an alliance led by the Hungarian Democratic Forum won the opposition's first seat in Parliament by 69.2 per cent to 29.9 per cent for the Communist candidate. In the parliamentary elections that must be held before June 1990, the old Communist party doesn't hold much hope of winning a majority. 'We have to face the music after forty years,' says Istvan Foldesi, advisor to the General Secretary of the Hungarian party.

Hungary now has a free press. A new law put forward in Spring 1989 allows any party or individual, including foreign business entrepreneurs, to found a newspaper or a radio or television station. Leslie Colitt of the *Financial Times* says the Hungarian press now provides 'a breadth and quality of domestic and foreign news coverage which would be difficult to duplicate in many Western countries'.

In 1989 an international stock exchange—the only one in Eastern Europe—was opened in Budapest. Since 1 January 1989, companies in Hungary have been entitled to sell any number of shares to anybody. An extraordinary new law allows certain public and private companies to be 100 per cent foreign-owned.

A measure of their seriousness is the extent to which Hungarians have turned to the West for help in restructuring their economy. They have engaged the New York-based brokerage firm Bear, Stearns & Company and the accounting firm Peat

Marwick, and Price Waterhouse, all with impeccable capitalistic credentials.

'Reform is moving so fast here, sometimes I can't believe it,' says Ivan Lipovecz, editor-in-chief of the respected *HVG* weekly. 'It's all of a sudden like a dam burst.'

Miklos Nemeth, a reform-minded economist trained at Harvard University, became prime minister in November 1988. He sees his mission as promoting private enterprise and democratizing Hungary. In August 1989, the Hungarian government pledged an 'irreversible shift' towards a market economy, and integration into the Western European economies.

Imre Pozsgay, the leading reform member of the Politburo of Hungary's former Communist party and the socialist (i.e., most left-wing) candidate to be president in 1990, says that the political system imposed on Hungary after World War II 'has proved to be a false path in its entirety.' He fully expects that Hungary will become a complete democracy by the mid-1990s. Furthermore, Pozsgay sees the present 'as a corridor—at the end of it is the European Community'. Helmut Kohl, the West German Chancellor, believes Hungary could be a member of the European Community by the year 2000.

However complicated the process, it seems clear that capitalism is coming back to Hungary.

Poland

With 37 million people, Poland is Eastern Europe's biggest country and the most important testing ground for *perestroika*. It is also a yeasty bundle of trends, contradictions, and paradoxes. In Poland change has been pushed bottom up rather than imposed top down as in the Soviet Union.

There have been two cultures in Poland: first, the government-sanctioned Communist society; second, the underground —sophisticated, complex, vibrant. The Communist world has never known anything like it before.

Polish Renaissance

At the start of the 1980s Solidarity was the soul of a Polish renaissance. After martial law banned Solidarity at the end of 1981, the renaissance did not die. The state's hold on ideas having been broken, there was a flowering of literature and the arts unequalled in the Soviet bloc.

In this second culture there are about 400 underground newspapers and magazines, with total circulation in the millions, and several hundred books published each year. As you would expect, there are political journals of many stripes. There are also punk-rock newspapers, children's magazines, a journal of alternative medicine. There are banned videos, even underground public opinion polling. Annual awards are given for the best of the underground books, music, acting, directing, and art.

There are about 200 unofficial art exhibits in apartments and church basements. At independent universities unexpurgated history is taught. There are an estimated 500,000 videocassette recorders showing forbidden films rented out by the underground. The banned film *Man of Iron*, about the birth of Solidarity, shown in recent years in the West, has now been seen by just about everyone in Poland. Street demonstrations are still banned in Poland; but everyone who was jailed for working underground has been released, and the underground flourishes.

Because the state lost its information monopoly, it must compete with the underground, by permitting more and more criticism in the official press. As a result, the circulation of the underground press has declined.

CNN for Breakfast

There are already lots of satellite dishes in the Warsaw area, and at least some Poles watch the latest news from America's CNN while having breakfast. CNN anchor Bobbie Batista is becoming a well-known personality in Poland.

Despite the 1987 crackdown on satellite dishes, requiring Polish citizens to obtain a permit to have one, Poland became the first Soviet bloc country with significant public access to Western satellite television, further weakening the control of the state.

In applying the 1987 restrictions to ownership of satellite dishes, a Communications Ministry office was quoted in the weekly *Polityka* as saying, 'How would our roofs look if everyone installed their own antennas? A certain order in the landscape has to be preserved.' How delicate.

While the state producer of television antennas cannot meet

demand and is hopelessly behind in developing satellite dishes, private entrepreneurs are making Western-attuned dishes for local installation and export. 'We are making the highest-quality dishes you can get in Europe, and our market for them is growing,' said Zdislaw Zniniewicz, founder of the private firm Svensat, a joint venture with a Swedish group. Svensat is now one of the largest private firms in Poland and the largest producer of satellite dishes in Eastern Europe.

The Year of the Political Earthquake

On 5 April 1989, after nine weeks of meetings between the government and representatives of Solidarity, they agreed in signed accords to restore the banned union's legal status and to restructure the parliament and have the first free and open elections in Poland since World War II.

A new body was created in the parliament, an upper house called the Senate with 100 seats. In an entirely open election in June 1989 voters were to chose the 100 members. The new Senate can veto legislation of the (already established) lower house, the Sejm. In the June 1989 election 65 per cent of the seats were reserved for candidates of the Communist candidates and their allies, and 35 per cent open to the opposition and independents. Beginning with the next election in 1995, all seats will be openly contested.

The idea was that Solidarity would be represented in both houses of the parliament as a 'constructive' opposition for four years, during which General Jaruzelski, having been elected to the now more powerful presidency, would, with a Communist-led government, take the hard measures required to prevent the economic collapse of Poland.

Then came the stunning, unforeseen Solidarity electoral landslide.

Solidarity candidates won virtually all the seats they were allowed to contest, taking 99 out of 100 seats in the Senate and all 161 seats of the Sejm (out of 460) for which they were permitted to compete.

One government official said bitterly that 'if Walesa had been photographed next to a cow wearing a Solidarity sign around its neck, the cow would have been elected'.

When the 161 deputies who belong to Solidarity were sworn in as members of the Sejm on 4 July 1989, it was the first time that an opposition party had sat in an Eastern European parliament since the late 1940s.

Later that month, on 19 July, the joint bodies of the parliament elected General Jaruzelski president by a one-vote margin. Most of the Solidarity members voted against him or abstained. (So unaccustomed was the parliament to an opposition that most of the session was devoted to a discussion on how to vote. It was finally decided that votes would be cast on signed cards.)

The June election shock was followed by the September drama of the installation of the first non-communist government in Eastern Europe since World War II. Solidarity stalwart Tadeusz Mazowiecki became prime minister, and eleven other Solidarity members joined the Council of Ministers (the cabinet). The Communist party got four seats on the Council (including defence and police); the man named foreign minister was an independent sympathetic to Solidarity, and the other seven seats went to the United Peasant party and the Democratic party. On 12 September 1989, the new government was approved by the lower house by 402 to 0, with 13 abstentions.

'For the first time in half a century Poland has a government that can be considered by millions of people as their own,' said Lech Walesa from Gdansk.

During the four days of Parliamentary hearings preceding the vote to approve the new government, the proposed economic ministers outlined 'the most far-reaching and radical free-market reforms ever proposed by an East bloc country'.

Leszek Balcerowitz, who was to become the deputy premier responsible for the economy, told the Parliament, 'We have an unrepeatable chance of implementing not only political but also economic change in the direction of a Western-style free market economy.' The new industry minister, Tadeusz Syryczyk, is a free marketeer, a follower of Milton Friedman. According to the new government plan all the state-owned factories and businesses (90 per cent of the economy) will eventually be auctioned off to private owners.

Beginning in 1993 a president will be elected by popular vote. Lech Walesa has said he might run for president in 1993. It is a way off, but he would be only fifty-two years old.

In the meantime, Solidarity and the Communist Party have to work together to attend to Poland's pathetic economy. Before and since the accords of April 1989 both Solidarity and the reform wing of the Communist party said they are prepared to support a radical restructuring of the economy, including a strong emphasis on free-market mechanisms and private enterprise. Because this will involve shutting factories, creating unemployment, and setting higher prices for now subsidized food, things will get worse in Poland before they get better.

Beyond sharing responsibility for the enormously unpopular economic measures to come, some in Solidarity favoured taking over the government. But Bronislaw Geremek, head of Solidarity's caucus in parliament, said that the majority view within Solidarity is that it should not assume power for at least another year, while the media and judiciary are cleaned up and preparations are made for fully democratic elections. 'It is not,' he said, 'that Solidarity is not ready to set up a government but rather that the necessary political context is not yet in place.'

The April accords also provide for greater press freedom, permit private schools (this mostly means that the Catholic Church will be able to run its own schools), extend health care (private as well as public), and commit the government to do more for the environment (pollution from Poland's heavy industry is the worst in Europe).

Poland's first independent opposition daily, *Gazeta Wyboreza*, went on sale on 8 May 1989, most of the staff coming from the underground press. Its editor is Adam Michnik, a political dissident and leading figure in Solidarity and now a deputy in the Sejm.

What all this amounts to is that Poland's Communists have surrendered their monopoly of power. In another era it would be a political earthquake, but today it is the direction the world is going.

Lech Walesa says that 1989 saw the 'beginning of the road to democracy and a free Poland, and hence we look with boldness and hope into the future'.

With the emergence of Gorbachev the hard-liners in Eastern Europe can no longer invoke Moscow to prevent liberalization in their countries.

Gorbachev's name is on everyone's lips. 'Should he stay on, if only for two years, and succeed, if only partly, with some of his reforms,' said one sympathizer, 'our hard-liners will have to shut up. Should he fail, we're sunk.'

Speaking of *glasnost* in the Soviet Union, the famous Polish writer Stanislaw Lem said, 'I think that if Gorbachev has it his way, this will be irreversible, and everything in all the other socialist countries will have to go the same way.'

A leading reform theorist at Poland's State School of Planning has gone so far as to say, 'The dream of an economic system better than capitalism is dead. There is no third way, no model between Stalinism and capitalism that works well. The only reasons to stop, short of returning to capitalism, are pragmatic—and political.'

Eastern Europe is heading in three directions: political pluralism, free-market economics, and, in the longer term, integration with Western Europe.

FROM BERLIN TO HANOI

It is obvious that this integration with Western Europe will be greatly affected by the free elections now promised for East Germany and Czechoslovakia. Surely in East Germany some party which wants closer re-union with West Germany will eventually emerge—and win. In Czechoslovakia the mood could be strongly anti-socialist from the start.

However the various elections go, the move to freer-market economics seems set. All central-planning socialist countries throughout the world are struggling with reform, and all (except Albania and North Korea) are experimenting with market mechanisms.

Even Vietnam, as rigidly Marxist a country as you could find, is shifting. After years of disastrous decline, it is trying market mechanisms to jump-start the economy.

In December 1986 Nguyen Van Linh, a leading seventy-two-year-old economic reformer, was appointed head of the ruling Communist party of Vietnam, the first real transfer of leadership in the fifty-six-year history of the Vietnamese Communist party.

Van Linh has begun to introduce limited capitalist measures. While party secretary in Ho Chi Minh City (Saigon) he managed to decentralize the economy and to introduce incentive schemes in agriculture and industry.

Hopes for economy change were accompanied by political liberalization. On 19 April 1987, Vietnamese went to the polls to elect a new national assembly. Voters were given a wider choice of candidates. Hence 829 candidates ran for 496 seats, and the number of electoral units were almost doubled to make candidates more accountable to a smaller number of voters.

All candidates had to be approved by the quasi-governmental Vietnam Fatherland Front, but for the first time candidates could be nominated by local party officials. At least three of the candidates running in the 19 April election in southern Vietnam had received doctorates from American universities during the Vietnam War.

Van Linh may emerge as a Vietnamese equivalent to China's Deng Xiaoping, introducing a host of bold market reforms to try to lift the nation out of poverty.

IS IT STILL SOCIALISM?

In Stockholm on 22 June 1989, the Socialist International at its 100th anniversary meeting, embraced the market economy and rejected nationalization of industry. Voting for this major revision of its basic principles were representatives from eighty left-wing and social democratic parties from around the world. International's president, former West German Chancellor Willy Brandt, said experience had convinced Socialist parties everywhere that they were mistaken in having 'strong confidence in the role of the state in the economic process'.

The essence of the economics of socialism is that the government owns the means of production and controls the distribution of goods. All over the world socialist countries are letting go of that control. Through privatization and leasing they are effectively transferring ownership of the means of production. Whatever the result is, it is not socialism, at least not technically. For more than 100 years the ideological competition in the industrial era has been between Marxism and capitalism. Shall we do it the capitalist way or the Marxist way? But now the industrial period is behind us. An extraordinary regrouping is occurring. We will hear more and more about 'free-market socialism', which, of course, is not socialism at all. The myth and (for some) romance of classical socialism may live long after the transformation of socialism itself. Myths do.

4

Global Lifestyles and Cultural Nationalism

Thanks to a thriving world economy, global tele-communications, and expanding travel, exchanges among Europe, North America, and the Pacific Rim are accelerating fast.

In the urban centres of the developing world signs of the international youth culture are almost everywhere. So enthusiastically are we swapping food, music, and fashion that a new universal international lifestyle reigns in Osaka, Madrid, Chelsea and Seattle.

It is consumer-driven: drinking cappuccino and Perrier; furnishing the apartment with IKEA; eating sushi; dressing in the United Colours of Benetton; listening to US/British rock while driving the Hyundai over to McDonald's.

'The world is becoming more and more cosmopolitan, and we are all influencing each other,' says designer Paloma Picasso.

For the companies that sell these new international products, that understand the world as one single market, it is an economic bonanza.

'There are already groups of consumers in New York, Stockholm, and Milan who show more similarities than consumers in Manhattan and the Bronx in New York itself,' says Leif Johansson, group vice-president of Electrolux's major appliances division. Electrolux's global territory is divided into a 'triad' format—the United States, Europe, and Japan. Each new product is aimed at all three markets.

Among the world's forty best-known brands are Coke, IBM, Sony, Porsche, McDonald's, Honda, and Nestlé, according to a survey of 3000 consumers in nine countries. These are 'the world's first true world brands,' says John Diefenbach, CEO of Landor Associates, which conducted the survey. Seventeen of the forty were US companies; fourteen were European; and nine were Japanese.

But even as our lifestyles grow more similar, there are unmistakable signs of a backlash: a trend against uniformity, a desire to assert the uniqueness of one's culture and language, a repudiation of foreign influence.

Examples:

- Europe today is at peace—except for the religious and cultural battles of Irish and Basque separatism.
- So concerned were Canadians about being culturally annexed by the United States that they came close to voting against the 1988 US-Canadian free-trade pact, an agreement very much to Canada's economic advantage.
- In northeastern Spain the Catalan language, forbidden during the dictatorship of Francisco Franco, has been reinstalled as the official language.
- The Welsh language is making a comeback.
- Quebeçois penalize individuals for speaking English, forbid English street signs, and continue threatening to secede from Canada.
- After twenty years of educating its people in English to accommodate to the world economy, Singapore has begun a 'Speak Mandarin' campaign—an effort to rekindle 'old values'.

Three of the protest movements look particularly violent and important:

- Long part of the USSR, the Soviet republics of Armenia, Azerbaijan, the Ukraine, and Georgia, as well as Latvia, Lithuania, Estonia, Moldavia—and many more to come—emphasize their ethnic identities and assert their independence from the Kremlin.

- In China, ten years of openness to all things Western culminated in student protests for democracy which were met with a bloody government crackdown and backlash against the deemed source of unrest—outside influence.
- One of the most visible forms of cultural backlash is the transnational revival of Islam initiated by the late Ayatollah Khomeini in Iran.

Though identified with Iran and Lebanon, Islamic fundamentalists assert their cultural and religious identities in Britain, Egypt, Indonesia, and Turkey. Liberal Britons were shaken by the reaction of some gentle ex-Pakistani Britons when Salman Rushdie blasphemed: they wanted him murdered. All through Islam—even in Bradford—there is a reaction against what is perceived to be an onslaught of Western influence.

Turkey's rich contradictions will present a textbook case. Although only a small percentage of the nation's 52 million (predominantly Moslem) people are fundamentalists, Turkey's geographic position makes it a link between Europe and the Orient. Writes *Washington Post* foreign correspondent Edward Cody, 'Imams in minarets look east toward Mecca while businessmen in office towers look west toward Brussels'.

Prime Minister Turgut Ozal is a business-oriented technocrat and a devout Moslem. Even as Turkey petitions to join the Common Market, its young college women are enthusiastically wrapping their heads in Islamic scarves, which have been banned at public universities as part of an official discouraging of religious practices dating back to the 1920s, when Kemal Ataturk introduced secular reforms. Enrolment in Moslem schools has multiplied six times in fifteen years. Which will win out? The Islamic revival or the European Community? Or a creative combination?

The more homogeneous our lifestyles become, the more steadfastly we shall cling to deeper values—religion, language, art, and literature. As our outer worlds grow more similar, we will increasingly treasure the traditions that spring from within.

THE EMERGENCE OF A GLOBAL LIFESTYLE

Trade, travel, and television lay the groundwork for the global lifestyle. The film and television media deliver the same images throughout the global village.

Air travel opens the avenues of exchange. From New York you can fly to France as easily as to California. Fly Concorde and you get to London as quickly as Houston. Full-page ads in the *New York Times* beguile Americans to shop at Harrods in London.

Technology will collapse the Pacific, too. Nearly 3 million Japanese visited the United States in 1988. Many were young honeymooners. Now the US government is developing a plane that flies from New York to Tokyo in just two hours.

The jet set has given way to an affluent, travelling middle class of honeymooners, grandmothers, families, students, business people of all nationalities. In the 1990s the volume of travel will really accelerate. Across the United States, 23,000 scheduled flights a day carried 450 million passengers in 1989. By the year 2000, there will be 750 million. Today one billion passengers fly the world's airways each year. By the year 2000, it will be 2 billion passengers, *double* the 1990 figure.

Every day 3 million people fly from one place on the planet to another.

World trade today is much more than buying and selling of goods among 60 nations; it is a thriving, interdependent, single global economy. We used to trade in the basics: raw materials; foodstuffs; steel. Today we trade everything. There is an explosion in the buying and selling of financial instruments (stocks, bonds, currencies), an explosion in the buying and selling of what we wear, eat, listen to and watch—what makes up our lifestyles. In a 'fax-it-to-me' world, it is as easy to do business with a supplier in Taipei as in Chicago.

Lifestyle images speed around the globe at the velocity of light, diffusing their contents everywhere. Since fashion can be faddish, speed is essential. If the information comes too late, you miss the fad. Today the message is getting through to places as disparate as Shanghai, Prague, and Buenos Aires. In all of them, hip young people follow the same code of international fashion (sometimes to the dismay of their elders).

FOOD, FASHION, AND FUN

Haute cuisine and haute couture notwithstanding, decisions about food, clothing, and entertainment involve no great commitment. They are delightfully superficial and fun. On this level people can afford to be open to all sorts of foreign influence. In what we wear and eat, we are blending, borrowing from each other, playing in each other's backyard:

- Americans annually import more than $3 billion worth of Italian clothing, jewellery, and shoes.
- Yuppies are an 'in' group in big West German cities, even though most of the young, upwardly mobile professionals do not understand the meaning of the English term.
- Yummies—young, upwardly mobile Marxists—are emerging in the USSR, imitating the clothes and music tastes of yuppies.
- Travel shows about exotic places—from Samarkand to Rio de Janeiro—are among the most popular programmes on British television. A lot of young Britons go on to visit them.
- Christmas is celebrated in Japan, even though fewer than 1 per cent of Japanese are Christian.
- Each day 200 varieties of cheese are flown to the United States from France.

Food, fashion, and music, the stuff of everyday life in Europe, the United States, and Japan, are taking on similar (some would say disturbingly similar) characteristics—especially in cities.

In Times Square, in the Ginza, and on the Champs Élysées sushi bars, croissant shops, and McDonald's compete for the same expensive real estate.

The Culture of Cuisine

West Los Angeles is the home of Gurume, a Japanese-run restaurant whose speciality—Gurume chicken—is Oriental chopped chicken and green beans in an Italian marinara sauce, served over spaghetti, with Japanese cabbage salad, Texas toast, and Louisiana Tabasco sauce. It is a symbol of what is happening to world lifestyle and cuisine.

Bangladeshi restaurants have gone up-market in London, Tex-Mex is all the rage in Paris, and the United States is importing sushi bars as if they were Toyotas.

'Three years ago the world had never tasted soft-shells [crabs] and now we export to twenty-two countries,' said Terrence Conway, owner of the John T. Handy Company, a Chesapeake Bay firm that in 1986 exported 270,000 pounds of crabs, mainly to Japan. (In 1988 the company was bought by a Japanese firm.)

Mexican cuisine is prepared kosher in Israel, where former Houstonian Barry Ritman's 'Chili's' restaurant comes complete with a Lone Star beer sign, armadillo art, and cactus garden.

Eating out in Britain used to mean fish and chips, just as in Middle America it used to mean steak and potatoes. Now it is Mexican, Chinese, Korean, Indian, Japanese, Afghan and Ethiopian. Between 1982 and 1986 overall restaurant traffic in the United States increased 10 per cent, but Asian restaurants saw business grow 54 per cent, Mexican restaurants 43 per cent, and Italian restaurants 26 per cent. In a one-block area of the Adams Morgan neighbourhood of Washington DC, you can eat Ethiopian, Jamaican, Italian, Mexican, French, Salvadorean, Japanese, Chinese, Caribbean, Indian or American.

A Big Mac by Any Other Name . . .

While America tastes Thai and Afghan, its fast food dominates the international scene. The Golden Arches are recognized from Aruba to Istanbul to Munich, Buenos Aires, and Taipei. Whatever the country, you can order a Big Mac.

Oversaturated in US markets, McDonald's is pursuing an aggressive global strategy. More than 10,500 restaurants operate in fifty countries, promising 'the same quality food, quick service, clean surroundings, and eating-out value that customers in the United States have enjoyed for more than 30 years'. More than 600 new McDonald's restaurants opened in 1988, at least that many in 1989. Worldwide 1988 sales exceeded $16 billion, 29 per cent from foreign operations.

- In Germany one can order Chicken McNuggets at nearly 300 McDonald's outlets. Britain has 289 McDonalds outlets, France 84, and Canada 568.
- The Golden Arches have become a fixture in Belgrade and Budapest.

- São Paulo, Brazil, has 16 McDonald's.
- Eastern Europe, where McDonald's is a big hit, and the Soviet Union, where the first McDonald's opened in 1989, are McDonald's biggest new growth markets.

In Beijing, within the sight of Mao's tomb, Kentucky Fried Chicken operates the world's largest fast-food restaurant.

Japan has more American food franchises than any country outside North America; between 1974 and 1984 alone the number increased from 265 to 1490. Today Japan has a total of 7366 US franchise outlets. Most—72 per cent—are restaurants, food or convenience stores.

'We sell the idea of good old America. Green pastures, fresh air, clean water,' says Shin Ohkawara, president of Kentucky Fried Chicken in Japan, which has 800 outlets. The colonel's global empire operates more than 7750 outlets in more than fifty-eight countries.

Japan imports 400 California wines, up from just 150 in 1986—and it will buy more because its tariffs are coming down. Coca-cola is by far Japan's number one soft drink.

Japanese ordered $580 million worth of sushi from the largest Japanese food chain, Kozozushi Honbu's sushi shops, in 1986. But they spent more on hamburgers; McDonald's 590 outlets in Japan brought in $950 million that year and sales now exceed $1 billion. McDonald's principal competition is from the Daiei Group of Western-style restaurants with sales of only $780 million—but it has 2000 shops.

The favourite foods of Japanese children are curry, rice, hamburger, and spaghetti. If a Japanese family needs to pick something up on the way home, it can stop at one of more than 3200 American franchised 7-Eleven convenience stores.

Japanese spend twenty-five cents of every food dollar eating out, says Kazutaka Kato of the Japan Food Service Industry Association. It is forty cents in the United States. 'In the next ten years,' he says, 'as women continue to join the work force and disposable income climbs, we expect that figure to climb to forty cents here.'

Culinary Imperialism?

Most Americans admire the entrepreneurial efforts of US fast-food makers. But the health-conscious are bound to feel uneasy about the massive export of foods high in fat, cholesterol, and sodium when American themselves are trying to limit such foods or even eliminate them.

So far there are few complaints abroad about America's 'culinary imperialism', or unhealthiness in its fast-food invasion. The French may grumble about fast food, but in the land that invented pâté, no one gripes about fat content. In the Communist bloc and the Third World the cholesterol backlash is nonexistent. Food and cuisine might pose health risks, but do not threaten people's deeper cultural values.

Traditionally the best restaurants have been French, but the global lifestyle trend has even opened the French to the influence of other cuisines, especially American: chocolate chip cookies, corn on the cob, strawberry shortcake, and California wines (in small quantities). The French Association of American Studies sold out a recent quarterly review on American cuisine.

In Paris, American-style restaurants are setting new trends in cuisine, from barbecued spare ribs to chicken sandwiches. Some play American music, and are decorated with American movie posters—ketchup is *de rigueur*.

'Everything about America is fashionable these days,' says Elaine Bourbeillon of the General Store, the first American food boutique in Paris, which sells peanut butter, cranberry juice, and buckwheat pancake mix. It has trouble keeping up with demand.

The Great Food Exchange

Food nourishes body and soul, gently introduces another way of life, and suggests how to embellish our native cuisine: Japanese businessmen in Tokyo order California roll, a type of crab and avocado sushi invented in San Francisco, while American chefs top off a grilled salmon with a butter sauce, laced with wasabi, that tingling Japanese condiment.

In the nonthreatening arena of cuisine we are attending an international bazaar of unprecedented abundance.

International Fashion

In a prospering global village, where ideas are instantaneously exchanged through travel and telecommunications, the sin of coveting thy neighbour's goods has become the multibillion-dollar international fashion business.

American businessmen are switching to Italian suits, Italian youths dress entirely in blue denim, and fashionable Chinese young people wouldn't be caught dead in a Mao jacket.

'Now people travel so much, they get inspired by the same thing,' says Laurie Mallet of WilliWear.

The French fashion magazine *Elle* publishes 16 international editions. After just two years the circulation of the American edition challenged venerable *Vogue*, for decades the arbiter of taste. *Elle* is considering coming out with four new foreign editions: in Turkey, Hungary, Taiwan, and Thailand (*Elle's* appearance is probably as reliable an index of growing disposable income as a fancy economic study). CNN's *Style* programme reports direct from the runways of New York, Tokyo, Milan, and Paris.

London's Harrods department store might as well be Bloomingdale's. At one point Harrods catalogue went out to 145,000 American customers, who could phone in their orders toll-free, an international combination of direct marketing and telephone sales. Now the Harrods catalogue, sent three times a year to UK charge customers, is available to overseas customers for a fee.

'The Time. The Date. The Place. The Sale. The Card. There is Only One Harrods. There is Only One Sale.' Full-page ads in the *New York Times* advertised Harrods' annual January and July sales to Americans. The 'card' is American Express.

If the tactics of genteel Harrods seem a bit aggressive, take note of this: More than 40 per cent of its sales are to overseas customers—to *every country in the world*. Its products are equally international.

Harrods fruit and vegetable department stocks French peaches, Dutch radishes, English strawberries, Californian asparagus, Russian button mushrooms, and East African lemon grass. Harrods, which operates shops in West Germany and Japan, is owned by Egyptians.

In sophisticated Milan, teenagers reject chic designers like Giorgio Armani in favour of Levi 501 jeans, deck shoes, and the preppy look seen in American movies, on TV, and in advertising. Children of wealthy families, these new-wave teens are called *Paninari*—from *panino*, the word for sandwich—symbolizing the American ideal of life in the fast lane. US-based The Limited has borrowed the name Paninari as a theme for its Forenza, European-flair line.

On the other side of the world, in China, where no one had worn red since the Revolution, bright stylish clothes, including revolutionary red, sheer stockings, and blue jeans, appeared in the 1980s. Chinese women wore spaghetti-strap sundresses, stirrup pants, even mini skirts. French designer Pierre Cardin presents fashion shows to thousands in stadiums in China.

Will China's fling with fashion survive the conservative mood after Tiananmen Square? If it does, it will be without the assistance of one high-profile designer—Yves Saint Laurent.

Saint Laurent's partner Pierre Berge resigned in protest as official advisor to Beijing's China Garments Research and Design Centre, which was to have connections to the world's fashion capitals and to train 100 to 200 design students each year.

Instead Berge urged French firms to help the 2800 Chinese students in France to find jobs. The Saint Laurent boutique on Paris's rue de Tournon was transformed into a headquarters for students and others seeking democracy in China.

The king of French fashion for three decades, Saint Laurent's hand is still extended to the rest of the socialist world. At the request of Raisa Gorbachev he exhibited his work in the Soviet Union in 1986.

In Tokyo, Des Moines, and São Paulo, the fashion-conscious fifteen-year-old is likely to favour clothes from one of the big international fashion retailers, Benetton, Esprit, or Britain's Laura Ashley, clothiers to the youth culture, outfitters of the global lifestyle.

Benetton

'The United Colours of Benetton' advertisements project the vision: The world is made up of different races and nationalities—all linked by the same colourful clothes, which symbolize peaceful, happy coexistence.

United as in the United States, multi-national as in the chain's home continent, Europe, and multi-racial, Benetton's 'All the

111

Colours of the World' theme creates an international flavour no other retailer can match.

Since its beginning in Italy in 1968 more than 4500 Benetton stores have opened in seven countries. At one point in its history a new Benetton franchise opened somewhere on the average twice a day. There are now more than 650 stores in North America.

After intense growth, the company is retrenching amid disputes with franchisees who complain that the stores are too close together and that ordering goods is difficult. Seven Benetton shops closed in 1987. In December 1987 the company brought in a consultant to administer American operations autonomously.

Benetton is nonetheless the world's largest knitwear maker and the largest consumer of virgin wool. Sales have increased from $78 million in 1978 (mainly in Italy) to $1 billion in 1987, when profits hit $108 million. Outside Italy, the United States is Benetton's largest market, followed by Germany and France. A Moscow store was due to open in 1989.

A key factor in the company's success is the use of high technology. Computers design clothes, ship products, and monitor consumer preference. Benetton employs more computer technicians than seamstresses.

Esprit

The Esprit customer, says company literature, 'is a young-minded woman who is fitness oriented, sporty, outgoing, happy and socially conscious. She has an easy confidence about herself and her sexuality, and enjoys "the difference" between men and women. She's never a sex object and youth to her is an attitude, not an age.'

With 125 stores in fifteen countries and boutiques within 100 department or specialty stores, and sales to thousands of other stores, Esprit is more than state of mind; it is one of the world's leading sportswear merchants. Esprit sold an estimated $1.2 billion worth of women's, men's, and children's apparel and accessories in 1988. Today there are seventy stores in the United States and fifty-five stores outside the United States, where two-thirds of sales are generated.

'Esprit is an international company,' says Doug Tomkins, co-founder of Esprit. 'The head of graphics is Japanese; our photographer is Italian; our architects are Italian and French. We have German, Swedish, English, Dutch, and Chinese designers. When we all get together, it's like a little United Nations.'

Esprit's corporate offices in San Francisco are located on a ten-acre compound where employees can take subsidized language classes, improve their tennis games, or lunch at subsidized prices at the Esprit Café.

Laura Ashley

Laura Ashley, Inc., exemplifies the English lifestyle. Wooden storefronts evoking Victorian London are filled with Laura Ashley dresses and fabrics in the mood of an English garden. Saleswomen, wearing the flower-print dresses they sell the customers, also offer fabrics, children's clothing, sheets, and wallpaper. No wonder it is one of Prime Minister Margaret Thatcher's favourite examples of British enterprise.

In 1953 the late Welsh designer Laura Ashley began silk screening on tea towels, which her husband sold to local stores. Although the first shop did not open until 1968, by the early 1970s there were stores in Australia, Japan, and Canada. A US shop opened in 1974; today there are 174 in North America. Worldwide there are 425 shops, and sales total about $400 million. There are factories in Wales, Holland, Ireland, and Kentucky.

Habitat/Conran's

British entrepreneur Terence Conran, founder of Habitat, sells sophisticated, contemporary, and affordable home furnishings in more than 100 stores worldwide. There are fifty-seven in the UK and scores across Europe. Habitat also operates in Japan, Singapore, Hong Kong, and the United States, where it is known as Conran's. The look is simple and functional, white walls and light woods. Conran's has seventeen US stores but hopes to expand to 200. For his success in retailing, Conran was knighted by the British government in 1983.

IKEA

'Champagne dining on a beer budget' is what the Swedish retailer IKEA promises. It sells unassembled furniture for 30 per cent less than the finished product would cost. IKEA operates eighty stores in nineteen countries from Western Europe to Saudi Arabia, the Canary Islands, Canada, and Australia. IKEA catalogues—more than 50 million worldwide—are published in twelve languages. Cartons come labelled in English, Danish, German, French, and Swedish. In 1988 sales totalled more than $2.6 billion; sales at three US stores alone were $93 million. A store in Budapest is scheduled to open in 1990.

Global Pricing

Global merchandising has led to global pricing—through electronics. A few years ago a fashionable New Yorker could fly to Milan and shop the temples of haute couture along the Via Napoleone at prices that saved enough to cover the hotel and airfare. No longer. And it is not just because the dollar is lower.

Today prices are regulated electronically to protect all outlets from currency fluctuations that could hurt business. Chanel, for example, adjusts prices in shops around the world to take into account shifts in currency values. A Chanel suit or handbag costs more or less the same whether it is purchased on the Avenue Montaigne, at the boutique in Hong Kong's Peninsula Hotel, or on Rodeo Drive.

The international operations of British, Swedish, Italian and American retailers—as well as of upscale designers—are increasing options for the vast majority of clothes buyers. But paradoxically, does the success of these businesses push the limits of homogenization? When the same shops are found in Honolulu, in São Paulo, and at the local mall, what happens to diversity, local colour, and texture?

The emerging global lifestyle walks a thin line between greater options and greater homogenization, which decreases options.

THE CULTURAL BALANCE OF PAYMENTS

Although Americans are still trying to increase exports, no one questions the enthusiasm with which they send TV shows, entertainment, music, and films to almost every country on the planet.

Film

In 1982 French Cultural Affairs Minister Jack Lang gave a rousing speech about what he termed 'US cultural imperialism'. Though he sometimes sounds remarkably like Lee Iacocca railing against Japanese auto importers, Minister Lang has a lot to be concerned about.

The French dominated the film scene in the 1950s and 1960s, but the United States does today. In 1986, 121 American films were released in France, compared with 158 French films. During the first three months of 1988 French films failed to capture 30 per cent of the French movie market. American movies held more than a 50 per cent share.

American films also seized 50 per cent of the Italian, Dutch, and Danish markets, 60 per cent of the German, and 80 per cent of the British market. But the largest market for Hollywood movies outside the United States is Japan.

Music and Entertainment

In France cultural imports dominate radio stations and rock video shows. In January 1987; twenty of the top fifty hit singles in France were foreign records.

'Mass culture from the US—from jazz to disco—has conquered the world. China is the last battleground, and we are putting up hardly any resistance,' said Li Delun, the musical director of the China Central Philharmonic Orchestra long before China's hard-line government had second thoughts about all that 'openness'.

Young Chinese love the jeans and rock music of Western society. Wham! was the first megagroup to play China in 1985. Rock music is the foundation of the international youth culture. Genesis, Billy Joel, and the Rolling Stones are stars worldwide.

It is not clear whether Western culture will disappear after the Chinese government's bloody crackdown against student protests. But before June 1989 there had been great latitude for *cultural*, if not political, self-expression:

- On Wednesday and Saturday evenings Chongwenmen Cultural Palace sponsored break-dance time.
- In May 1988 nearly 300 youths participated in Beijing's first government-sponsored break-dance competition.

115

- More than 1000 senior citizens took part in Beijing's first Old Folks' Disco contest in April 1988.

In Japan, meanwhile, lovers of American style demonstrate little restraint in their wild embrace of American cultural icons —from nightclubs to Disneyland.

In the early 1990s twenty-five rock and roll clubs called Studebaker's and outfitted with fixtures and furniture imported from the United States will open in Japan.

The first All-American Disneyland to open outside the States was, of course, in Japan. 'We finally decided that we wanted it to look and feel like an experience in the States,' says Toshio Kagami of Tokyo Disneyland, where many street signs are in English. 'Now we consider that the biggest factor of our success.' In the early hours of 1987, 130,000 Japanese braved near-freezing temperatures to ring in the New Year at Tokyo Disneyland. It was the single busiest day of the year. Minnie Mouse wore a kimono.

EuroDisneyland, the $2 billion fourth Magic Kingdom, opens at Marne-la-Vallée, just outside Paris, in 1992. Along with increasing tourist traffic, it will create 8000 jobs. Country houses owned by British aristocrats are turning themselves into American-style theme parks.

Publishing

Thanks to satellite transmissions, the *Wall Street Journal*, *Financial Times*, *USA Today*, *Die Zeit* of Hamburg, *China Daily*, the *Economist*, *Time*, and *Newsweek* are published the same day on several continents. The *Economist* is read by people in 170 countries. Only one-quarter of its readers are in Britain. Its pages are sent each Thursday by satellite for printing in Singapore, California and on America's east coast; they take longer to reach its British printing works by road.

At the Newsroom in Washington, DC, you can buy magazines, newspapers, records, tapes and books in 100 different languages.

Television

Seventy-five per cent of all imported television programmes come from the United States:

- *Dallas* is seen in ninety-eight countries.
- In New Zealand 40 per cent of television programming was American in 1986.
- The American shows *Matlock* and *Spenser for Hire* tied as the number one shows in South Africa in January 1989.
- Mickey Mouse and Donald Duck—their voices dubbed in Mandarin—are seen weekly in China.
- *Sesame Street* was seen in eighty-four countries in 1989.
- On Wednesday nights in Shanghai, more than 70 per cent of the television audience tunes in to watch *Hunter*, an American police show.

Obviously the United States is an aggressive TV exporter, but it has little experience *importing* TV shows (except for a few from Britain). The United States has much to gain in the way of quality arts and cultural imports. That might help balance its cultural trade surplus.

Global television already exists potentially in Europe's multi-national satellite television stations. But they, too, are subject to the pull of global lifestyle, the counter pull of cultural nationalism and the nuances of language.

A single such broadcaster beaming out programming can reach a huge international audience. But country by country, that audience may well prefer local programming. That is the lesson that British broadcasters have learned.

The first pan-European television news program, Britain's *Independent Television News*, aired on British-owned Super Channel beginning in 1987. It reached a potential audience of 20 million cable viewers in fourteen nations. The news was read in slightly slowed-down English, to accommodate millions of viewers with a working, though not native, knowledge of English.

Even that was apparently not enough. The Independent News went off the airways in November 1988. Super Channel lost $100 million in its first two years. Rupert Murdoch's Sky Television, which reached 10 European countries did not do much better. Most Europeans prefered national satellite stations with entertainment dubbed in local slang.

Viewers worldwide will apparently be able to watch as many US television programmes as they can stand. But the day when one megabroadcaster will beam out the same homogenized programming worldwide will—mercifully—never come. The reason is cultural nationalism. CNN is available (mostly in hotels) in eighty-three countries.

Many Polish citizens are better informed than their Soviet neighbours. Poles with satellite dishes can choose among twenty-one channels broadcast from North America and Western Europe, including the BBC World Service and US-based CNN.

Although they have left the USSR, 100,000 Soviet Jews in Israel have not abandoned Soviet TV. They watch the news via satellite.

The potential impact of television in the world's most populous countries is staggering.

'Latin America is the region of the world with the highest level of imported TV programmes,' says Rafael Roncagliolo, director of the Lima-based Center for Studies about Transnational Culture. 'About 60 per cent of the programmes are imported, and 80 per cent of those come from the United States.'

Ocobamba, Peru, a tiny village of 400 people, had battery-powered television sets before running water, regular mail service, and even electricity. 'Before phones, people in this part of the world want television,' says Carlos Romera, director of Peru's National Institute for Research and Training in Telecommunications.

The Tuareg, the largest tribe of nomads in the Sahara, delayed their annual migration for ten days in 1983, in order to catch the last episode of *Dallas*.

In the relatively poor countries of China and India, where 40 per cent of the world's population resides, people are bombarded with images from the developed West.

India has 400 million potential television viewers. There are approximately 100 million TV sets in China with an estimated audience of 600 million. As early as 1986 one out of every two homes, in Beijing and Shanghai, had a TV set, reports the *World Press Review*.

The potential of global television, and the massive export of American television shows, lead to least-common-denominator programming and the homogenization of culture? Will it threaten the differences that make individual countries interesting? Will it facilitate the tendency for powerful countries like the

United States to impose their values on Third World and other countries? Or will it bring backlash?

'If we accept a cheeseburger culture, it's only gonna give us a stomachache,' says Richard Pawelko, a filmmaker from Wales and critic of American mass culture. It may mean more than a bellyache.

A lot of sophisticated people even in developed countries feel that technology has invaded their lives and that 'everything is just moving too fast'. Is it any wonder that some people in developing countries feel more resentful still?

In Iran, where modernity is associated with the West and dubbed 'Satanic', people threaten violence—in the name of religion—to fend off outside influence and express their frustration.

America's 'cultural imperialism', writes columnist Georgie Anne Geyer, 'infiltrates a country through radio and TV, through tourists and Peace Corpsmen; it walks into an ancient and tormented country such as Iran on the cat's feet of supposedly good-willed men from Sioux City, who are in reality "Satan", bringing with them Big Macs and women's rights and relativistic and tolerant values.'

Unlike cheeseburgers and jeans, the globalization of television is explosive and controversial because it conveys deeper values the way literature does. Entertainment, through the medium of language and images, crosses over the line of superficial exchange and enters the domain of values. It goes right to the ethos of a culture, addressing the fundamental spirit that informs its beliefs and practices.

ENGLISH AS A UNIVERSAL LANGUAGE

The most important factor accelerating the development of a single global lifestyle is the proliferation of the English language. Language is a great agent of homogenization; it is the frequency on which culture is transmitted. If English is gaining a lock on global language, the implications are clear: The cultures of English-speaking countries will dominate.

English is becoming the world's first truly universal language. It is the native language of some 400 million people in twelve countries. That is a lot fewer than the 800 million people or so who speak Mandarin Chinese. But another 400 million speak English as a second language. And several hundred million more have some knowledge of English, which has official or semi-official status in some sixty countries. Although there *may* be as many people speaking the various dialects of Chinese as there are English speakers, English is certainly more widespread geographically, more genuinely universal than Chinese. And its usage is growing at an extraordinary pace.

Today there are about 1 billion English speakers in the world. By the year 2000 that figure is likely to exceed 1.5 billion.

- Two hundred and fifty million Chinese—more than the entire population of the United States—study English.
- In eighty-nine countries English is either a common second language or widely studied.
- In Hong Kong nine of every ten secondary school students study English.
- In France state-run secondary schools require students to study four years of English or German; most—at least 85 per cent—choose English.
- In Japan secondary students are required to take six years of English before graduation.

Language study is compulsory for Soviet children; most study English. In Norway, Sweden, and Denmark English is compulsory. Within Europe, Holland has the highest concentration of English proficiency outside Britain. Since Portugal entered the European Community, the demand for English classes has replaced the demand for French.

There are 1300 English-language schools in Tokyo, and 100 new schools open a year. Berlitz offers both British and American English at 250 language schools in twenty-six countries. Worldwide 80 to 90 per cent of Berlitz students study English. Between 1983 and 1988 English enrolments increased 81 per cent.

Media and Transportation

English prevails in transportation and the media. The travel and communication language of the international airwaves is English. Pilots and air traffic controllers speak English at all international airports. Maritime traffic uses flag and light signals, but 'if vessels needed to communicate verbally, they would find a common language, which would probably be English,' says the US Coast Guard's Werner Siems.

Five of the largest broadcasters—CBS, NBC, ABC, the BBC, and the CBC (Canadian Broadcasting Corporation)—reach a potential audience of about 300 million people through English broadcast. It is also the language of satellite TV.

The Information Age

The language of the information age is English. Even computers talk to each other in English.

More than 80 per cent of all information stored in the more than 100 million computers around the world is in English.

Eighty-five per cent of international telephone conversations are conducted in English, as are three-quarters of the world's mail, telexes, and cables. Computer program instructions and the software itself are often supplied only in English.

German was once the language of science; today more than 80 per cent of all scientific papers are published first in English. Over half the world's technical and scientific periodicals are in English, which is also the language of medicine, electronics, and space technology.

International Business

English is the language of international business.

When a Japanese businessman strikes a deal anywhere in Europe, the chances are overwhelming that the negotiations were conducted in English.

Manufactured goods indicate their country of origin in English: 'Made in Germany', not *Fabriziert in Deutschland*. It is the language of choice in multi-national corporations. Datsun and Nissan write international memorandums in English. As early as 1985, 80 per cent of the Japanese Mitsui and Company's employees could speak, read, and write English. Toyota provides in-service English courses. English classes are held in

Saudi Arabia for Aramco workers and on three continents for Chase Manhattan Bank staff.

The international language of Iveco, the Italian truck maker, is English. Philips, the Dutch electronics firm, conducts all board meetings in English. The French company Cap Gemini Sogeti SA, one of Europe's major software producers, made English its official language.

Even in France, which has little regard for any language but its own, a leading business school will now teach in English. École des Hautes Études Commerciales now offers its classic two-year advanced business management course in English. It is the first time a major French school of higher education will teach in a foreign language.

When the operator answers the telephone at the Paris head-quarters of Alcatel, the second largest telecommunications in the world, it is not in French, but, 'Alcatel, Good Morning'. When the French yield on language, something compelling is happening.

Diplomacy

English is replacing the dominant European languages of cen-turies past. English has replaced French as the language of diplomacy; it is the official language of international aid organ-izations such as Oxfam and Save the Children as well as of UNESCO, NATO, and the UN.

Lingua Franca

English serves as a common tongue in countries where people speak many different languages. In India, nearly 200 different languages are spoken; only 30 per cent speak the official lan-guage, Hindi. When Rajiv Gandhi addressed the nation after his mother's assassination, he spoke in English. The European Free Trade Association works only in English, even though it is a foreign tongue for all six member countries.

Official Language

English is an official or semi-official language of twenty African countries, including Sierra Leone, Ghana, Nigeria, Liberia, and South Africa. Students are instructed in English at Makerere

University in Uganda, the University of Nairobi in Kenya, and the University of Dar es Salaam in Tanzania.

English is the ecumenical language of the World Council of Churches, the official language of the Olympics and of the Miss Universe competition.

Youth Culture

English is the language of international youth culture. Young people worldwide sing the lyrics of U2, Michael Jackson, and Madonna songs without fully understanding them. 'Break dance', 'rap music', 'bodybuilding', 'windsurfing', and 'computer hacking' are invading the slang of West German youth.

Will English-Speakers Learn Anything Else?

There is worry in Britain that the British are by far worse speakers of foreign languages than any other people in the European Community. An attempt is being made to stimulate teaching of French and German in the new schools curriculum.

The Americans say that one-third of their children in high school are now studying a foreign language. That looks tragically small, but it is the highest proportion for seventy years.

The trend in America is the opposite of that in Britain. It's right away from French and German. 'There's quite a shift from the traditional European languages to Asian languages,' says William F. Cipolla, director of New York University's language and translation department.

The percentage of American college students studying Japanese doubled between 1980 and 1987, to a total of 23,454. Chinese-language study increased 48.6 per cent to 16,891; Russian 41.6 per cent to 33,961.

While Spanish-language study increased only 8.4 per cent, it still attracts the largest number of college students—411,293. In 1970 Spanish replaced French as the most widely taught foreign language in US colleges and universities.

English has infiltrated many languages. Franglais is the combination of English and French. Other results are Spanglish, Sovangliski (with Russian); and Hinglish (with Hindi). Peculiar English, as she is spoken in Japlish (much used in Tokyo), makes

English words popular even if they do not quite make sense: T-shirts sprout slogans like 'I feel Coca-Cola'. Japlish is spreading on many humorous billboards and shopping bags.

Foreign diplomats in Washington, DC, can take a course in colloquial American English at the Smithsonian Resident Associate Programm. Where else would they learn 'Let's do lunch', 'networking', and 'knee-jerk' among the 1000 Americanisms taught?

English is the inevitable future of Europe. It is displacing French and German as the most widely spoken language among Europeans. The reason is 1992, and the trend has only just begun.

One of the greatest appeals of English as the world language is that it is easy to speak badly.

'English is the international language,' says Akira Nambara of the Bank of Japan. 'Or, I should say, broken English.'

But just as English becomes the universal language, there is a backlash against that same universality. People are insisting on keeping traditional languages and cultures alive.

CULTURAL NATIONALISM

From Alor Star in Malaysia, to Soweto in South Africa, to Xian in China, young people embrace the products of Western culture. In Nairobi, Cairo, Buenos Aires, and Kathmandu, you can hear the sounds of American music on almost any street corner. But the mass export of Western culture—especially US culture —and the spread of English as a universal language have not come without a cultural backlash.

Against the backdrop of rock music, blue jeans, and American television, a new cultural and linguistic chauvinism is emerging:

- The English language can be found on the street signs of major thoroughfares in Tokyo but is prohibited in the French-speaking province of Quebec in Canada, a country where English is the official language.

- The Catalan language, outlawed during Francisco Franco's regime, is in the midst of a renaissance.
- In Wales parents who never learned Welsh themselves are sending their children to Welsh schools.

In the Third World the universality of English is coming under increased scrutiny. In the Philippines, Malaysia, and Sudan, English has been restricted in the schools. More than a dozen countries have tried to limit its use. Chances are they will have about as much luck as the Académie Française, which has consistently failed to protect the French language from an onslaught of foreign words, mostly English.

Nevertheless, language is the pathway to culture. If the inhabitants of a Third World country sense that an outside culture is gaining undue influence, they will feel their values are threatened and may respond with cultural nationalism, vigorously asserting their language and/or religion, just as they would counter a political or military invasion with renewed political nationalism.

The Case of Islam

In the revolutionary Islamic state of Iran, the force inflaming cultural assertiveness is religion, not language. Millions of Shiite Moslem followers of the late Ayatollah Khomeini are reasserting traditional religious principles and repudiating all Western (especially American) influence as corrupting to the conservative rule of Islamic law.

For Iran, the West is synonomous with all that is modern and secular (technology included) and is therefore godless, even 'Satanic'. The United States and Iran have engaged in a battle of cultures that has sometimes turned tragically violent. Britain has been horrified by Moslem reaction to a book by a British citizen living in Britain.

Like other forms of religious fundamentalism, the Islamic movement embraces the primacy of Scripture—the word of Allah set down by Mohammed, his Prophet. When some blasphemous references to the Prophet appeared in *The Satanic Verses*, a work of fiction by Salman Rushdie, a Sunni Moslem living and working in London, an outraged Ayatollah Khomeini urged his followers all around the world to execute the author. The Western values of freedom of speech and of the press clashed with the Islamic definition of respect. But the seeds of that clash had been germinating for at least a decade.

A lot of Pakistani immigrants who had seemed to be well-integrated into Britain—gentle small shopkeepers, hard working newsagents, parents of students at British universities—appeared on the streets of British cities, waving banners which demanded death to Rushdie. Some bombs were placed outside shops selling the book.

The US had an even bigger shock when Iran's revolution unleashed a wave of anti-American sentiment, culminating in the siege in early 1979 of the US Embassy the following November. Fifty-two Americans were held captive by Iranian revolutionaries for 444 days. They were released in 1981 during the beginning moments of the Reagan administration, partly because westernized Iranians had told Khomeini that Reagan was a right-wing nut who might throw bombs back at them.

According to former hostage Moorhead Kennedy, the US State Department was bewildered that the issue of religion could have provoked the shah's overthrow and the embassy takeover. In the State Department's grand scheme of things, Kennedy concludes, 'There is no wedge of the pie for religion. Therefore, it lacked significance. . . . Nothing in its long experience prepared the foreign service for a transnational religious movement of the kind led by the Ayatollah Khomeini.'

We are only now beginning to understand the depth of cultural nationalism. It is a challenge that will not be faced exclusively by developing countries.

Today's generation of Japanese young people, for example, are enthusiastic about traditional Japanese clothes, food, and culture. 'The young are writing *haiku* poems,' says London's *Economist*, 'just as their grandparents (but not their parents) did.'

The more we influence each other, the more we shall seek to maintain our traditions. Not with the violence of some Iranian revolutionaries but with a good bit of their zeal.

In the face of growing homogenization, we shall all seek to preserve our identities, be they religious, cultural, national, linguistic, or racial.

Wales

The Welsh, Quebeçois, and Catalonians described here are other contemporary examples of ethnic and regional groups engaged in the struggle to preserve their cultural identities in an increasingly homogeneous world.

It is easy to forget that Europe's nation-states were made up of scores of ethnic groups—Flemish, Bavarian, Provençal, Andalusian, Catalonian, and Welsh, among them.

In Wales, where virtually everyone speaks English, the Welsh language (Cymric) is making an emotional comeback after becoming nearly extinct. At the end of the 19th century, 80 per cent spoke Welsh. By the 1930s the percentage had declined to 30 per cent. After the 1945 war, the percentage seemed to be dropping below 20 per cent. Since the 1970s, however, there has been a widespread movement to revive the usage of Welsh:

- Adults learn Welsh in intensive courses called Modified Ulpans which meet five evenings a week.
- The Welsh Nursery School Play Group Movement teaches Welsh to children between the ages of two and a half and five.
- The nonpolitical Welsh League of Youth with 750 branches and more than 45,000 members encourages young people to learn the language.
- Englishmen who have bought country or second homes in Wales, intending to retire to the lovely country, have found militant Welsh nationalists burning them down.

Today there are Welsh radio stations and newspapers like *Y Cymro* and *Y Faner*. A Welsh-only television service was established in 1982.

'The more TV becomes a global medium, the greater the threat to minority languages,' says Emlyn Davies, programme controller for the Welsh-language station. 'My son is thirteen years old. He loves the rock group Queen. As long as he discusses Queen in Welsh, I don't regard that as a threat to his culture.'

Parents make great sacrifices to send children to Welsh schools, sometimes driving them twenty miles each way to attend. Nearly 400 primary schools (about 20 per cent) use the Welsh language as the main medium of instruction. About 1000 schools teach it as a second language; only 343 schools teach no Welsh at all.

Half the population of rural Wales attends the Eisteddfod festival of Welsh ceremonies, music, and poetry contests held every August. 'Most participants agree that it is only there that their identity as Welshmen is annually renewed,' reports Bud Khleif in *Language, Ethnicity, and Education in Wales*.

Junior Eisteddfod, a miniature version of the festival for children, holds annual contests in music, poetry, singing, and drama. One year the winning student refused to be interviewed in English.

The Welsh revival shows how cultural and linguistic identity can be deeper than politics. Wales has not been independent for *five* centuries.

Wales today is a country, but not a state; it has a capital city, but not a government; its own postage stamps, but not its own currency; a flag, but no embassies; an indigenous language, but no indigenous laws.

In a 1979 referendum 20 per cent of the Welsh electorate voted that they wanted greater independence from the United Kingdom. As that vote indicates, Welsh nationalism is more cultural than political. It is centred mainly on the language which was once regarded as almost dead.

Quebec

In the Canadian province of Quebec, 85 per cent of the 6.5 million inhabitants speak French. For decades there has been talk of Quebec separating from the rest of Canada. In 1976 the Quebec separatist movement achieved partial victory in being elected as Quebec's government, responsible nevertheless to the federal government. Almost immediately after, Quebec passed Bill 101 obligating citizens to speak French at work and banning English commercial signs. 'Language police' issued fines to violators. The law also requires that children attend French schools, unless one of their parents attended an English school in Quebec.

In 1980 a referendum to separate from Canada was defeated, 60 per cent to 40 per cent. Today Quebeçois are still evaluating the economic costs of linguistic nationalism.

In the eight years following Quebec's language law, a quarter of a million people, including 14,000 senior corporate executives, and almost all from the English-speaking community, left the province. One of Quebec City's two English dailies has folded. The Sun Life Assurance Company was one of the first to pull its business out of Quebec and was frank about the reason:

the language law. Banks and brokers moved to Toronto, and real estate prices slumped.

Quebec's linguistic nationalism is preserving the French-Canadian heritage: Investment from France has increased, and enrollment in French universities has soared from 20,000 before 1960 to 130,000 in 1988. But do the costs outweigh the benefits?

In 1987 the Quebec Court of Appeals decared the French signs mandated by Provincial Law 101 legal. In 1988, however, the Supreme Court of Canada reversed the lower court and ruled the law unconstitutional. Quebeçois are scrambling to create a compromise solution that will please both the court and Quebec's French-speaking majority.

During 1987 seventeen businesses were fined for displaying signs in English and in violation of the French-only Provincial Law 101:

- When a merchant hung a MERRY CHRISTMAS sign, he was told by the 'language police' to change it to French or take it down.
- When two employees of a fast-food restaurant were overheard speaking English, the government sent undercover agents to investigate possible violation of the French-at-work law.
- A Montreal grocery store that posted advertisements in both English and French was fire-bombed.

In 1987 Quebec signed the Canadian Constitution, officially stating that it no longer sees itself separate from the rest of Canada. But at last word, the French-only Parti Quebeçois is working to rebuild the separatist movement.

Catalonia

Castilian Spanish is Spain's official language. But not in Catalonia, an autonomous region of 6 million people, where Catalan has been proclaimed the official language and is in the midst of a major revival. Nearly 70 per cent of the people speak Catalan, and 85 per cent understand it. Catalan newspapers, magazines, books, and folk traditions were outlawed during the reign of Francisco Franco. They are now flourishing again.

Language is the basic characteristic of Catalonia's personality and the personality of its people. For centuries, Catalonia and its

capital, Barcelona, have been known as the economic heart of
Spain, representing 20 to 25 per cent of the Spanish economy.

**'Without my language I have no culture, and culture is the best
weapon man has against oppression',**

says Joan Brossa, a Catalan poet. 'Generalissimo Franco and his
fascists knew this well. They tried to steal our language from us,
but they failed. Now I think the worst moments for us have
passed. It is Franco who is dead, and not Catalonia.'

- The renaissance has been a great stimulus for news-
  papers such as *Avui* and magazines like *El Mon* and *Serra
  d'Or*.
- Publishers like Ediciós 62, Editorial Empuries, and
  Editorial Laia are three of the seventy-five firms in the
  Guild of Catalan Language Editors. Ediciós 62 is trans-
  lating William Faulkner, Graham Greene, F. Scott Fitz-
  gerald. Readers are eager for Catalan translations in
  science fiction and business, too.
- *La Vanguardia*, Barcelona's main daily, prints features in
  Catalan.
- There are twenty-one radio stations broadcasting in
  Catalan, as do three television stations at least several
  hours a day.

On Sundays at noon people spontaneously gather in front of the
Barcelona Gothic Cathedral, and on Sunday evenings Catalans
gather on the Plaza Sant Jaume, to participate in traditional
dances.

Today's Catalan renaissance grows out of centuries of tradition. Catalans have been allied with Spain since the days of
Christopher Columbus. But after losing their independence to
Philip V in the 18th century, they sought greater autonomy,
often with language as a unifying force. The literary Renaixensa
of the 1850s and 1860s celebrated the language in poetry and
festival, further encouraging linguistic nationalism.

Catalonia achieved political autonomy in 1932 before falling to
Franco during the Spanish Civil War. Political and social institutions were abolished; language and culture, repressed.

In 1980, for the first time in forty-eight years, Catalans were free to elect representatives to their own governing body, the Generalitat.

'We accept, we agree that we are Spaniards, but we are Spaniards in a different form than the other Spaniards. We are Spaniards being Catalans,' says Jordi Pujol, president of the Catalan government. 'We want to remain Spaniards, but we also want our language, our culture, our traditional political institutions, and our reality as a different people to be accepted in Spain.'

Catalonia today represents probably the best balance between individuality and nationality, the most positive model for maintaining individual identity while participating in the collective. An old Catalan proverb states, 'A country that defends its language defends itself'. Another minority people in Spain, the Basques, are much more liable to commit bomb outrages in their nationalist cause.

Singapore

In Singapore, the city-state racing to be internationalized, there is increasing anxiety about Westernization. The loss of 'core Asian values' and 'preoccupation with self rather than community' among the younger generation have Prime Minister Lee Kwan Yew worried. 'That we can become a pseudo-Western society,' he said in a recent speech, 'would be a disaster.'

He created the Speak Mandarin campaign to reduce Westernization by discouraging the use of English and what he regards as Pidgin Chinese.

The Soviet Union

Nationalism is surging forward in the Soviet Union, the greatest multi-national country the world has ever known. There are fifteen republics, 104 ethnic groups, and 100 languages—and thirteen time zones.

In the *glasnost* era a wave of nationalism is spreading across the huge Soviet nation:

- As early as 1986 Kazakhs rioted in Central Asia when a Russian replaced a local party boss.
- In 1987 some 800 Tatars demonstrated in Red Square over

the loss of their Crimean homeland in the 1940s, when Stalin deported them to Central Asia.

- Two old Christian nations, Armenia and Georgia, have held numerous demonstrations, escalating to riots. The Armenians feel persecuted by the mainly Islamic republic of Azerbayan next door. One area in Azerbayan is inhabited mainly by Armenians, and there have been a lot of racist murders here.
- The old Baltic republics, Estonia, Latvia, and Lithuania —which were independent until 1940—have declared their independence and done just about everything except secede from the Soviet Union.

In the name of *perestroika*, the Baltic republics are invoking Gorbachev's reforms to assert their long-suppressed nationalism. Early in 1989 the legislature of Estonia voted to make Estonian, a language related to Finnish, the official language, replacing Russian. In what sounds like a replay of the language wars of Quebec, Russians there would have to learn Estonian. The Estonian law is more liberal, though; signs on streets and in business could contain small Russian translations. Later in 1989 the Moldavian parliament declared Moldavian the official language. Moldavian is actually a dialect of Rumanian written in the Cyrillic alphabet.

Several other republics—Armenia, Georgia, and Azerbayan —are also considering laws to replace Russian with the local ethnic language.

Cultural nationalism runs deep. When it is challenged, or when there is a new opportunity for its expression, it will rise to the surface.

Global Lifestyle and Human Rights

'The emerging global culture is not all T-shirts and fast foods, thank God,' writes Walter Truett Anderson, a writer with Pacific News Service and author of *Rethinking Liberalism*. 'It is also a widening acceptance of principles of human rights. Such principles are becoming global norms, fragile ones to be sure, often honoured in rhetoric and brutalized in practice, but nonetheless, understandable statements of what peoples all over the world can demand for themselves, and can expect to be demanded of them by others.'

The Vienna accords on human rights—following the Helsinki accords of 1975—was signed by thirty-five nations in early 1989, promising to permit human rights such as freedom of information, of religion, of association, and of emigration. The accord was signed by the Soviet Union, the United States, and Canada as well as all European nations (except Albania). It is not going to be obeyed by all of them but it will have some effect.

The trend toward a global lifestyle, and the countertrend toward cultural assertion represent the classic dilemma: how to preserve individuality within the unity of the family or community.

The more humanity sees itself as inhabiting a single planet, the greater the need for each culture on that globe to own a unique heritage. It is desirable to taste each other's cuisine, fun to dress in blue denim, to enjoy some of the same entertainment. But if that outer process begins to erode the sphere of deeper cultural values, people will return to stressing their differences, and suffer a sort of cultural backlash. Each nation's history, language, and tradition are unique. So in a curiously paradoxical way, the more alike we become, the more we will stress our uniqueness.

The Welsh, French-Canadians, and Catalans are not the anomalies; they are the bellwethers. The cultural integrity of these countries has been threatened far longer than the rest of us have experienced. As we partake of the global lifestyle, we will begin to assert our cultural nationalism much as they have.

In 1992 an economically integrated Europe will be accompanied by an outbreak of cultural assertiveness for the rest of the 1990s. It will inflame and enhance the global renaissance in the arts and literature, in poetry and dance and song.

5

The Privatization of the Welfare State

Few leaders in history may be said to have changed their country's basic direction. Margaret Thatcher is one of them. She reversed the movement toward socialism in the United Kingdom. She alone believed that 'what has seemed the march of history could be halted or reversed'.

She never made any secret of her desire to 'bury socialism'. Her ideological objectives were to turn Britain into a nation whose citizens own their own homes and hold stock in its corporations. Mrs Thatcher now says that the Conservatives' task is to lead the nation into the 1990s.

'We intend to spread the ownership of homes, shares, and pensions even more widely than we've already done. We shall continue to sell state industries back to the people,' reads the 1987 British election Tory platform pledge. 'We want to give more power back to people to conduct their own lives. In 1979, less than 7 per cent held any shares in British industry, while less than 50 per cent owned their homes. Now, more than 20 per cent own shares, more than 66 per cent own their homes.'

Margaret Thatcher hit a chord with the British people. By the Autumn of 1987, after her third smashing reelection, even the Labour party was copying her.

BRITAIN AS MODEL

Between 1980 and 1988 more than 40 per cent of Britain's state sector was transformed to private enterprise. For this reason alone it must be considered the primary model in the global shift from the welfare state to privatization.

- More than 1 million former tenants in public housing became homeowners.
- Sixteen state-controlled enterprises, including British Telecom, British Gas, the Trustee Savings Bank, Jaguar and British Airways, were privatized.
- More than 600,000 former government employees now work in the private sector.
- In the process an astonishing 400,000 workers bought shares in their companies, on very favourable terms.
- Privatization has gathered more than $11 billion into the UK treasury.

'It's the biggest story of the 20th century,' says Madsen Pirie, president of the Adam Smith Institute in London, a free-enterprise think tank. 'Bigger even than the collapse of Keynesianism. It marks the reversal of 100 years of collectivism.' Even Soviet socialism hasn't been around that long.

The Tory Programme

After her landslide election victory in 1987 Prime Minister Thatcher declared that since she had succeeded in reviving free enterprise and competition, her aim now was to dismantle 'municipal socialism'.

'We will free tenants from their dependence on council landlords,' Mrs Thatcher said, 'we will free parents to choose the schools they want for their children.'

In 1987 she vowed to broaden homeownership from 62 per cent to 75 per cent of British households, increase competition within the National Health Service, and set stricter standards for welfare recipients.

She said that the most important task of Parliament was to raise the quality of education. New education laws would allow local schools to break away from Labour-dominated local governments to become 'independent state schools'.

True to her conservatism, Mrs Thatcher would increase the number of commercial television channels, while establishing a Broadcasting Standards Council to monitor sex and violence on television.

Is there strong opposition to this powerful lady? By 1989 there was the usual mid-term swing back in British opinion polls against the government of the day. But the swing against her three years before the obligatory general election (1992) was not a great as it was two years before her re-election victories in 1983 and 1987. Within the Tory party, the Cabinet is all Thatcherite, and no one, in the words of ex-Minister John Biffen, is about to go on 'a frantic and frenetic search for new measures of liberalism'.

'Our purpose as Conservatives,' said the prime minister, 'is to extend opportunity and choice to those who have so far been denied them.'

Not content to point to her record or to consolidate her gains, Mrs Thatcher is a crusader who believes in extending her revolution.

Prime Minister Thatcher takes herself very seriously. 'Our third election victory was only a staging post on a much longer journey. I know with every fibre of my being that it would be fatal for us to just stand where we are now,' she said. 'Whose blood would run faster at the prospect of five years of consolidation? Of course, we secure what we've achieved. But we move on, applying our principles to even more challenging grounds.

'It is interesting that no party now dares to say openly that it will take away from the people what we have given back to the people.'

Labour Party Copying Her

Neil Kinnock, the Labour party leader, has met this problem by changing the nature of his party. Mrs Thatcher's programme to increase homeownership and privatize state-owned industry has found favour with many traditional Labour voters. Kinnock has therefore begun to copy many of Thatcher's policies.

Kinnock has urged his party to examine its socialist principles in light of the new 'realities' brought about by nine years of Prime Minister Thatcher's 'popular capitalism'. The Labour party, he concludes, must choose whether to adjust to 'a changing economy, a changing electorate' or become a party of 'permanent condolence senders'. In 1988, some 8 per cent of its members quit, the biggest exodus since 1981.

Kinnock is keenly aware of how outdated Labour's traditional message sounds to the working class in Thatcher's England.

'What do you say to a docker who earns $400 a week, owns his house, a new car, microwave and video, as well as a small place near Marbella? You do not say, "Let me take you out of your misery, brother".'

Labour has long since abandoned its call for a state-managed economy: Mr Kinnock concedes that Mrs Thatcher's market economy is 'an adequate system' for providing what consumers want. The opposition party has begun to accept that many of Mrs Thatcher's changes are here to stay.

At a Labour party conference a resolution to nationalize everything that has been, or would be, privatized by the Tories was defeated nearly two to one.

The debate in the Labour party has changed from how much of Thatcherism should be rejected to how much should be *accepted*. But the party does not initiate many new ideas of its own. A report authored by Kinnock, 'Moving Ahead', admitted the Labour party lacked credibility on the economy and argued the party should combat Thatcherism by arguing in the same terms of 'individual self-interest and prosperity'.

Kinnock's admirers say that he has now convinced the electorate that a Labour Cabinet would no longer consist of 'ministers hell-bent on spending like drunken sailors'. He now appears as a man who would implement Thatcherite policies but with more compassion.

Kinnock's critics say that episodic successes in by-elections and opinion polls (and European Community elections) will, just as with the Democratic party in the United States, seduce the Labour party into thinking it can regain power without really changing.

Shareholders' Democracy

Mrs Thatcher has said she regards the extension of share ownership as one of the achievements of which she is most proud. It is the most original part of her programme and has leveraged the most change.

Between 1979 and 1989 the number of people owning shares in Britain has almost tripled, from 7 to 20 per cent of the adult population. Many bought stock with the privatization of the giant utilities British Telecom, British Gas, British Airways and in late 1989, the ten water authorities of England and Wales. Waiting in the wings: British Electricity, the largest utility of them all.

During the flotation of British Telecom stock, the trade union movement urged British Telecom workers not to buy shares. But 96 per cent did.

One of the great success stories was National Freight Consortium (NFC). At the time of its sale about 10,000 NFC workers bought shares. Now more than 27,000, virtually the entire work force, hold stock. And shares are worth a phenomenal forty-seven times the original price. Since it was sold to a management led consortium of staff and pensioners in 1982, the pretax profits of this trucking group have increased ninefold, and its reputation with customers has improved dramatically. 'When National Freight was owned by the state it was appalling. Our dealers had to bribe drivers to get deliveries made,' says Sir John Egan, chairman of Jaguar, itself privatized in 1984. 'It's a very good contractor now.'

The most outspoken enthusiasts for privatization are top managers of companies that previously were under state control. They have escaped from a rigid system that subjected them to constant official interference—political, social, and economic obligations irrelevant or contrary to their commercial objectives.

In 1988 Britain experienced a symbolic crossover. For the first time in history more British citizens were holders of shares than were members of unions.

Water and electricity privatization are proceeding in this Parliament. Potential areas for later privatization include forestry, prisons, railways, coal and the post office. Madsen Pirie even foresees the government's selling off land it owns. With a potential price tag of $336 billion, selling off such land could keep the privatization business going, at the current rate of $7.5 billion annually, for another forty years.

At the Conservative party's conference in October 1988, Energy Minister Cecil Parkinson pledged that Parliament would take the coal industry private. 'From the days when the miners' leaders thought they owned the government—to the day when every miner owns part of his own mine,' he said to a standing ovation. 'That's the change. That's the British revolution.'

Forward to the Year 2000

By May, 1989, Margaret Thatcher, the grocer's daughter who became the first woman prime minister in England's history, marked a new achievement: She became the longest continuously serving British prime minister this century.

During her stewardship most Britons grew wealthier. Average real earnings have risen by a quarter, while in much of Labour's 1970s they stood still. First-time stock owners, buying shares in the privatization of state-owned enterprises, tripled to 8 million. Two-thirds of Britons own their homes, up from 50 percent in 1980. Unemployment was down from a record high of 13 per cent to a seven-year low of 5.9 per cent in 1989.

If she were to serve a full fourth term, she would complete it at age seventy-two and be within three years of overtaking Sir Robert Walpole (1721–1742) as Britain's longest-serving prime minister—and still be younger than Winston Churchill was when he first became peacetime prime minister.

GLOBAL PRIVATIZATION

Where Mrs Thatcher has led, more than 100 countries have followed. That is why she attracts more admiring crowds abroad than she does at home. It was she who began the process of rolling back the frontiers of state. From Chile to Turkey and from Brazil to Bangladesh, from Italy to Tanzania, state governments are selling enterprises to private owners. Their motives range widely. Some do it for policy reasons; others, just to raise money.

- During the 1980s, the *Australian* and *New Zealand* Labour governments have removed exchange and price controls, abolished subsidies, restored free-market competition, reduced state intervention and state ownership—after their nominally conservative predecessors had been moving in the opposite direction.

- *Nigeria* is planning to sell its stake in 160 state-owned banks, breweries, and insurance companies and the country's electric utility.

- *Turkey* plans to denationalize its 263 state companies.

- *Pakistan* has privatized more than 2000 rural rice, flour and cotton mills. In 1990, the government of Prime Minister Benazir Bhutto will sell off some large state companies including Pakistan International Airlines.

- The new government in *Argentina* is making privatization a central plank of its economic reforms. ENTel, Argentina's state-owned telecommunications company, will be sold in June 1990.

- The *Mexican* government has reduced the number of state-owned companies from 1155 in 1982 to fewer than 700. It has sold a state chain of five-star hotels and withdrawn from the automobile industry with the sale of Vehiculos Automotores Mexicanos and Renault de Mexico. In May 1989 Mexico announced it would sell its majority share in the country's leading airline, Mexicana, to Mexican and foreign investors. The sale of the state telephone company is next.

- Soon after Corazon Aquino assumed power in the *Philippines*, she promised an ambitious privatization programme. She pledged to sell off any state-run company 'found unnecessary or inappropriate to maintain'. She said she 'wanted government to get out of business, and fast'.

- *Canada's* province of Quebec has a minister of privatization and *New Zealand's* Labour government had something like one.

Nations of Stockholders

In Britain privatization is pushed as 'popular capitalism'. 'We are determined to make share ownership available to the whole nation,' reads a Conservative party manifesto. 'Just as with cars, television sets, washing machines and foreign holidays, it would no longer be the privilege of the few; it would become the expectation of the many.'

The democracies of Western Europe seem intent on becoming nations of shareholders as well. In *France*, for example, the number of private shareholders has tripled since the end of 1986, when the first state-owned company, a glassmaker was privatized.

At the Paris Bourse, individual shareholders now account for an impressive 80 per cent of the value of transactions. In the last three years 138 companies—worth a combined $20.4 billion and employing more than 300,000 workers—have moved to the private sector. The sale of Paribas, the merchant bank, attracted an astounding 3.81 million investors.

The socialists, who returned to power in 1988, have not renationalized any of the privatized companies.

In *Portugal* in July 1987 Anibal Cavaco Silva won the most dramatic general election in Portuguese history. His platform: to reverse all the nationalization of the 1970s. He immediately announced plans to privatize the state-owned breweries, a tobacco company, cement and pulp manufacturers, and banks.

The prime minister's plan faced some legal barriers: the Communist-inspired Constitution of 1976 declared the nationalized companies to be 'untouchable'. But a new mood in Portugal today favours privatization and private investment. Young business people, the prime minister believes, have 'different attitudes, are more innovative, open to risk and less inclined to wait about for government handouts and subsidies which solve nothing'.

The *Netherlands* is famous worldwide for a lavish welfare state, but a new prime minister has earned popular favour by reversing that tradition. Ruud Lubbers at forty-two became the youngest prime minister in Dutch history. He is the first Dutch premier to begin paring down the caretaker state, cutting government spending, shrinking the budget deficit, and trimming taxes—all at once. Even civil servants' wages have been cut. In 1986 he began his second term, clearly part of the conservative tide that has swept Western Europe. In 1989 he won again, increasing the number of seats for his party in the Dutch parliament.

The Dutch prime minister believes that the way to finance an increasingly expensive welfare system is to move away from the caretaker state and toward what he calls a 'caring society'—in which the individual takes more responsibility for providing social services, thereby relieving the financially strapped government. 'There was a tradition in our financially good times to let the government subsidize everything, at a hundred per cent, and I guess we have gone a little too far,' he said.

In *Turkey* in 1986 the government announced plans to de-nationalize 100 per cent of its 263 state companies. 'The people, instead of the state, from now on will play the leading role in industry and services,' said Prime Minister Turgut Ozal, who had long promised such a programme to 'change the economic and social landscape of Turkey' and 'help us attain the levels of the advanced Western countries.'

Shares in the state enterprises will be offered first to employees, then to people living nearby, and then to Turkish workers abroad. The remainder of the shares will be offered to foreign investors via the Istanbul Stock Exchange, which opened in 1986.

The privatization trend is sweeping *Canada*. The government has sold two aircraft companies, a telecommunications company, and most of Air Canada. It is considering selling shares in Petro-Canada.

The province of Quebec has been the most aggressive in selling off its commercial ventures. Since 1986 the Liberal government of Quebec Premier Robert Bourassa has sold an airline, a sugar-beet refinery, a fish processor, a gold-mining company, and controlling interest in a large forest products company, totalling about $600 million.

'We don't want the state to intervene as much as it did in the past,' says Pierre Fortier, Quebec's minister of privatization. 'We want to be more of a catalyst than an entrepreneur.'

Chile has moved into privatization further and faster than any other Latin American country. The reason: its close ties with the Chicago School of economics, well known for its free-market advocacy. Between 1973 and 1975, 350 small- and medium-size companies were turned back to their original owners. Nearly 100 banks and other companies worth $916 million were sold between 1975 and 1983. In 1986–87 shares in 23 companies were sold, raising approximately $500 million; the sales included a telecommunications group; the national telephone company (CTC); the electrical company, Endesa; the computer company called Ecom; and Lan Chile, one of two national airlines.

Chile has sold 65 per cent of a nitrate mining company, 49 per cent of an electricity generating plant and a medical and chemical laboratory, and 100 per cent of the electric utilities serving the

Santiago and Valparaiso metropolitan areas. In 1987 the government of Chile completed the sale of 100 per cent of Pacific Steel, a holding company primarily engaged in integrating steel production and exploitation of iron ore deposits and one of the largest companies in Chile. Its 1986 sales totalled $319 million, including $120 million in exports, mostly ore to Japan. About 9000 people bought stock in Pacific Steel, including 4000 of the 6500 employees. The company provided loans to encourage employees to buy stock.

Jorge Bugueno, sales manager of the iron ore subsidiary, says it was difficult at first to stir interest in stock purchases among mine and plant workers. But share prices rose. And after dividends equal to two months' salary were paid, interest picked up.

Privatization Popular in Africa

After independence from European colonial powers, African countries usually nationalized companies or created unwieldy state-owned companies. Today those trends are being reversed. Nationalization is no longer fashionable; the new buzzword is 'privatization'.

- Nigeria is planning to sell its stake in 160 state-owned banks, breweries, insurance companies and utilities.

- Kenya intends to divest the government's interest in more than 400 enterprises wholly or partly owned by the state.

- Marxist Mozambique has privatized more than 20 industrial plants since 1985.

- Tanzania, once a model for African socialism, is seeking foreign managers to take over state-run hotels and game lodges.

- Leninist parties that run the governments of Angola and Benin are preparing to sell money-losing state companies. Angola is pushing to privatize its state mining, fishing, and construction companies.

- Togo started to privatize 18 companies in 1988. This West African country was the first to try privatization and has pushed it the farthest. 'We have decided to have a completely liberal economy; the state will not put another franc into the state companies,' says Koffi Djondo, Togo's minister of state enterprises and industry.

In the 1980s an estimated 5 per cent of Africa's state-owned companies were privatized. There is still a long way to go. Privatization is likely to be limited in many African countries by the shortage of local capital and management skills and a variety of other political and economic obstacles.

But the ground has been broken. Over the past few years African countries have begun to turn their backs on central planning and state control. As experience in privatization grows and success stories spread, more will embrace experiments in reversing nationalization.

The United States and Privatization

The United States has privatized a few railroads but has not been a big player in the privatization game because it did not nationalize very many companies in the first place.

At the state and local level, however, the privatization trend continues strongly: As of mid-1989, 36 per cent of local governments hire private contractors to collect garbage and repair streets. One of the most recent manifestations is the contracting out of the management of prisons.

At the national level there is increasing talk of the US privatizing the Postal Service and the Social Security system, or at least opening the doors to private-sector alternatives.

A leading advocate of a private Social Security system is Peter Ferrara, who was a member of the White House Office of Policy Development during President Reagan's first term and now writes on Social Security issues for two conservative think tanks, the Cato Institute and the Heritage Foundation.

Individual retirement accounts, life insurance, disability insurance, health insurance, and other vehicles perform the same function as Social Security benefits which the British call old age pensions. 'Why can't workers be allowed to choose among these private-sector alternatives instead of social security?' asks Ferrara.

Forcing workers to invest in Social Security is 'a rather heavy restriction on freedom of workers to control their own incomes', Ferrara believes. He complains that state old-age pensions are a system of replacing what could be 'a private financial industry represented by the private alternatives, replacing a private, competitive, flexible, decentralized free market'.

'What is needed is a new compact between the generations, modernized for the twenty-first century,' says Ferrara, who thinks that the elderly should get their benefits but that young people should be free to choose other options (like private pension schemes) as 'part and parcel of the basic free-market cause now sweeping the world—the expansion of economic freedom and growth through less government'.

Privatizing the Postal Service

Many Americans believe that the US government's monopoly over letter mail is an economic anachronism whose days are numbered.

Postal workers' wages are 40 per cent higher than those of the average US worker. Service is slow and unreliable; 9 per cent of all third-class mail never reaches its destination, and more than 80 per cent of second-class mail arrives late. The number of postal employees, nevertheless, has grown by more than 100,000 since 1981.

The cost of first-class stamps has also continued to rise—from six cents as recently as 1970 to twenty-five cents in 1988, more than twice the rate of inflation during the past two decades.

Unlike Britain's Royal Mail, the US Postal Service itself has actively pursued privatization. More than 10 per cent of its budget now goes to private operators for transportation, sorting and rural delivery. The American way will eventually be followed throughout Europe and the Pacific Rim. President Reagan's Commission on Privatization in 1988 recommended that the federal government sell Amtrak and the Postal Service.

When you consider the business done by private carriers like Federal Express and United Parcel Service, plus fax machines and electronic mail, it is clear that the US Postal Service is already at least halfway to privatization.

Privatizing Unemployment Insurance

Two British writers have proposed an intriguing twist in the privatization picture. Michael Beenstock of London's City Uni-

145

versity and Valerie Brasse take on the task of reformulating unemployment insurance in a book entitled *Insurance for Unemployment*.

Premiums for unemployment, they argue, should reflect the real risk of becoming jobless. The cost of insuring your life or your house depends upon the risks. Why should that not be the case with your job? At present, an accountant (whose risk of losing his or her job is not great) is subsidizing the high-risk construction worker. Under a private scheme the individual would be free to buy as much insurance as he wanted. Competing insurance companies could offer cheaper, more efficient service than a state monopoly.

There are all kinds of problems with this scheme, but it does suggest that the enthusiasm for market forces is touching almost every aspect of our lives.

Privatization is an idea whose time has returned. The postwar tide toward state ownership of business activity is being reversed.

The Rise of the Market Place in Italy

Italy has been losing more than 100,000 industrial jobs a year for a decade. The old blue-collar Communist following is dwindling as factories are automated and the service sector booms. Small businesses with 100 workers or fewer now employ about two-thirds of Italian industrial workers. That leaves the Communist party hard pressed to reach its traditional constituency.

In Italy, however, the decline of Communist party and union clout does not translate as a loss for the left overall. In Italy, unlike Britain or West Germany, there is no talk of a basic ideological shift toward conservatism. In June 1987 about half the voters chose leftist parties. Still, Italy's Communist party lost more than 1 million votes to rivals across the spectrum, from Christian Democrats on the right to the Proletarian Democrats on the left.

'This was not a simple defeat but a broad rejection of the party's image and credibility,' said Stefano Draghi, an analyst for the Communist party's secretary. Even more disheartening for the party, some of the biggest losses were incurred in the northern industrial cities once known as the Red Belt. Many young voters defected.

Today's transformation of Soviet socialism does not help

matters much, either. 'If Gorbachev were Italian, he would vote Socialist,' says Massimo Pini, a Milan businessman closely allied to the Socialist party.

In the new Italy, ideologies take a backseat to business. A surprising number of Italians seem genuinely convinced that what is good for Fiat, or Montedison, or Olivetti, is good for Italy.

For many Italians today, industrialists and entrepreneurs are the nation's superstars and role models, as well known as the best soccer players and as glamorous as the leading film and television stars. Their thoughts and actions are chronicled in society and sports columns as well as in the political and financial pages of newspapers and periodicals.

Bocconi, Milan's business university, was once the least prestigious university in Italy. Among upwardly mobile families engineering used to be the prestigious degree. Today Bocconi is the top. Founded only fourteen years ago its graduate school now turns down nine out of ten applicants.

Today's well-off Italians include so many restaurant owners, artisans, small businessmen, taxi drivers, and other kinds of self-employed 'small people' that sociologists and journalists speak of the new 'Italian dream' as a reincarnation of the 'American dream', while Italy's well-to-do have joined the upper echelons of the global elite.

ITALIANS—RICH PEOPLE, proclaimed a recent cover of *Mondo Economico*, a respected economic journal. The story reported that Italians are among the world's conspicuous consumers, spending huge amounts on jewellery, expensive cars, and other luxury items and taking vacations in exotic places.

The young leftists of the late 1960s and 1970s have become middle-aged entrepreneurs and business leaders eager to make up for lost time and lack of training. They are crowding into a growing number of business schools offering mid-career management courses. Their younger brothers and sisters never even went through a leftist phase. Even union leaders agree that 'profit', once a dirty word, has become respectable in Italy.

Scandinavia

In Scandinavia the welfare state has earned the famous characterization 'cradle to grave'. People are born in state-run hospitals, go to state-run day-care centres, receive state grants for the university, attend state-training programmes if they lose their jobs, and finish their days in state old-age homes.

Now that people are living longer, that model cannot be afforded. In all rich countries, the cost of paying old-age pensions has already soared. In 1949, the maximum annual social security tax in the United States was just $60. By 1958, it was $156, and by 1965 it was $348. Now it is $3600.

The cost of old-age pensions will sky-rocket when the enormous number of babies born in 1946–65 reach pensionable age of 65 in 2011–2030. Ferrara believes that today's young workers won't get their promised social security benefits in the US. If they do, this would require that pay-roll taxes in the US more than double, putting the total combined US employer and employee pay-roll tax as high as 35 per cent, compared with 14 per cent today.

Something of the same sort of 'old-age pensions crisis' is likely to occur everywhere, but Scandinavia will have a special shock.

Healthcare costs for the old make this worse.

The welfare state is popular with most Scandinavians, but taxes to pay for these services are not. Tax dodging is pervasive, especially in Sweden (which has had the world's highest income tax rates). There are also complaints about declining standards in health care and education. Throughout Denmark, Norway, and Sweden, there is a marked sense of disenchantment. Many people are demanding tax reform measures similar to those recently enacted in the United States. Many people wonder whether so much government welfare is truly good for them.

In Sweden these sentiments have been manifested in a new centrist political force that supports both free enterprise and some government assistance.

The people's Liberal party, headed by Bengt Westerberg, has nearly tripled in size since 1985, winning some 13 per cent of the vote in the 1989 election. The Social Democrats hung on to power, but Westerberg and the Liberals grabbed the headlines.

'We in the Liberal Party stand on two legs,' says Westerberg, 'one is a hard belief in the free market and individual liberty; the other is a belief in social justice.'

Westerberg does not oppose social services but believes the giant public sector smacks of 'big brother'. The state is unable to provide services efficiently, he argues, and is squeezing off private initiative. His solution is to allow private companies to compete with public monopolies in such fields as day and health care.

What does this new force represent? Some observers see Westerberg as the next nonsocialist prime minister. 'He came out of nowhere to take over the party,' say Daniel Tarshys, a Liberal parliament member and a professor of political science. 'His combination of market economy and caring society worked.'

In Sweden, which carried the welfare state the farthest, government spending rose from 31 per cent of its gross domestic product (GDP) in 1960 to a peak of 67 per cent in 1982—the highest proportion in any developed country (61.5 per cent in 1988). Yet Sweden's economy has remained quite strong. That challenges the conventional wisdom of the 1980s: that a big public sector puts a drag on economic performance. But the Social Democrats' commitment to an efficient capitalist private sector has enhanced rather than choked growth. While Sweden's capitalist sector maximizes output, its public sector redistributes the wealth through taxes and transfers.

The 'Swedish model' consisted of five main ingredients:

1. A fairly tight fiscal policy
2. Nonintervention in the production of goods; market forces deciding which companies fail or thrive, and ownership of industry in private hands
3. A policy to reduce wage differentials
4. Job creation schemes to deal with unemployment
5. Improvement of labour mobility through grants to help workers move and secure retraining. (When an unemployed worker refuses to accept retraining, he does not get full unemployment pay.)

This model served Sweden well until the middle of the 1970s, when it was hit hard by the oil crisis and the economic shift from an industrial to an information base. Since then the Swedes have been earnestly re-examining their approach. When asked recently which Western country might be the most interesting economic model for the Soviet Union, Gorbachev's economic adviser, Abel Aganbegyan, unhesitatingly said, 'Sweden is the most interesting to us'.

THE DECLINE OF THE WELFARE STATE IN THE UNITED STATES

Perhaps the best example of the push for privatization in the United States is the nationwide movement toward getting people off welfare and into private-sector jobs. To date, some thirty-nine states have enacted workfare programmes. Congress has mandated that all states must have such jobs programmes by the end of 1990.

It is a dramatic reversal of a fifty-year cycle of increased government assistance in the United States, which began with the New Deal's Social Security Act of 1935 and culminated in Lyndon Johnson's Great Society.

Workfare is a practical response to the majority of Americans who complain the welfare state has gotten out of hand.

The new pro-work sentiment is well expressed by the National Governors Association (twenty-eight Democrats, twenty-two Republicans): 'It is our aim to create a system where it is always better to work than be on public assistance . . . the provision of genuine employment opportunities represents the surest route out of poverty for our nation's poor families and children.'

New Values/New Policies

Workfare policy reflects a new mix of American values:

1. The belief that people are better off working than depending on government resources
2. The trend for middle-class and well-to-do mothers to work
3. The emergence of a new social contract—that people who accept welfare benefits owe the government a good-faith attempt to get a job.

It is a classic example of the convergence of changing values (it is acceptable to require women to work) and economic necessity (the need to 'balance the budget' in combination with the need to fill many vacant jobs created by labour shortages).

Unlike the New Deal and Great Society programmes, conceived in Washington and imposed top down on the nation, workfare has emerged experimentally state by state. Revised, tested, and tinkered with, workfare has evolved a lengthy, successful track record.

There are about 11 million people on welfare, called Aid to Families with Dependent Children (AFDC). The 1988 AFDC budget was $16.6 billion. Monthly AFDC payments vary state by state from a high of $784 for a family of four in Alaska to a low of $136 in Mississippi.

Welfare is a direct result of couples not marrying, of fathers failing to support their offspring. Thus 90 per cent of adults on welfare are mothers with dependent children; 67 per cent of all welfare recipients are children under eighteen.

Even before workfare, Americans were asking many painful questions about the impact of welfare on individuals, families, the nation.

Does welfare destroy the incentive to work? Promote teenage pregnancy? Discourage marriage and a stable family life? Does it encourage a cycle of dependency on government assistance that is passed from one generation to another?

Losing Ground

No one has raised these questions better than Charles Murray, author of *Losing Ground: American Social Policy, 1950–1980*. He contends that those whom the welfare state sought to assist were worse off in 1980 than they were before the Great Society programmes.

In 1968, 13 per cent of Americans could be classified poor, argues Murray. In 1980—after the United States had quadrupled social welfare expenditures—the percentage was still 13 per cent. Yet from 1950 to 1980 social welfare costs increased thirteen times.

It is one thing to complain that welfare costs too much. It is quite another to conclude, as Murray has, that welfare expenditures are not buying any real social change. But page by page, statistic by grim statistic, Murray reaches an unsettling conclusion: The more America spent on the welfare state, the worse off the poor became.

Needless to say, Murray's conclusions have proved controversial; several liberals have debated with Murray, disputing his contention in person and in print.

But those who support workfare—the great majority of both liberals and conservatives, blacks and whites—do so because they agree with Murray's sad conclusions, controversial or not.

Reformulating Questions

Even as Americans raise their voices in favour of welfare reform, there are unprecedented demands that federal and state governments do more to 'help' homeless people and others. The welfare state, then, is not entirely dead.

Somewhere between do-gooder liberalism (which may do very little good) and hardhearted conservatism (which can really be out-and-out racism in fiscal clothing) are the questions people really want answered:

What are a government's legitimate responsibilities toward those who cannot help themselves?

And how can you help people without making them dependent on the government in the process?

The answer is to assist as many welfare recipients as possible to find jobs in the private sector, to privatize the welfare system.

Workfare in the States

Massachusetts

At the forefront of American workfare is the Massachusetts programme that has saved taxpayers more than $281 million. A voluntary plan enacted in 1983, it has helped 60,000 former welfare recipients into jobs paying an average full-time salary of $15,000 per year, well over twice the average AFDC benefits.

'I don't think our programme is liberal or conservative,' says Governor Michael Dukakis, who, even before losing a bid for the presidency, knew what it is like to need a job. After his first term as governor, he was defeated in 1978. Dukakis spent part of his exiled years studying welfare, which he calls the 'Middle East of domestic policy'. When re-elected governor in 1982, he had a welfare reform plan (called Employment and Training, or ET) at the ready and—this was important—put it into the hands of a director with a background in job training, rather than welfare.

The programme works like this: When a Massachusetts welfare recipient takes a job, she keeps state-paid medical insurance and receives state-paid child-care benefits and transportation allowances for a one-year transition period. Once they are in the private sector, 75 per cent are still off welfare one year later.

More than 10,000 Massachusetts firms have hired participants. Eighty per cent of placements are in the private sector, unsubsidized by government funds.

Although the programme has a good record, some critics dismiss ET's success. Economics Professor Barry Schiller argued that the success of the Massachusetts programme is 'really the product of a robust economy'. Unemployment in Massachusetts stayed at 3 per cent for much of the 1980s, the lowest in the United States.

Other critics of the Massachusetts programme ask: If you create a generous workfare programme—medical benefits, child care, education—won't you create incentives for the working poor (who are already job-ready) to sign up and go on welfare?

The governor's office answers critics with claims that it is saving taxpayers a bundle—$8000 per year in AFDC, food stamps, and Medicaid for every person who goes off welfare; cost per placement averages $5600.

'For every dollar we invest . . . we save $2 in reduced welfare benefits and increased tax revenue,' according to Public Welfare Commissioner Charles Atkins.

Michigan

In Michigan, where the sunset industrial economy has forced men and women with good-paying auto jobs onto welfare and driven unemployment to as high as 12 per cent, workfare is working nonetheless. That might silence those who claim Massachusetts's success is attributable only to its low (2.5 per cent at one point) unemployment rate.

Michigan Opportunity and Skills Training (MOST) provides child care and medical insurance, like the Massachusetts programme. It is different in that it 'pays' employers to hire clients. That is to say, employers who hire and pay regular salaries to welfare recipients get the welfare cheques up to half of the wage paid for a period of six months.

MOST cost $53 million in 1988 and saved the state a net of $81 million. Since the programme started in 1984, 150,000 welfare recipients have been placed in full-time jobs for a total savings of $730 million.

Other States

The Oklahoma Education Training and Employment Programme, begun in 1982, has placed nearly 45,000 participants into unsubsidized employment. Illinois's Project Chance put almost 160,000 people, mostly mothers with children under six, to work by March, 1988. In California, which has the country's largest welfare population, a new welfare reform act was authored by two state legislators known for being ultra-right and ultra-left.

A respected 1986 study by the Manpower Demonstration Research Corporation (MDRC) concluded that workfare 'worked'. It studied 35,000 people in eleven states and concluded that the hardest-to-place people benefitted most from workfare. It also concluded that at least half of all employable welfare recipients should be able to be holding jobs or be in training within a few years. Decreasing the welfare population by half is no mean feat. Even if a substantial initial investment is required, reducing the welfare rolls by half would save a huge amount of financial and human capital.

The Mood of America: Working Women

The workfare issues emerged in the midst of a major reassessment of American attitudes about working women. The prevailing view of the 1970s, recalls the respected columnist William Raspberry in a 1986 column, was that 'forced work' constituted an unacceptable assault on human dignity. 'AFDC mothers had the right—perhaps even the obligation—to stay home with their children,' he writes. Today most women, whether high, middle, or lower income, are working. Policy makers are now willing to suggest low-income mothers should work once their children reach school age.

When New York State announced a job programme for welfare recipients with young children, Ilene Margolin, the governor's assistant secretary for social services and the mother of a three-year-old, noted that half of all women with children under six years old work.

'So why not offer the opportunity to welfare mothers?' she asked. The programme included day care.

The New Social Contract

The rise of workfare in America is a fundamental change in the relationship between a government and its citizen, a renegotiation of the social contract. Lawrence M. Mead, associate

professor of politics at New York University and author of
Beyond Entitlements: The Social Obligations of Citizenship, believes
society should 'set clear standards for able-bodied welfare recipients'.

He believes assistance should be granted, but not without
conditions. 'People on welfare must begin to live by the same
rules of reciprocity—giving something in order to get something
—that other nondependent Americans live by,' he says.
'Welfare must begin to mean obligations as well as rights.

'We, the government, will assist you financially; you, the
welfare recipient, in turn, must make a good-faith attempt to get
work.

'I think the idea of a work requirement has become an essential part of the welfare system,' says Mitchell I. Ginsberg, dean
emeritus of Columbia University's School of Social Work.

How do welfare recipients react to this new social contract?
With enthusiasm, says one official. Michael J. Dowling, New
York State's deputy services commissioner, says, 'The first thing
they say to me when I ask what we can do is, "Are you crazy?
I want a job. Help me get a job." Workfare is designed to do
that.'

Bipartisan Support

Workfare programmes afford liberals and conservatives the
opportunity to carve out common ground. For conservatives
there's the work ethic and the new social contract: Workfare is
not a handout, but a two-way street. For liberals there's the
emphasis on job placement and training, the voluntary nature of
most programmes.

That consensus is expressed by New York Governor Mario
Cuomo, often considered ultra-liberal. In redefining 'compassion' and 'callousness', he stated, 'dependence on government subsidy from generation to generation' is 'callous'. Job
training, he believes, is more compassionate.

For both liberals and conservatives there is the satisfaction
that jobs get people out of poverty.

Origins of the Welfare State

The term 'welfare state', properly defined as a government that
spends funds to help protect citizens and promote their social

well-being, is relative. The American 'welfare state' is considered almost laissez-faire in Scandinavia.

Caring for people's welfare dates back to primitive societies and certainly to ancient Greek and Roman times. Tithing among the early Christians and the Moslem zakat partly financed charitable contributions to the poor.

But large-scale government assistance is only about 100 years old. Germany's Chancellor Otto von Bismarck introduced government-financed social insurance in 1883. Under Bismarck's plan, certain employees who became sick and could not work received medical care and cash benefits from a fund that both employers and employees paid into. In 1889 a law was passed granting a pension to virtually all German workers at age seventy.

Historians say Bismarck's real motivation was 'to check socialism and avert revolution'. Nevertheless, the result was the first modern example of state protection against life's economic insecurities.

Today a generous welfare state is in force in the Scandinavian countries, the Netherlands, Australia, and New Zealand, even though these countries are in the process of rethinking and reconceptualizing their approaches to welfare. By American standards, it is also extensive in Europe, where most countries provide health insurance or health care and some pay for higher education. About 140 countries have some sort of welfare programme. From 1945 to 1980, welfare programmes were expanding. Now the trend is rapidly reversing.

Reinventing the Welfare State

The 1984 and 1988 landslide presidential victories for the Republican party do not represent a turning away from people in need, as the liberal wing of the Democratic party might interpret them, as the victories are, however, a repudiation of the liberal way of social welfare. Most people do not want the government to spend massive amounts of money on programmes that do not work. Instead they want government funds paired with private funds and specifically directed at well-targeted opportunities, situations in which people have exercised initiative or can readily do so, like the Massachusetts welfare mothers. Government and its private partners can invest seed money like venture capitalists to amplify people's efforts.

Across the world, there is now a clear shift of emphasis to the individual from class or group (poor blacks, unwed mothers). In the past it has been: We are going to do this, or should do that, for *them*. Now the focus is shifting to the individual. What works best is a tailored programme to match individual strengths and needs, to have government in concert with the private sector respond to each individual, not to classes and groups and categories.

THE WELFARE STATE'S MEGATRENDS

Led by Margaret Thatcher, positioning herself in the path of a confluence of shifting values, 20th-century welfare statism is being reconceptualized everywhere.

The basic shift is from central government to individual empowerment:

From public housing to home-ownership
From monolithic national health service to private options
From government regulation to market mechanisms
From welfare to workfare
From collectivism to individualism
From government monopoly to competitive enterprise
From state industries to privatized companies
From state industries to employee ownership
From government Social Security plans to private
  insurance and investment
From tax burdens to tax reductions

As we move toward the next century, governments all over the world are in the process of reconceptualizing society's responsibility to its citizens, especially those citizens who truly cannot help themselves.

This process of working out what will replace the welfare state—working out what the post-welfare state will look like—will surely continue for the decade left in this century.

6

The Rise of the Pacific Rim

Five hundred years ago the world's trade centre moved from the Mediterranean to the Atlantic. Today it is moving from the Atlantic to the Pacific. The cities of the Pacific Rim—Los Angeles, Sydney, and Tokyo are taking over from the old, established cities of the Atlantic—New York, Paris, London.

Asia's Pacific Rim region is twice as large as Europe and America combined. Today Asia has half of the world's population. By the year 2000 it will have two-thirds, while Europe will have only 6 per cent. Asia is a $3 trillion-a-year market growing at the rate of $3 billion a week. Any way you measure it—geographically, demographically or economically—the Pacific Rim is a powerful global presence.

The Pacific Rim is a vast region stretching from the West Coast of South America northward and across the Bering Strait to the USSR and southward all the way to Australia, all the countries touched by the Pacific's waters.

But the driving force behind the shift from Atlantic to Pacific is the economic miracle of Asia. In this chapter, the term Pacific Rim stands for the Asian Pacific Rim, unless otherwise noted.

The Pacific Rim is emerging like a dynamic young America but on a much grander scale.

'The Mediterranean is the ocean of the past, the Atlantic the ocean of the present, the Pacific the ocean of the future,' said John Hay, US secretary of state at the turn of the last century. Today that prophecy has become a reality. The five most important points to remember about the Pacific Rim are:

1. The shift to the Pacific Rim is economically driven—and at a pace that is without precedent.

2. The shift will prove cultural as well. The countries of the Pacific Rim speak more than 1000 languages and have the most varied religious and cultural traditions in the world.
3. Although Japan is the region's economic leader today, the East Asia region—China and the Four Tigers (South Korea, Taiwan, Hong Kong, and Singapore) will eventually dominate.
4. The Pacific Rim's economic thrust is being reinforced with a commitment to education. As early as 1985, a higher percentage of young Koreans attended schools of higher education than young Britons.
5. In a global economy the rise of the Pacific Rim need not signify the decline of the West unless the West ignores the significance of this trend and fails to capitalize on it.

America's Pacific Rim states (California, etc.) are well positioned to capitalize on the shift into the Century of the Pacific.

A MASSIVE ECONOMIC SHIFT TO THE PACIFIC RIM

Because we have heard so much about the Pacific Rim it might be tempting to believe we understand its significance. To do so would be a great mistake. Most people do not realize that this massive economic shift will reshape the world totally. And few of us have any idea how to capitalize on it.

Today the Pacific Rim is undergoing the fastest period of economic expansion in history, growing at five times the growth rate during the Industrial Revolution.

'Asia looks like the best thing to happen to the world since America,' said a recent article in the *Economist*.

But one symbol of this change is difficult for many—especially Americans—to digest. In the late 1980s, for the first time in decades, no US institution is among the world's twenty-six largest banks, according to figures compiled by *American Banker*, a financial newspaper. A decade ago there was just one Japanese bank among the top ten. In 1989 Japanese banks captured the

159

first twelve spots and seventeen of the top twenty-five. New York's Citibank, the largest US bank, ranked twenty-seventh. Bank of America, once the world's largest bank, came in forty-fourth.

Thirty years ago the Pacific Rim's gross national product equalled only half of the United States' and one-third of Europe's. By 2000 its GNP will about equal North America's and probably exceed Western Europe's.

The millennium will see the world's GNP roughly divided into four quarters: the Pacific Rim, Europe, the United States, and the rest of the world.

The export-driven economies of the Pacific Rim are growing three times faster than much of the rest of the world. Between 1975 and 1988 the Four Tigers increased their share of the world's total export of manufactured goods from 4 per cent to 11 per cent. Between 1985 and 1987 they increased their share of world export of consumer electronics goods from 15 to 30 per cent. Eight of ten jobs in Taiwan depend on exports. Two-thirds of Singapore's total output of goods and services are exported. The foreign-exchange reserves of the Four Tigers (South Korea, Singapore, Taiwan, and Hong Kong) now total $100 billion —and are growing.

The Pacific's growing economic clout is clearly visible in US trade patterns. The United States today sells more to South Korea than to France and more to Taiwan than to Italy and Sweden combined. As early as 1986, US per capita sales to Taiwan were $286—higher than to Japan ($222) or France ($131).

In 1960 America's trade with Asia was about half its trade with Western Europe. Since 1983 the US Pacific trade has exceeded its Atlantic trade, and in 1988 US trade with Asia was 50 per cent larger than that with Europe, reaching $300 billion in 1988.

At this pace US trade with Asia will be *twice* the trade with Western Europe sometime in the 1990s.

Taiwan must expand trade with China—which reached $2 billion in 1988—or fall behind its Tiger competitors. Most Taiwanese entrepreneurs are eager to bury the hatchet and get on with the moneymaking. There are more than eighty factories at least partly owned by Taiwan in just the two provinces of Fujian and Guangdong on the mainland of China, according to newspaper reports from Tokyo and Beijing. Dozens of shoe, textile, and electronic-parts factories have moved to China from Taiwan in the past three years.

THE SHIFT IS CULTURAL, AS WELL AS ECONOMIC

'Since the avant-garde Japanese designers took over opening day of the ready-to-wear showings, Paris fashion has never been the same,' reads the *Washington Post*'s description of Paris's autumn fashion shows in 1987. 'They have influenced designers all over the world.' IN PARIS, A BOW TO THE JAPANESE, read the *Post*'s headline six months later for the spring 1988 showing.

The most famous Japanese designers showing in Paris are Rei Kawakubo, Issey Miyake, and Yohji Yamamoto, but there are now eight who show in the company of Saint Laurent and Givenchy. Kawakubo owns or franchises 249 retail outlets in Japan and 84 internationally.

In the 1950s New York seized leadership in the arts from Paris.

The 1990s will show Tokyo playing the leadership role in fashion, design, and many of the arts.

'The Japanese look is not trendy; it's here to stay,' says Bernard Portelli of the Okyo hair salon in Washington, DC. 'French style—it's over. There's nothing new, nothing in food, nothing in clothes. They're all following the Japanese.'

'Paris is still imbued with the spirit of 1789,' according to French architect Richard Bliath. Tokyo is 'the only city with an architecture of here-and-now.'

'The future belongs to the Japanese,' says Manhattan interior designer Jay Specter. 'When I am in France, I am fascinated by the culture, by the decoration, the furniture, the art. But I can't help feel that a great deal of it belongs to yesterday. Japan, to me, looks like tomorrow . . . like a view into the 21st century.'

Japan has opened scores of new museums since the 1970s and Tokyo has nine symphony orchestras.

Museums in the United States are now spending more of their resources to showcase Japanese art, an implicit acknowledgement of its growing influence in the West. The Los Angeles County Museum of Art spent $12.5 million on a pavilion for

Japanese art, and there is a new Japanese gallery at the Metropolitan Museum of Art in New York City.

Contemporary Japanese artists are attracting increased interest. 'There is an unprecedented coincidence of curatorial activity in this country that is looking to Japan,' says independent New York curator Alexandra Munroe.

The first major US show of new Japanese artists in eighteen years opened in June 1989 at the San Francisco Museum of Modern Art and will travel to five American cities.

Japanese cultural influence in the West is apparent in the ascendancy of Japanese architect Arata Isozaki, who designed the Los Angeles Museum of Contemporary Art, the interior of the Palladium in New York City and the expansion of the Brooklyn Museum.

Singapore has learned the value of emphasizing culture as part of a strategy to attract more visitors. In 1988 it opened the Empress Palace, a major new cultural centre whose first show featured 312 artefacts from the Qing Dynasty on view for the first time outside China.

Hong Kong has become the home of a vibrant arts scene, especially rich because it embraces both Chinese and Western culture, from Cantonese opera to the Hong Kong Philharmonic Orchestra. Hong Kong hosts the best international arts festivals in Asia and the past five years has witnessed an extraordinary boom in arts building, including the new Cultural Complex.

Hong Kong's showpiece Academy of the Performing Arts teaches dance, drama, music, and technical arts, including both traditional Chinese and Western approaches. It stresses an inter-disciplinary approach: Music students study movement, dancers study drama, and all must learn some technical skills.

The Chinese are great film fans: per capita cinema attendance in Hong Kong (eleven times a year) is third highest in the world, while mainland China ranks an astonishing twenty-one visits a year for first place (the USSR is second with fifteen). And the Chinese show every indication of becoming giants in the business. In 1988 China produced 158 feature films, and 31 Chinese films won prizes in international film festivals.

'Together, Hong Kong and China will emerge as the new fashion centre,' predicts Eddie Lau, high-fashion clothes designer. 'When China takes over Hong Kong, we will have an identity to match with our skills. China will need designers to reach out to the world, and they will find them here.'

'I think the Pacific will emerge as a major force in the arts over the next 200 years in the way European arts have had a tremendous period of hegemony that is just finishing,' says avant-garde director Peter Sellars of the Los Angeles Festival.

EAST ASIA: GIANTS OF THE 21ST CENTURY

Although Japan is the Pacific Rim's most developed country, East Asia and Southeast Asia are the world's fastest-growing regions. China and the Four Tigers have a great cultural and commercial heritage. If China continues along the capitalist road, it could eventually threaten economic Japanese leadership later in the 21st century.

In the Pacific Rim the economic strategy is beating Japan at its own game.

Countries like South Korea, which were impoverished three decades ago, now challenge the United States and Japan with exports of automobiles, television sets, ships, computers, and VCRs, and make Europe look positively anaemic.

South Korea, Taiwan, Singapore, and Hong Kong have revolutionized the theory of economic development by showing the world how to skip over much of the industrialization phase and plunge right into the information economy. They are expected to continue growing in the 1990s at annual rates ranging from 7 to 10 per cent, compared with about a 3 per cent growth for the United States.

The economies of the Four Tigers were initially built on cheap labour, but today they are turning to high-end computers and other complex tasks at which the United States and Japan were dominant. New growth areas like Thailand, Malaysia, Indonesia, and the Philippines, which have lower labour costs, will take over the low-end economic tasks. Indeed Thailand and Malaysia are already exporting some high-tech goods.

Hong Kong: Jewelled Gateway to a Giant Dragon

Modern Hong Kong artfully combines Confucianism and laissez-faire with all the convenience of Manhattan: a trading centre of high-tech buildings; advanced financial and communications systems. With a per capita GDP of above $9000, Hong Kong is twice or thrice as rich as Greece or Portugal.

Hong Kong is already one of the great financial centres of the world. By the mid-1980s Hong Kong counted '284 insurance companies, 142 mutual funds, 900 stock brokerages, 1300 registered securities dealerships', according to a *Wall Street Journal* report. Virtually all major banks have offices there. Hong Kong has the second-largest financial-futures market in the world, and its stock exchange ranks eleventh in capitalization. Hong Kong is a leading exporter of toys and textiles and has the world's second-busiest container port.

But today Hong Kong's importance is further underscored because Hong Kong is the gateway to China.

In just ten years China moved from being Hong Kong's forty-sixth most important trading partner to its first. Hong Kong is China's premier foreign investor, accounting for 75 per cent of China's foreign projects. That is why the transfer of Hong Kong to China should not interrupt its growth, despite Hong Kong's understandable nervousness after Tiananmen Square.

As 1997 (when Hong Kong reverts from British to Chinese control) approaches, Hong Kong's population is understandably sceptical about China's promise that Hong Kong can remain a free-market democracy. Thousands have already immigrated to Canada and the US.

But China and Hong Kong are mutually dependent. Hong Kong must maintain its privileged access to the Chinese giant if it is to beat out the other newly industrialized countries (NICs) as a top manufacturing centre and the top financial centre. China needs Hong Kong to keep pulling in foreign investment:

- China receives some 30 to 40 per cent of its foreign-exchange earnings either from or through Hong Kong.
- China has invested $6 to $10 billion into Hong Kong —more than the United States' $5 billion investment.
- Since 1985 China has been Hong Kong's biggest trading partner; the United States is second, and Japan third.

'There is almost no Hong Kong industry that does not have a foot in China now,' according to one Western diplomat. Some industries have vacated Hong Kong almost entirely; more than 50 per cent of toy operations have moved across the border.

In the province of Guangdong, Hong Kong capitalists and Chinese Communists are working together in a great economic collaboration.

Eighty per cent of the total investment in Guangdong is from Hong Kong. Hong Kong manufacturers employ more than 1 million workers in China's Pearl River delta, while the entire manufacturing workforce of Hong Kong consists of only 900,000 people. More than 2 million Chinese have migrated to Guangdong Province for work.

'This is the place to get into China,' said T. W. Wong, deputy director general of the Federation of Hong Kong Industries.

South Korea: Heir to the Samurai's Crown

Twenty years ago a nation of poor farmers, South Korea has become the most advanced of Asia's NICs. In 1965 a war-ravaged Korea had a per capita GNP of $120 a year. By now it is passing $4000. Although other Tigers have higher incomes per head, South Korea's large population of 43 million, together with the diversity of its production, makes it a bigger economic power.

South Korea's economy is now larger than either Denmark's or Austria's.

In 1988 South Korea's exports reached a stunning $59.7 billion, including Hyundai cars, Daewoo computers, and Samsung video recorders—40 per cent of which went to the United States. Since 1965 industrial production has increased fifty-fold, the volume of exports a hundred-fold. Exports soared 30 per cent in both 1986 and 1987. No wonder South Korea has been called the hardest-working country on earth.

In 1987 the Korean Development Institute projected that Korea's per capita GNP will surpass $5000 by the end of this century. That seems far too conservative. Real GNP continues to rise *10 per cent a year*. At that rate total GNP doubles every seven years. By UN standards, Korean income distribution is among the fairest in the world. Every developing country in the world is trying to figure out how South Korea does it.

With this stunning track record South Korea is poised to threaten Japan's pre-eminence in many industries. And neighbouring Japan is watching it with growing unease.

'Japan and the Japanese have a lot of respect for American and European economic prowess. But they are deathly afraid of the Koreans,' reports *Tokyo Business Today*. 'While the Republic of Korea usually gets lumped in with Taiwan, Hong Kong, and Singapore as one of the NICs, Korea is developing the strongest and most diverse economy of the four.'

Staking its future on automobiles, as Germany did in the 1950s, and Japan in the 1970s, South Korea will be among the top five auto-producing countries by the end of this century. (Top five in 1987 were Japan, the United States, West Germany, France, and Italy; South Korea was number ten.) In 1987, 800,000 cars were produced, eight times as many as in 1982. Two-thirds were exported. By 1993 Korea's five automakers want to double production.

South Korea is home to the world's largest steel plant and its largest dry dock. Having already stripped Japan of a sizable chunk of market share in industrial products, South Korea is pushing ahead into the information era. South Korea spends 2 per cent of GNP on research and development, compared with 3 per cent of GNP for the US and Japan. But South Korea is planning to increase R&D spending to 5 per cent by 2001. Korean companies invested $2.5 billion in semi-conductors in 1987 and 1988.

Korea has captured the low end of the American TV and VCR market from the Japanese. In 1987 South Korea's electronics production reached $17.4 billion—up 44 per cent from 1986. Electronic exports totalled $11.2 billion. The electronics industry may become the largest sector of Korea's total manufacturing sector exceeding automotive or machine tools, according to Korea's Institute of Electronics Technology.

Though the distinction is lost on most Westerners, the cultures of South Korea and Japan are quite different. And Korea's dislike of Japan, after a brutal forty-year occupation, is well known. But one thing is certain: Korea is even hungrier for success than Japan and plans to beat the old samurai at his own game. By the year 2000 Korean government planners aim for one-third of all exports to be high tech: computers, software, semi-conductors, communications equipment, and biotechnology products.

In words that echo those of rival Japan twenty years ago, Kim Young Soo, executive vice-president of Samsung Semiconductor & Telecommunications, says, 'We have no natural resources. Technology is our only survival.'

Professor Hsieh Shih-hui, of Japan's Tokai University, predicts that Korea will overtake Japan in income per head by the year 2010.

As recently as 1986 the average Korean wage was only $1.55 per hour. Korea's workers—who put in an average of fifty-four hours a week—have won wage increases of about 40 per cent between 1986 and 1989. Yet productivity has nearly kept pace with wage growth and is the envy of Asia. Between 1982 and 1986 Korean productivity increased at an annual 8.4 per cent, compared with 7 per cent in Taiwan and 3.5 per cent in Japan.

Korea's economic success is even more impressive considering it spends 6 per cent of its GNP on defence—about the same as the United States and far more than Japan's 1 per cent. The reason, of course, is the continued presence of armed Communist North Korea. But the voices advocating reunification are growing stronger. 'If we unite as one people, we can become a more powerful competitor,' says Professor Ji Byung-Moon at Kwangju's Chonnam University.

Singapore: Super City-State

Singapore, a city-state of 2.6 million people in an area smaller than New York City, is wealthy and well educated. It is a stronghold of political stability in a region that has suffered some of the worst political strife in the 20th century. Lee Kuan Yew, a benevolent dictator, has forged a nation that is independent, capitalist, prosperous, stable, and relatively free of corruption.

Singapore enjoys high growth (10 per cent in 1988), low inflation, full employment, positive balance of payments, large financial reserves, and one of the highest savings rates in the world—42 per cent in 1988. In the ten years ending in 1988 per capita income increased from $2810 to about $7500. In 1988 per capita GNP reached $8772. The main cloud on the horizon is the acute shortage of labour. Singapore's work force is only 1.1 million.

'Singapore is organized and run like a business,' says Gary Fowler, who surveyed five other Southeast Asian countries before deciding on Singapore as the site for Silicon Systems, the silicon chip-making company he manages. Tax incentives, factory space, and quick governmental action all played into his final decision.

'Our tax exemptions go to companies that help us gain a few points in the technology race and maintain our 15 to 20 years' advance over other countries in the region,' said Peng Yuan Hwang, Singapore's Economic Development Board chairman, in 1985.

Today multi-national companies, including IBM, Johnson & Johnson, and a total of more than 600 US companies, account for most of Singapore's industrial capacity and exports. Apple Computer makes most of its 11e computers in Singapore, where labour accounts for only 2 to 3 per cent of manufacturing costs. Two-thirds of the disc drives used in the US today are made in Singapore.

But the government is trying to grow its own local entrepreneurs with tax breaks, low-interest loans, and venture capital funds.

'We can't keep piggybacking on the multi-nationals,' says Eddie Foo, managing director of Singatronics, a local electronics manufacturer. 'They have no loyalty, no commitment to us. To survive, we must develop our own firms, our own technology, our own marketing.'

In 1980 Eddie Foo took over Singatronics, a $2 million calculators and electronics games business. After investing in a modernized manufacturing operation, the company went into medical electronic instruments. Its Healthcheck products now account for 25 per cent of the $33 million in annual sales.

'Within the next five or ten years, the real heart of our economy will be advanced technology developed right here in Singapore,' Vincent F. S. Yip, executive director of the government-backed Science Council of Singapore, told *High Technology* magazine.

Tragic irony may provide yet another economic boost. China's crackdown against the students and its new hardline mood may attract more investment into Malaysia and Thailand—countries for which Singapore, not Hong Kong, is the natural gateway.

Taiwan: The Little Giant

Taiwan is pleased to do business with any one of the 120 countries whose governments do not recognize it and is eager to work with one that even Taiwan refuses to acknowledge—mainland China.

What this island of 20 million inhabitants lacks in diplomatic recognition, it makes up for in economic clout. Per capita GDP exceeds $6000 a year, which is probably twelve times mainland China's. Overseas trade (exports plus imports) exceeded $110.3 billion in 1988, ranking it the world's twelfth-largest trader, neck and neck with Sweden and South Korea. Taiwan's trade surplus has grown from $1.8 billion in 1981 to $10.9 billion in 1988.

Taiwan held about $74 billion in foreign exchange reserves in 1988, the world's largest after Japan with $87 billion, but Japan has six times more people.

Politically, socially, and economically 1987 was a benchmark year for Taiwan. Martial law was lifted for the first time since 1949, as was the ban on rival political parties. Dramatically, some long-standing barriers between Taiwan and the mainland were at last dissolved, and travel between the two was permitted.

But even before this thaw, trade with the mainland through third parties had already reached $2 billion a year. It will increase monumentally, as soon as China stabilizes. Labour-intensive industries, such as footwear, apparel, and low-end consumer electronics products, have already moved manufacturing operations to China, through citizens of third countries, such as Hong Kong.

Taiwan's objective is a massive shift in its economy from easy-to-make, labour-intensive products, such as clothing, footwear, and toys, to high-value electronic items. In the meantime, Taiwan's agricultural base declined from 32 per cent of GDP in 1952 to a European-like less than 6 per cent today.

Like Japan and Britain, Taiwan is investing in the United States. By March 1988 Taiwan's US investment had reached $1.25 billion.

In contrast with conglomerate-dominated Japan and Korea, small business is the key to Taiwan's economy. In 1987 there were 316,712 factories in Taiwan, up from 28,800 in 1968. Small industries like these are able to shift gears rapidly in response to a changing world and market conditions, giving Taiwan a real competitive edge.

In the fast-paced Pacific Rim, the economic advantages belong to the swift.

China

China is the oldest continuous major world civilization. Records date back 3000 years. In the past 100 years, however, China has undergone a metamorphosis as great as any modern power.

In 1949 Chairman Mao established a Communist regime in China. Thirty years later, Deng Xiaoping introduced the primitive beginnings of market mechanisms. The Chinese, who had been considerable capitalists before 1949, took to the free market with considerable enthusiasm.

- Shanghai's first free-market site along the Jiao Road opened in 1979 with 30 stalls. Now there are more than 500 and 30,000 customers a day.
- In some years of the 1980s China's GNP growth touched 10 per cent, about the highest in the world.
- Exports rose from $30.9 billion in 1986 to $45 billion in 1988 and China became the USA's twelfth-largest trading partner.
- Some 12 million businesses engage in free enterprise. About 225,000 employ more than eight people (big business by Chinese standards). There are about 20 million jobs in the private sector.
- Members of China's elite class of factory owners can become very rich men in a country where per capita income is officially down at $300 (though really perhaps $500).

China's rapid progress unleashed forces the government could not manage or contain. Corruption was rampant. Inflation in the first five months of 1989 ran at an annual rate of 25 per cent. Young people embraced Western styles (see Global Lifestyles chapter) and the disparity between the poor majority and a new layer of nouveau riche grew increasingly visible. Hardest to confront was the new demand for democracy.

As the world knows, China's long march toward freedom hit an impasse on 3 and 4 June 1989, when government troops attacked unarmed students protesting against corruption and demanding greater democracy. Hundreds, perhaps thousands, were killed.

In the months following the bloody crackdown, China faced global condemnation. Embassies and multi-nationals withdrew personnel, dependants and investments. The World Bank and others suspended billions in loans—$6 billion held back by Japan alone. China's tourism earnings plummetted, an estimated $1 billion of much needed foreign exchange lost in 1989. Investors from Taiwan and especially Hong Kong recoiled in horror. And everyone tried to figure out what was happening.

Would hardliners like Premier Li Peng consolidate their authority in a power struggle after—or even before—top leader Deng Xiaoping's demise? Would the student leaders who escaped to the West mount a successful movement in exile as Sun Yat-sen had done before 1911? Would their aim be reform or the overthrow of the Communist regime? What role would wealthy overseas Chinese play in the country's future? How could Hong Kong trust in China's promise to keep it capitalist and free after the June 1989 massacre?

Today China presents a lot more questions than answers and the reports read in the West are rife with ambiguity.

Deng keeps promising that economic reform will continue, while Li Peng calls for more central planning. Deng chooses as his successor Jiang Zemin—the Shanghai party chief, known for his pro-western economic policies—yet permits cultural revolution-like harassment of students and workers suspected of being sympathetic to the pro-democracy protestors.

The freshman class of Beijing University in autumn 1989 will total 800, down from 2000, and students must endure a year-long indoctrination process before beginning classes. Some seniors will have to work in the countryside for a year before getting a job.

Gold Coast

Western businesspeople wonder about the fate of China's 'Gold Coast' programme which targetted coastline provinces like Guangdong and Fujian for the rapid development of low-wage, export-oriented industries, China's version of the Four Tigers model. With the help of Hong Kong entrepreneurs, Guangdong, China's premier exporter, shipped $5.5 billion in goods in 1987. The same year it attracted $5.3 billion in foreign investment, more than half of China's total.

Guangdong is home to 60,000 businesses and China's richest consumers. The average person in Guangdong earns $100 a month, twice the income of neighbouring Hunan province and about the same per capita income as Thailand (often called Asia's Fifth Tiger), and Turkey, which has petitioned to join the European Economic Community.

About 5 per cent of the prosperous regions of eastern China earn more than 10,000 yuan—$2700—each year.

Virtually all the 30,000 residents of the coastal city of Shishi, north of Xiamen in Fujian province have refrigerators and television sets. In Xiamen, the private sector accounts for 42 per cent of industrial output; in Shishi it is 82 per cent.

Long before Tiananmen Square the gap between the Gold Coast and the poorer interior was apparent. The government did not want to kill the 'golden goose', as a *Washington Post* article called the coast, but did want to try to tame it. To try to slow inflation and industrial growth, it cancelled or postponed thousands of construction and investment projects.

Although Beijing has arrested some corrupt officials along the Gold Coast, its inhabitants have escaped most of the post-Tiananmen Square indoctrination classes. They have largely been left alone to do what they do best—make money.

Even though 80 million Chinese have shifted from farming to industry, China is still an agricultural economy. 800 million are farmers, one out of every three on the planet. Thanks to policies rewarding small farmers, rural income has increased threefold in a decade. But one-tenth of China's people are still unable to feed or clothe themselves adequately. An authoritarian reversal will not help them.

A question of policy

Deng seems to want to maintain economic freedom while curtailing political freedom. He can observe China's neighbours for models of that very combination—there is Singapore and until only recently Taiwan and South Korea.

The lesson from the Four Tigers seems to be that economic freedom lays the foundations for greater political freedom. Hope for the long-term future is what fuels many of the West's dealings with China now.

Resisting pressure from Congress, President Bush imposed only limited sanctions on China, arguing that to do more would hurt its 1.1 billion people more than its hardline government. Students and dissidents want to keep the pressure on, though. 'Easing sanctions against China, that is oxygen for Li Peng's government,' said Chen Yizi, one of the highest ranking officials to escape China and an associate of deposed liberal Zhao Ziyang.

Washington seems to be following the advice of that old cold warrior President Richard Nixon, who says greater reprisals will push the Chinese into 'angry isolation' and 'dash the people's chances for further economic progress and *eventual political reform*'.

Instead, he argues, the West should 'influence its leaders to get the economic reforms back on track and also to go forward with peaceful political reforms'.

Indeed that seems to be the dominant strategy: World Bank President Barber Conable announced in autumn 1989 that he hoped to release World Bank loans held back in June. Japanese business interests were returning to China, too: 80 per cent of the 333 Japanese firms that left China returned three months later.

The pro-democracy effort should be carried out through private channels, Nixon argues. One such intermediary is Anna Chennault, the Chinese-American widow of the Major General Claire Chennault and champion of the old line Nationalist cause during the 1950s and 1960s. A long-time Bush friend, she has access to China's top leadership and has travelled often to China.

Though sensitive to China's need to save face, she is frank in private. If China is to play a role in world affairs, she tells its leaders, they must honour accepted standards of international conduct, including human rights.

China's millennium

Whatever questions remain—and there are many—there is also widespread agreement that China's economic surge in 1976–89 was extraordinary.

The biggest economic gains so far have come mostly with Hong Kong's collaboration. Once China stabilizes and begins moving forward again, its relationships with Taiwan will move to centre stage. China's economy, already jump-started, will feel the thrust of a dual rocket burst—both Hong Kong and Taiwan.

The 1988 report of a prestigious US-government commission predicted China's economy would be second only to that of the United States in just two decades.

In 1980 China's economy was only about half the size of Japan's and about one-third the size of the Soviet Union's. By 2010 it may exceed both, the Commission on Integrated Long-Term Strategy predicted. Calculations, based on figures from the Rand Commission are conservative—based on less than 5 per cent growth a year. China's has been growing about 10 per cent a year in recent years.

The tragic events of Tiananmen Square and its economic aftermath do not invalidate this prediction. Even if hardliners consolidate power and revert to the thug-like tactics of the cultural revolution, they do so without popular support. Chairman Mao and his wife mobilized gangs of students in the mid-1960s to do the dirty work of the cultural revolution, but today's students have put their bodies on the line for greater democracy.

The government has won points by acting on student demands to clean up corruption. But a return to centralized planning will cut economic growth and cause shortages of consumer goods, increasing popular unrest. As the old regime dies out, literally, it will be replaced one way or another by a new generation which has tasted economic incentives and longed for the political freedom to match it.

The whole world is moving toward greater democracy and China will follow. It took ten years for the pendulum to swing from the excesses of the cultural revolution to Deng's early reforms. Even if hardline power encrusts in a worst case scenario, it should take far less time for it to swing back.

As China's hardliners must realize, this is 1990, not 1968. China has opened up to the world. Its people are better educated and more sophisticated. Its diplomats and students have seen the West. Residents of the Gold Coast regularly view Taiwan and Hong Kong television. Hundreds of millions have seen the world on television. The intimidation tactics of the cultural revolution, though powerful, will not work as well in this new environment.

Deng Xiaoping says that by 2050 his nation will be a 'middle-developed country'. It should know by now how to do better than that. China must compete with Malaysia and Thailand to pick up the NIC's throwaway industries—like toys and textiles. The government will need eventually to liberalize rather than to 'manage' the economy. When it does it will face even greater demands for political freedom.

The long-term course is set. China cannot go back. It cannot stay where it is for very long. The great giant has been unleashed.

Malaysia

After the recession of 1985–86, government spending was cut, foreign investment regulations relaxed, and a start was made in selling off state enterprises to the private sector. Malaysia is now enjoying robust economic growth. The fastest growth of the decade (8.7 per cent) was recorded in 1988. The economy should do at least that well in 1989 and 1990. Total exports increased by 26 per cent and 23 per cent respectively in the past two years (that rate of increase means a doubling of exports in three years).

While predominantly an agricultural nation, Malaysia has become the world's third largest manufacturer of integrated circuits, behind the US and Japan. An extraordinarily high 53.8 per cent of Malaysia's manufactured exports are semiconductors and other electronic goods. It is also experiencing rapid growth in the manufacturing of air-conditioners, radios, and television sets.

The Malaysian government is preparing a big privatization programme on a scale that few governments have attempted. To be carried out in the 1990s, almost 500 companies have been named for initial privatization, with 1400 potential candidates. The sale cuts across the whole of the economy: utilities, manufacturing, finance, agriculture, transportation, construction. The National Electricity Board will be the biggest sale. In the sales, 30 per cent of the shareholdings will be reserved for Malays. With this commitment to the free marketplace, plus a good education system and a per capita income already passing $2000, which is higher than Thailand's, Malaysia will become increasingly popular with foreign investors.

Thailand

In 1988 Thailand's economy grew 10 per cent, tying it with Singapore as Southeast Asia's fastest-growing economy. The

Asian Wall Street Journal has called the Thai stock market 'one of the world's hottest'. Thailand offers low wages, a large, inexpensive work force, apparent political stability, and a pro-business environment that welcomes foreigners. Another plus: Thailand permits more personal freedom than virtually any country in Southeast Asia. No wonder it is attracting investors from Europe, the United States, Japan, and all four of the Tigers. Is Thailand on its way to becoming Asia's fifth economic tiger?

It looks that way. Just a few years ago 80 per cent of Thailand's export earnings came from a few primary commodities like rice, rubber, and tin. But in 1985 manufactured goods overtook agricultural products as Thailand's main source of export earnings. Thai exports increased 36 per cent in 1988 to $16 billion. Manufacturing exports have averaged more than 40 per cent annual growth for the past few years. Earnings from tourism are very impressive. In 1987, 'Visit Thailand Year', 3.5 million tourists contributed $2 billion to the economy, its most important source of foreign exchange.

Although manufacturing and services now dominate its GNP, Thailand remains a largely rural society; 60 per cent of Thais are still engaged in farming. In 1965 only 13 per cent of the population lived in towns and cities. In 1985 the number was still only 18 per cent. By comparison, 38 per cent live in cities in Malaysia, and 73 per cent in Brazil.

Thailand's per capita GNP reached $1045 a year in 1988 but is unevenly spread. It is likely to go higher quickly, because the productivity of its young people is starting.

'Productivity is higher in our plants here than in Japan because the workers are only about twenty years old, much younger than in Japan,' says Makoto Ikeda, director of Minebea's operations in Thailand.

'We're thinking ahead. Korea and Taiwan first exported textiles, then moved to electronics and computers. That's the direction we want to go,' says Damri Darakananda of Saha-Union. Darakananda started Saha-Union as a joint venture in 1961 with YKK of Japan. The company is now Thailand's largest exporter of manufactured goods, ranging from textiles to Nike shoes.

In 1988 the government said it believed that within ten years Thailand would be a developed country. It may not take that long. In 1988 almost 4900 new factories were opened in Thailand, and total investment reached $1.33 billion. Investment funds specializing in Thailand are now listed in New York, London, and Singapore.

Thailand will achieve a lot of industrialization by 1993, predicts Edward Chen, an Asian studies expert at Hong Kong University.

This rush to industrialization has one sophisticated observer frustrated. Thailand seems determined to become a NIC, the *Economist* complains. With that conventional objective, it is ignoring its greatest potential—services. Thailand might be wise to be the first country to bypass industrialization completely and evolve from an agricultural economy right into a service economy, a SSE—*straight to services economy*.

Thailand is doing well, says Kamchorn Sathirakul, governor of the Bank of Thailand, because it is following the Buddhist precept of *majhima patipada*, the middle path, avoiding extremes.

BEYOND ASIA

The Soviet Union has a massive presence on the Pacific Rim; its Siberian east coast stretches for 2200 miles north to south along the Pacific from Alaska to Japan.

Soviet President Mikhail Gorbachev wants to be part of Asia's economic miracle. He has invited his Pacific neighbours to help develop Siberia. To achieve 'miracle' status, the Soviets must also import both technology and investment from the United States or Japan. To win economic allies, the Soviet must 'accept the present political and strategic balance in the region instead of continually looking for ways to change it', writes Richard Holbrooke, a former assistant secretary of Asian affairs and managing director of Shearson Lehman Hutton. That is the only route, he believes, for future Soviet participation in the economic boom of the Pacific Rim.

As the Pacific Rim heats up economically, Australia and New Zealand have been trying to think Asian. During much of its history Australia identified with Britain because of its roots in the British Commonwealth. Since World War II its people have rather favoured the United States, which, after all, saved Australia from the Japanese, in 1942.

But now, as we move to the century of the Pacific, Australia is beginning to feel its role as a key part of the Pacific Rim economy and is slowly beginning to identify with Japan and its emerging Asian partners.

The country has some overborrowed internal entrepreneurs, but a free-enough market to make their shares cheap. It is thus ripe for foreign investment. In the fiscal year ending June 1988 Australia attracted nearly $4 billion in direct foreign investments, 20 per cent coming from Japan. Australia's tourism industry is among the fastest-growing in the world.

Once we enter the next millennium we will feel the impact of more of the countries in the Pacific Rim—Mexico, Ecuador, North Korea, Vietnam, and all the others—but today the focus is on Asia.

IN THE WORLD ECONOMY, EDUCATION IS THE PACIFIC RIM'S *COMPETITIVE EDGE*

In the new economic order the countries that invest most in education will be the most competitive.

In the Pacific Rim—where economic growth is much more rapid than in mature Western economies—the need for well-educated people is recognized.

An extraordinary number of young Asians came to the US for education. In the United States 44 per cent of Asian-Americans hold college degrees, compared with about 25 per cent in the US adult population.

In an information society, college pays off in the marketplace. Although Asian-Americans are only 1.5 per cent of the US population, their incomes match or exceed those of non-Hispanic whites. Chinese, Japanese, Indian, and Filipino families earned an average $26,535 a year, which is the average white family income, according to a study by the US Civil Rights Commission. Korean families earned a bit less than that—$25,234. Among foreign-born Asians, only Vietnamese, at $15,859, fell substantially below the average white family. Japanese families in America exceeded white family incomes by nearly $9000 a year.

How much are the countries of the Pacific Rim investing in education?

Japan

In Japan, 94 per cent of students stay in school beyond the legal age of sixteen as opposed to 86 per cent in the United States—an impressive showing compared with the United Kingdom, for example, where less than half stay on.

The Japanese have the highest proportion of science degrees of any country in the world, 68 per cent of all degrees awarded, compared with 25 per cent in the United States.

Japanese students attend school 240 days a year (versus 180 in the United States), 5½ days a week. Most of them feel even that is not enough. Nearly 50 per cent of middle-school children supplement their studies with *juku*—entrance-examination tutorial schools. Most experts agree Japan's economic success is linked to the rigour and efficiency of its primary and secondary schools.

Japan's university and other higher education system is weak. 'The American higher education system is the best in the world,' says Julia Ericksen, vice-provost of Philadelphia's Temple University, the first US college to establish a branch in Tokyo. 'The Japanese recognize that.'

That is one reason why the Japanese have quietly gone about trying to purchase several small US colleges, often in rural areas. The long-range plan is to create environments for more Japanese students to study in the United States.

Korea

Like the Japanese, Koreans put a high premium on advanced education. About one-third of Korean young people go on to university. In Korea 85 per cent of the seventeen- to eighteen-year-old age group stay in secondary school, more than in Britain (46 per cent) and France (75 per cent).

Since 1985, more young Koreans than young Britons have attended schools of higher education.

Half of Seoul's adult population either attends or has graduated. But education does not end with college; Korean firms provide on-the-job training for white-collar workers.

Korea has the highest number of PhDs per capita in the world, according to Ms Jacqueline Y. Pak of the Il Hae Institute, a Seoul think tank. The Daewoo Group alone needs to hire 1000 PhDs by 1990. Many no doubt will be American-educated Koreans.

South Korea turns out 32,000 applied-science graduates a year in areas like engineering, more proportionately than America and nearly as many as Japan. However, for every 10,000 people in the South Korean labour force, there are only 32 engineers. In the United States there are 160 per 10,000, and in Japan there are an extraordinary 240. The amazing thing is that even when the per capita income was about the same as Korea's is now, Japan still had about 240 engineers per 10,000 people.

When the government could not meet the demand for schooling because of 'lack of financial resources', says a publication by the Korean Economic Institute, the private sector 'stepped in'. Now 206 of Korea's 256 universities are *owned* by companies like Hyundai, Daewoo, and Korean Air.

Taiwan

Korea's and Taiwan's commitment to education exceeds or matches that of every developed country except the United States and Japan.

In the United States 44 per cent of high school graduates attend college; 39 per cent, in Japan; 30 per cent, in France; 26 per cent, in Italy; 18 per cent, in Germany; 15 per cent, in the Netherlands; and 7 per cent, in the United Kingdom. In Korea about 36 per cent go on to higher education; in Taiwan about 30 per cent.

In Taiwan 80 per cent of the seventeen- to eighteen-year-old age-group stays in school, and the proportion is growing. However, only one-third of graduating high school students can be accommodated in local institutions of higher learning. The result is a brain drain.

More than 7000 Taiwanese students—often the very best—go abroad to study each year. On average, only 1600 return. Taiwan has sent nearly a total of 100,000 students to the United States for graduate degrees. Of the 10,000 who earned PhDs, 85 per cent have remained in America.

The Education Challenge

Mainland China has the same problem. Of the 36,000 Chinese students who have gone to the United States to study, only 8800 have returned since 1979.

The Pacific Rim countries face enormous challenges in education. Populous countries—China, Indonesia—must devise new ways to educate millions of students. These students will increasingly reach out to both the United States and Japan. For the United States it will provide an opportunity to extend influence in the region, especially compared with Japan.

Through cooperative—sometimes telecommunications—education ventures, the United States can help the Pacific countries to educate Asians in Asia, not just the US. Since the British speak English, they can profitably join in.

AMERICA'S PACIFIC PRESENCE

The United States should not think of the Pacific Rim as a distant, exotic locale.

America's West Coast states constitute a major part of the region, are well positioned to capitalize on the century of the Pacific, and can play a pivotal role in its development:

- Mount Edgecumbe High School in Sitka, Alaska, requires students to study either Japanese or Chinese for a year and to take at least one other class on the Pacific Rim. More than one-third of the students are involved in the school's Pacific Rim programme. Governor Steve Cowper wants Pacific Rim classes in all Alaskan schools.

- One of every six jobs in Washington State is linked in some way to trade. 'The Japanese are ready to move for greater involvement in the United States and we are probably as ready as any state to work with them,' says John Anderson, former director of Washington State's Department of Trade and Economic Development.

- A San Francisco bank recently became the first US bank to open a full-service branch in China. Bank of the Orient's growing twenty-person office in Xiamen, 300 miles north of Hong Kong, is the first US-owned independent banking operation in China in almost forty years.

California: American's Megastate

For all practical purposes California is a Pacific Rim *country*, not a state.

Measured apart from the rest of the United States, it has the world's sixth-largest economy. Only the United States, the Soviet Union, Japan, West Germany, and France produce more than California. By 2000 California will have moved into fourth place. California's gross state product reached $600 billion in 1988, averaging an astounding 10 per cent-a-year growth for the past five years. This means it can double its income in seven years, quadruple in fourteen.

California is the leading US exporter of both manufactured and agricultural goods and is a leader in aerospace, defence, tourism, construction, and high technology. One-third of America's high-tech companies are in California, as are about one-third of its biotech firms.

California has more scientists and engineers than the next two most scientifically peopled American states combined.

New York's days of banking leadership are apparently numbered. The top twelve savings and loan institutions are headquartered in California; three are in Los Angeles, and two in Beverly Hills. Between 1980 and 1986 deposits in Los Angeles rose a whopping 65 per cent to $145 billion, while New York City banks increased only 7 per cent to $192 billion.

California is a mecca for Japanese interests. There are more than 750 subsidiaries of Japanese firms and 9 Japanese-affiliated banks whose assets total more than $10 billion. More than 40 per cent of total Japanese investment in the United States is in California. Eight of Japan's largest car companies have headquarters in the LA area; so does South Korea's Hyundai.

California is the US's undisputed gateway to the Pacific Rim. Aggregate trade through the state's ports has increased from $8.7 billion in 1970 to $118 billion in 1987; 80 per cent is with Pacific Rim countries. California is Japan's largest trading partner next to the United States itself—$41.5 billion in 1987, about half the total for the other forty-nine states. And the state leads the United States in overall foreign investment; $100 billion passes through California each year.

In 1986 and 1987 about 35 per cent of all trade between the United States and Asia passed through California ports.

The ports of Los Angeles and Long Beach are America's largest handlers of containerized cargo and have surpassed New York ports in vessel arrivals. The $550 million Greater Los Angeles World Trade Centre opened in May 1989. It will encourage more growth.

Los Angeles

With a population of more than 7 million, the Los Angeles metropolitan area is the second-largest city in the United States and growing. Number one, New York with 8.8 million, is losing population. By the year 2000 the city of Los Angeles, with an anticipated 8.8 million, will surpass New York, with a projected 8.4 million.

'LA's time has come,' says New York architect Norman Pfeiffer, of Hardy Holzman Pfeiffer Associates. 'The city reflects the Pacific Rim and Asia the way New York reflected Europe 200 years ago.'

Los Angeles has emerged as one of the world's most innovative and trend-setting cities in areas like art, architecture, clothing, beauty, food, music, pop culture, and, of course, movies. The art galleries in Hollywood, West Hollywood, and Santa Monica have made Los Angeles America's premier contemporary art market—after New York.

'The dynamism of LA is admired by all the young artists here,' says Ronald Chase, a painter who has worked in San Francisco since 1974. 'Anyone who goes down there cannot help but be impressed.'

A quarter of a million LA businesses employ some 6.5 million people, the greatest concentration of mathematicians, scientists, engineers, and skilled technicians in the country. Los Angeles creates $250 billion worth of goods and services a year. Today 10 per cent of LA jobs relate to overseas trade; by 2010 that figure will increase to 20 per cent.

San Francisco

San Francisco, it seems, will not give Los Angeles much competition in the California race for Pacific capital.

'The Pacific is now the dominant lake, and the Number 1 city on the Pacific Rim is Los Angeles,' says James P. Miscoll, executive officer for Southern California for the San Francisco-based Bank of America. 'We all love San Francisco, but the vast majority of our business is here in Los Angeles.'

Japanese and other Asian investors favour Los Angeles, which offers much more space, a pro-growth attitude, and, perhaps most important, a vast wave of Asian immigrants, along with the people, the climate, and the market. The ports of Los Angeles and Long Beach have taken most of the booming Pacific trade away from San Francisco and Oakland.

San Francisco is painfully aware of the battle with Los Angeles for the Asian trade and is not about to give up yet. The San Francisco area's key business asset: It creates more new business per capita than the Los Angeles area.

Immigration: Bridge to the Pacific

Asian immigration into California generates new vitality and creates important links across the Pacific. 'It is fashionable to describe Los Angeles International Airport as the Ellis Island of the 1980s,' writes Tom Brown, dubbed 'Pacific Rim reporter' at the *Seattle Times*. 'At least 84 languages are spoken by children in LA public schools.'

- Monterey Park, a suburb of Los Angeles with about 65,000 people, is known as Little Taipei, after the capital of Taiwan. Half its residents are Asian—the highest proportion of any city in America.
- Just west of downtown Los Angeles, along Olympic Boulevard, are countless blocks where virtually every sign is in Korean. In parts of Orange County, Vietnamese is a common tongue.
- The Los Angeles area is home to more Koreans than any place outside Korea and to more Filipinos than any place outside Manila. The LA area offers 300 Thai restaurants, 500 sushi bars, and 600 Korean eateries.

America's fastest-growing state, California will have a population of 33 million by the year 2000. Its strategic location, near the lucrative Pacific Rim markets, will be its greatest natural resource in the coming years.

Washington State

Washington State in the Northwest of the United States is beginning to exploit the commercial opportunities of its location on the Pacific Rim—Seattle has a thirty-six-hour advantage in shipping time over Los Angeles. 'We are the closest port of call in the US for Oriental imports, which helps tremendously,' says Carol Jones, vice president of merchandising at Code Bleu.

Seattle is using that advantage to become a fashion head-quarters. Seattle Pacific Industries, a $160-million-a-year business, includes labels like Union Bay, Reunion, Heet. Other Seattle companies include Generra Sportswear, Inc, Shah Safari, Code Bleu, Fresh Squeeze, and M'otto. For the most part, clothes are designed in Seattle and manufactured in Asia. Seattle is America's fourth-largest apparel market.

Three times a year the Seattle industry holds the preline show, so named because it precedes the main trade shows in New York and Los Angeles. The Seattle show increasingly dictates what young men wear.

Enrollment in the University of Washington's East Asian Studies programme has increased 53 per cent since 1984. It is so popular some students must wait a full year to enroll and then must attend classes twice as large as those at other universities.

'When eighteen-year-olds, particularly in this region, are beginning to think about career opportunities and their liveli-hood, they're far more likely to see it in terms of a connection to East Asia,' says John Haley, director of the Jackson School of International Studies at the University of Washington.

THE RISE OF THE EAST NEED NOT MEAN THE DECLINE OF THE WEST

The extraordinary ascent of the Pacific Rim signals great oppor-tunity for Westerners willing to do business with Asia. For the balance of this century and into the next, the great new commer-cial opportunities will be in Asia, with Tokyo and Los Angeles vying to become the world's number one city.

Instead of bemoaning this, peoples of the Atlantic community need to analyze what commercial advantages exist for the West in the Age of the Pacific and to determine how to exploit them properly.

For these key reasons the rise of the East need not mean the decline of the West:

1. The Pacific's economic development creates new markets for Western products and services—if vendors are prepared to learn the system.
2. Despite the overwhelming stories heard to the contrary, the Asian countries of the Pacific Rim began in 1987 and 1988 to dismantle trade barriers and open their doors to Western products.
3. The higher exchange value of the yen makes it attractive for the Japanese to set up facilities abroad. Because Japan's second language is English, many of them will be in English-speaking countries.

Americans and Europeans are good at lamenting the East's growing economic power but a bit slow to recognize the silver lining.

New Markets for the West

US and European business interests tend to ignore the competitive advantage their products have over Japanese goods among the Pacific's newly industrialized countries. Instead, they tend to lump Japan together with the NICs just because they all have large trade surpluses with the United States and Europe. In reality, because of their own trade problems with Japan, the NICs have some incentive to 'buy American'—or at least not buy Japanese.

'American businessmen are not aggressive in taking advantage of our natural favouritism toward American products,' says John Ni, of Taiwan's Industrial Development and Investment Centre. The Taiwanese government implores companies and consumers to buy American whenever possible. (Because of its huge trade deficit with Japan, Taiwan bans Japanese-made cars.)

Taiwan already looks toward the other edge of the Pacific Rim for investment opportunities. Taiwan money is behind some thirty small California firms in Silicon Valley, estimates K. Y. Lee, vice-president for product strategy and marketing for the Acer Group, a Taiwan-based personal computer maker.

American-owned firms in Singapore account for more than half of Singapore's exports to the United States.

Whether measured by wealth or by population, the East provides prosperous new markets for those willing to go after them. The very low birthrates of European countries do not translate into future growth markets for American business.

By the year 2000 there will be 11 million net new consumers in Europe. In the Pacific's wealthiest countries alone, Japan and the Four Tigers, there will be more—13 million. Plus 68 million in the next wave of developing countries—Thailand, Malaysia, Indonesia, and the Philippines. China could have 100 million with disposable income.

Yet the United States invests *ten* times more money in Europe than in Japan. Not Asia, just Japan alone. Over the longer term, the trend is exaggerated. During the next thirty-five years Europe's population will level off, while Asia grows 50 per cent.

Just as millions of Asians, known for their high savings rate, grow rich, the concept of 'disposable income' is catching on in Asia—with the governments' blessing.

Their wealth amassed, Japan and the Four Tigers are prepared to evolve into more mature, consumer-driven economies.

Upscale consumer items, such as designer clothing, speciality foods, furniture, household goods, and appliances, will be best sellers in Asia in the future, says Reymond Voutier, executive chairman of the Los Angeles Asiontrade Centre.

Korea's increasing wealth has brought the desire for imported luxury items like Burberry trench coats, Wilson tennis rackets, and Sanyo stereo equipment. In Seoul's Hyundai Department Store, Korean's nouveau riche can find them all.

Japan is now doing what many Westerners once thought impossible: relying on domestic demand for a good part of its 5.7 per cent 1988 GNP growth rate. In 1988 US exports to Japan increased nearly 34 per cent over 1987, to $37.7 billion worth.

In addition to competing with Japan in other Asian markets, the United States would do well to maintain its often ignored yet substantial market share of Japanese food imports against competition from the NICs. In 1988 alone US agricultural exports to Japan increased 34 per cent.

Teenage Japanese boys list their favourite food as pork, ice cream, and sherbet, according to a survey by the Ajinomoto

Company of Tokyo. Girls like hamburgers, pudding, and ice cream.

For 122 million well-off Japanese, mineral water has become a new necessity. In the first five months of 1987 consumers bought nine times as much mineral water as in all of 1986, according to Japanese customs officials. Perrier, Evian, and Canadian Rocky, not American waters, are the winners.

French and German wines together hold a 68 per cent market share in Japan. American wines from California have tripled their market share in the past five years but only to 15.6 per cent.

In November 1988, when the French Beaujolais Nouveau was released, Japan Airlines flew five Boeing 747 cargo planes to France, filled them with 540 tons of wine, and headed back to Tokyo. Other countries' vintners and businesses in general should draw inspiration from France's November release of (usually mediocre) Beaujolais Nouveau. It is one of the great marketing gimmicks of all time.

In addition to prospering Asian markets, the West should keep its eye on the buying patterns of giant China.

Only a handful of American business people bought the US Census Bureau's report on consumer trends in China. But more than 700 Japanese companies ordered the $500 study. It should not surprise Americans that China imports twice as much from Japan as from the US.

The United States and other Western countries will have to become much more aggressive exporters if they are to profit from the century of the Pacific.

They are starting to do so—more than 50,000 US products are now sold in Japan. 'That's where the money is,' says Maureen Smith at the US Department of Commerce. 'Trade barriers are starting to come down, and the [Japanese] consumer is starting to spend like crazy.'

Polaroid has 70 per cent of the instant film and camera markets in Japan. Warner-Lambert's Schick accounts for 71 per cent of safety-razor sales. Coca-Cola is the soft drink of choice for 62 per cent of the Japanese. Japan's craving for foreign food and other consumer products is well known. Less appreciated is its need for sophisticated high technology.

Imatron, a San Francisco company, makes computerized axial tomographic (CAT) scanners. Imatron sells about ten CAT scanners, which cost around $1 million each, a year in the United States and believes it can sell five to ten in Japan—a 50 to 100 per cent increase in sales.

In Banff, Alberta, in officially bilingual Canada, another language is overwhelming what little French is used—Japanese. Japanese tourists account for 40 per cent of Banff hotel guests; they are by far the biggest spenders visiting Canada. Menus at the Banff Springs Hotel restaurant are printed in Japanese. A local department store carries picture books with Japanese texts. Kyosen Ohashi, a Japanese television personality, operates one of his OK Gift Shops in Banff.

Something for American ski resorts to think about, already the Japanese skier is developing a prejudice in favour of the *Canadian* Rockies.

The Fall of Asia's Trade Barriers

American exports to Japan have long been understated—both by those seeking protectionist laws in the United States against Japanese and other Asian goods and by business 'leaders' trying to cover for inferior products or inefficient marketing.

If Westerners are to find competitive advantage in the Pacific region, they must take a look at what has really been happening on the trade front.

Between 1980 and 1986 American exports to Europe's four largest economies—West Germany, France, Italy, and the United Kingdom—dropped 7 per cent while those to Japan rose 21 per cent. Although US sales to Europe picked up steam after 1986, sales to Japan grew also. In 1988 the United States sold more to Japan ($37.7 billion) than to West Germany, France, and Italy combined.

US agricultural products, always best sellers in Japan, will reach an extraordinary benchmark in 1989. For the first time total sales to Japan will hit $8.3 billion, surpassing total combined sales to all twelve members of the European Economic Community at about $7.3 billion. Furthermore, the largest single importer of US wheat is China.

The Japanese spent $583 per head on US products in 1984, 6

per cent of their income, calculated Kenichi Ohmae, the chief of McKinsey & Company's Tokyo office, while Americans spent only 2 per cent of theirs—$289 on Japanese products a year.

American goods made headway in all Asian markets in 1987 and 1988. American exports to the Four Tigers rose more than 40 per cent between July 1987 and July 1988 (Taiwan's $1.5 billion gold purchases not counting).

US exports to Taiwan increased from $5.5 billion in 1986 to $7.4 billion in 1987. Then changes in 1988 set the stage for a huge increases. In February of that year Taiwan reduced tariffs on some 3500 items (by an average of 50 per cent): The sticker price of a Mercury Sable automobile fell by about $4000, and a General Electric refrigerator by about $500. In 1988 US automakers shipped 17,518 vehicles to Taiwan, compared with 3735 in 1987.

In 1988 Taiwan became the United States' fifth-largest trading partner. Total American imports reached $12.1 billion, more than a 200 per cent increase since 1986.

During 1987 and the first half of 1988 South Korea cut tariffs on 800 goods by an average of 40 per cent. In 1988 US imports reached $11.3 billion, a big 77 per cent increase over 1986.

Why have we read so little about the great breakthroughs in US-Asia trade during 1988, when US exports to Korea, Taiwan, Hong Kong, Singapore, and China increased an average of 40 per cent? European exports to these areas can start booming too.

The Yen's Rise Can Mean Opportunities for Americans and Europeans

In a truly interdependent economy it is harder to distinguish the winners from the losers. The strength of the mighty yen has Japanese companies looking to the United States and Europe for 'cheap' labour: just the way an American or European entrepreneur might have sought out offshore manufacturing in the Third World a decade ago, and as Britain did earlier in its empire.

The number of Japanese-affiliated plants in the United States reached 837 in May 1988, an increase of 287 over 1987, according to the annual survey of the Japan External Trade Organization.

Taiwanese ventures in the United States have led to the Taiyuen Textile Company's $35 million automated spinning mill, Multitech Industrial Company's agreement with Texas Instruments to produce computers in Austin, and Formosa Plastic's twelve US plants.

More than 300,000 Americans work for Japanese companies; 100,000 Japanese work for American ventures in Japan.

Tokyo's Ministry of International Trade and Industry predicts Japanese investment will spawn an additional 840,000 American jobs in the next few years, 1 million within ten years. Forty American states have liaison offices in Japan. And more Japanese factories will be coming to Europe.

When American banks from New York to Los Angeles need money, Japanese banks are there to lend it. In 1986 Japanese banks underwrote almost half of the United States' municipal bonds—$18 billion worth. In the first half of 1988 Japan invested more than $9 billion to buy ninety-five foreign companies, many in the United States, says the Industrial Bank of Japan.

'They don't want to see our society [the United States] go down because we're their biggest customer,' says Robert S. Ingersoll, former ambassador to Japan. Japanese portfolio investment in the United States totalled $160 billion by spring 1989.

The Japanese have become major research funders at major US universities. Sixteen chairs have been endowed at the Massachusetts Institute of Technology, at about $1.5 million apiece by the Mitsubishi Corporation and Mitsui & Company, which regularly spend some $4 million a year for access to research.

The Hitachi Chemical Company, in exchange for a $12 million donation, will use the majority of the space in a University of California at Irvine biotech laboratory.

The Japanese are investing additional millions in US-based research, according to the Japan Centre for International Exchange:

- Toshiba invested $3.5 million to support digital radiography work (combining computer technology and X-ray equipment for detailed medical diagnoses) at the University of Arizona.
- Two other Japanese companies are supporting development of a synthetic material that could improve catalytic

191

converters in cars at the Georgia Institute of Technology in Atlanta.
- MIT and Johns Hopkins set up offices in Tokyo to solicit Japanese funding.

Influence in the Pacific

Japan is the main trading partner for more than half the Pacific Rim countries. Japanese imports from Korea, Taiwan, and Hong Kong rose by almost 50 per cent in 1987. That same year Japan surpassed the United States to become the world's largest donor of government aid to developing countries, and two-thirds of that aid went to Asian nations. In 1988 total Japanese foreign aid reached $10 billion, and Japan has promised $50 billion over the next five years. Total US military and economic aid has been estimated at $500 million.

Japanese investment in Asia Pacific more than doubled in just two years to $6 billion. Sony now makes many of its consumer products, including compact disc players, in seven different Asian nations.

In 1988 an average of one Japanese company set up shop in Thailand on each weekday. In Thailand alone, the number of investment applications by Japanese companies nearly quadrupled between 1986 and 1988, to 200 projects worth $353 million. In 1987 the second-largest investor in Thailand became Taiwan—replacing the United States.

Business Week put it this way: 'After decades of looking to America for economic growth, the nations of East Asia are shifting their economic focus to Japan, despite deep and often painful memories of . . . its military occupation.'

Trade and aid are important avenues of influence, but so is education. There are some 26,000 foreign students in Japan, the majority from Taiwan, South Korea, and China. Japan wants to increase the total to 100,000 by the year 2000.

In this critical arena, US influence exceeds Japan's. There are more than 60,000 students from China, Taiwan and Hong Kong in the United States especially in California. In 1988 at least 20,000 Japanese attended US high schools or colleges.

Europe needs to grasp the implication of this. European business has to recognize that its domestic market is shrinking. Europe can never lose sight of the fact that Asia will have 80 million new consumers by the year 2000. The growing income millions of them already possess and the East's fortunate association of European goods with quality are Europe's advantages.

Are Western interests prepared to concede the entire Pacific region to the Japanese? Or is the West going to engage Japan in battles of influence and economics in the 1990s and into the 21st century? At stake are both social influence and market share in the world's fastest-growing region.

If the West's influence decreases, it will have only itself to blame, for ignoring Asia's markets, for lumping together Japan and the NICs, for sometimes becoming paranoid over Asian investment instead of welcoming the inflow.

In the end, as ever, what we are moving toward is an increasingly interdependent world.

'Asia's surge should hold no fear for the West,' reports the *Economist*. 'Its exports will mean cheaper, better goods for consumers to buy. Its growing affluence will mean growing markets for other countries to sell to. Its escape from poverty and war-rubble should lift the spirits of man—and serve as guide and inspiration to those left behind.'

Asia's Pacific Rim has demonstrated for all to see that a poor country can develop, even without abundant natural resources, as long as it invests enough in its human resources.

7

The 1990s: Decade of Women in Leadership

The 1990s will be the most challenging decade the business community has ever confronted. Corporations, large and small, from the United States, from the newly wealthy Asian countries and from Europe, soon to be the world's largest market, will be tripping over one another to exploit new opportunities abroad while trying to maintain their domestic advantage.

Just when the West was about to write off the Soviet Union as impossibly bureaucratic and medieval, the Soviets 'discovered' leasing, incentives, and the profit motive. Call it 'market socialism'. And China is home to 1.1 billion potential consumers.

American and European business are ready to meet these challenges with new leadership that will revitalize business and inspire global competitors much as Japanese management did in the 1970s. To a great extent that leadership will come from women.

Most of the facts and figures in this chapter are American, because the emancipation of modern businesswomen started there. But Northern Europe follows the American megatrend closely in this. All that prosper will have to, which may set big problems for Islam and smaller ones for Japan.

THE DECADE OF WOMEN IN BUSINESS

Corporations as we have known them were created by men for men. After World War II America's and Europe's veterans exchanged their military uniforms for factory overalls and grey flannel suits. But the bureaucratic, authoritarian military model from the 19th century remained the organizational system by which they governed themselves. Yet since World War II the number of working women has increased 200 per cent.

For the last two decades US women have taken two-thirds of the millions of new jobs created each year in the information era. They will continue to do so far into the millennium.

The days of women as some sort of minority in the work force are over. American women without children are now *more* likely to work than men. Today about 74 per cent of men work. But 79 per cent of women with no children under eighteen work. So do 67 per cent of women with children, almost as high a percentage as men. Half of women with small children work, too.

In business and many professions women have increased from a minority as low as 10 per cent in 1970 to a critical mass ranging from 30 to 50 per cent in much of the business world, including banking, accounting, and computer science.

The Circulation of *Working Woman* magazine grew from 450,000 in 1981 to 900,000 in 1988, surpassing *Fortune, Forbes,* and, finally, at 850,000, *Business Week.* The only business periodical with a larger circulation is the *Wall Street Journal.*

In the US, women are starting new businesses twice as fast as men. In Canada one-third of small businesses are owned by women. In France it is one-fifth. In Britain since 1980 the number of self-employed women has increased three times as fast as the number of self-employed men. As workers, professionals, and entrepreneurs women dominate the information society.

To be a leader in business today, it is no longer an advantage to have been socialized as a male.

Although some corporations do not fully realize it as yet, men and women are on an equal playing field in corporate America. Women may even hold a slight advantage since they need not 'unlearn' old authoritarian behaviour to run their departments or companies.

Like their male colleagues (who probably did not serve in the military either), they must learn to coach, inspire, and gain people's commitment. They must set personal examples of excellence.

195

After two decades of quietly preparing, gaining experience, and being frustrated with the male establishment, women in business are on the verge of revolutionary change. Older, wiser, more numerous, and well represented in the fastest advancing industries like computers, finance, and advertising, women are ready to break through the 'glass ceiling', the invisible barrier that has kept them from the top. As the nineties progress, conventional wisdom will concede that women and men function equally well as business leaders, and women will achieve leadership positions denied them in years past.

FROM MANAGEMENT TO LEADERSHIP

Along with male colleagues who share similar values, women will build on the foundations of corporate heroes, historically men; innovators like the late Bill Gore (founder of W. L. Gore & Associates) and Jan Carlzon (CEO of Scandinavian Air Systems) and women entrepreneurs like Britain's Laura Ashley. All these shunned traditional hierarchy and built highly profitable companies through vision, commitment, shared power, and responsibility—values which women managers and like-minded male colleagues believe in.

As the entrepreneurial eighties blossomed, as women flooded the labour market, dominating the cutting-edge information sector, millions of new businesses, founded by men and women alike, threw out the rule book and experimented with alternative corporate practices, philosophies, and structures.

A decade later their efforts have crystallized into a coherent, consistent approach to the people side of business, which can be summarized as follows:

The dominant principle of organization has shifted: from management (once needed in order to control an enterprise) to leadership (now needed in order to bring out the best in people and to respond quickly to change).

This is not the 'leadership' individuals and groups so often call for when they really want a father-figure to take care of all their problems. It is a democratic yet demanding leadership that respects people and encourages self-management, autonomous teams, and entrepreneurial units.

There is a big difference between management and leadership. Leaders and managers differ in orientation, mission, assumptions, behaviour, organizational environments, and ultimately results.

Leadership is the process of moving people in some direction mostly through 'noncoercive means', says John P. Kotter of the Harvard Business School, author of *The Leadership Factor*.

'We have a lot of managers—short-term, control-oriented, report-oriented,' says Russell E. Palmer, dean of the University of Pennsylvania's Wharton School of Business. 'Leaders think longer term, grasp the relationship of larger realities, think in terms of renewal, have political skills, cause change, affirm values, achieve unity.'

Outside the military management model, men and women are equally capable of inspiring commitment and bringing out the best in people.

Although capital and technology are important resources, it's people who make or break a company. To harness their power, leaders inspire commitment and empower people by sharing authority. Responding to labour shortages with flexibility, they enable their firms to attract, reward, and motivate the best people. But effective leadership will also need to monitor the external environment, tracking trends, markets, technological change, and product cycles in an increasingly global 1990s.

New Tasks; New Work Force

The tasks of business have changed, and so has its work force. That is perhaps the main reason why the organizing principle of business has shifted from management to leadership, opening the doors to women.

The management model is not to be despised; it served the industrial era and served it well. After World War II a male work force with a high school education or less manufactured the goods that made the United States the world's leading economic power. To achieve that success, it needed management—to be told what to do and to follow orders unquestioningly. Creativity on the assembly line was about the last thing anyone wanted.

The work comprised tasks that were outer-directed, mechanical, and easy to supervise. It made sense for power and information to be centralized in the hands of managers and executives not on the shop floor.

Four decades later, with the information economy dominating the developed world, it is an entirely different workplace.

If the male was the prototypical industrial worker, the information worker is typically a woman.

In sheer numbers women dominate the information society. Eighty-four per cent of American working women are part of the information/service sector. Of the people whose job title falls under the category of 'professional'—versus clerical, technical, labourer—the majority are women. Forty-four per cent of adult working American women (ages 25 to 64) are college-educated, compared with 20 per cent in 1965.

The jobs of people in the information, service, finance, computer, biotechnology, and health care sectors are not performed on an assembly line and cannot be managed as though they were.

It is almost impossible to 'supervise' information work. Mental tasks have replaced mechanical ones. 'Work' is what goes on inside people's heads at desks, on airplanes, in meetings, at lunch. It is how they communicate with clients, what they write in memos, what they say at meetings.

'Now we are managing people paid for their knowledge. We have never done that, and we don't know how to do it,' says Peter Drucker.

Today's Well-Educated Work Force

Because so much is written about the decline in education *standards*, it is easy to overlook the dramatic increase in educated people in the US in the past twenty years.

One quarter of the work force aged twenty-five to sixty-four consists of college graduates or better, *twice* the percentage twenty years ago. Another 20 per cent has one to three years of college, more than double the old ratio. That means nearly half—45 per cent—the work force is college-educated. In addition, 40 per cent are high school graduates. That leaves just 15 per cent who are adult-aged high school drop-outs. Twenty years ago it was 41 per cent.

Well-educated people have more options. 'Whereas manual

workers have been tied to their job by fear, lack of skills and ignorance, young people today have horizons; they can move,' Peter Drucker says.

'It's a more educated, affluent work force,' says Mark Sussman of Jackson, Lewis, Schnitzler & Krupman, a New York employment law firm. 'They don't feel that a job is an asset they're lucky to have. They have greater expectations.'

The Loyalty Factor

A recent survey confirmed what executives have complained about for years. Seventy per cent of managers report employees —especially young executives—do not exhibit the same loyalty to their companies that was the norm in the 1950s, concludes a study by Egon Zehnder International, a Zurich-based consulting firm with offices in New York City.

Success magazine, which surveyed the young people themselves, found they thought loyalty *was* important—but never as important as personal growth.

'Have skills, will travel' seems to be the motto of the job-jumping baby boom generation, confirming the stereotype of the selfish yuppie. But the fast pace of social and technological change has forced young people to adapt and change. The average American entering the work force today will change careers—not jobs, *careers*—three times, according to the Labour Department. Private experts believe successful executives of the future will need to count on as many as five different careers.

How can a company encourage greater loyalty? asked a recent survey of 100 senior-level executives of the largest public companies in America, and 74 per cent answered: better leadership. And some went on to define it.

But what kind of leadership do these executives have in mind? The best leaders do *expect* loyalty but also act in such a way as to inspire it and earn it. Women who have had to 'prove' themselves in the business world are well aware of this unwritten rule.

The New Corporate Archetype: More Like Women?

Michael Maccoby, author of *The Gamesman* and *The Leader*, postulates a new corporate archetype that tracks well with the *Success* executive profile. A 'self-developer', he says, is an individual who values independence, dislikes bureaucracies, and seeks to balance work with other priorities like family and recreation.

In *Why Work?* published in 1988 he describes a new generation of professional engineers whose main corporate objective is 'self-development'. They recognize that corporations cannot be relied on to take care of people and that their only security lies in the skills they take to their next job.

In old-fashioned businesses self-developers have been less likely to reach the top of corporations than Maccoby's 'gamesman' who is driven to succeed yet 'plays' the corporate game dispassionately to win. In modern businesses, leaders will need to inspire new generation self-developers who balance different priorities in their lives.

The tendency—often attributed to women—to want to balance the top priorities of career and family (along with other personal interests) is generational, not gender-specific.

Most self-developers are baby boomers, around forty and younger. The archetype is most prevalent among people in their early thirties and twenties.

The Leadership Challenge

Considering the complex tasks of the information era and its elite labour force, the business leader's job is quite a challenge.

He or she possesses no authority over people whatsoever. The military puts deserters in jail. In business, when you are deserted, you get two weeks' notice—maybe. Disobey a military order and you face a court-martial. In a seller's market, if your first lieutenant disagrees with your approach to the client, he or she can go out tomorrow and get another job that probably pays better anyhow.

A corporation is a voluntary organization.

Managing through authority is out of the question. Workaholics simply burn themselves out. Loyalty is a quaint memory of the industrial past, a bone in the throat of hundreds of thousands of coal miners, auto workers and steelworkers who thought it went both ways.

The military management model can command authority; business leadership must win loyalty, achieve commitment, and earn respect.

If people are not loyal and you have no authority over them anyhow, how do you accomplish anything?

Paradoxically, people who are difficult to supervise and free to leave, people who think for themselves, who question authority are a leader's best source of information and only hope for achieving organizational goals.

This sophisticated resource cannot be ordered, but it does respond to democratic leadership, financial incentives, and a company that recognizes that people also belong to another institution—the family.

The new work force will help your company achieve objectives if it can achieve its own personal goals as part of the bargain.

An effective leader creates a vision that tells people where a company is going and how it will get there and becomes the organizing force behind every corporate decision: Will this action help us achieve our vision?

'We learned that you cannot expect an employee to function at his optimum unless the manager has been successful in conveying the big picture to him,' says T. Stephen Long, vice-president of marketing at Trans Hawaiian, a $26 million-a-year tourism and transportation company in Honolulu.

More important is 'selling' that vision to the people who will actualize their own goals—for achievement, security, and creativity—by achieving the corporation's. Without their energetic participation, little can be accomplished.

Incredibly, some 'experts' and business gurus believe that treating people like partners and team members is patronizing or that the whole, enormous paradigm shift from authority to commitment, from management to leadership is merely a 'trend'. Pretty soon, they tell the hapless old-line managers who long for the past, the dust will settle and we'll be back to good old-fashioned coercion.

Revisionists in academia and the media fail to recognize what people who run businesses face every day: A highly skilled specialist can leave the company *anytime* to work for the competition—or raid the client list and start his or her own business.

201

WHY WOMEN WILL LEAD

Women have reached a critical mass in virtually all the white-collar professions, especially in business.

Twenty years ago women who worked as executives, lawyers or doctors were decidedly in the minority. Although large numbers of young women started getting educated for leadership positions in the 1970s, their entry into the professions was more of a trickle than a steady flow. The upward curve was modest. If the percentage of women lawyers, for example, increased from 12 per cent to 14 per cent, it was hardly worthy of comment. It would be ages before women could account for half of a major profession, or so it seemed in 1975, even 1985.

In 1990 the workplace is a very different world.

Since 1972 the percentage of women physicians has doubled. The percentages of women lawyers and architects have nearly quintupled.

Women have achieved, if not a majority, a substantial proportion of the previously male-dominated careers in the information and service industries, the jobs from which business and social leadership emerges.

Women hold some 39.3 per cent of the 14.2 million executive, administrative, and management jobs, according to the Bureau of Labour Statistics, nearly double the 1972 figure. Nearly one-third of computer scientists are women.

In finance women have reached the halfway point. More than half of all officers, managers, and professionals in the nation's fifty largest commercial banks are women. Women make up 49.6 per cent of accountants, compared with 21.7 per cent in 1972. About one quarter of Wall Street's financial professionals are women.

Even in the male-dominated manufacturing world, women have made great strides. Between 1983 and 1988 the number of women executives, administrators and managers in manufacturing swelled from 403,000 to 647,000, thereby increasing women's share of the top manufacturing jobs from 20 per cent to 26.3 per cent.

More than one-third of Procter & Gamble's marketing executives are women. An average of 35 per cent of Arthur Andersen & Company recruits are women. At the Gannett Company, Inc, almost 40 per cent of the company's managers, professionals, technicians, and sales force are women, and 25 per cent of its newspaper publishers are women.

In decades past, the few women appointed corporate officers were relegated to positions as assistant treasurers or corporate secretaries. Today 83 per cent of the female officers in Fortune 500 and Service 500 companies, responding to a survey by the executive search firm Heidrick & Struggles, held the title of vice-president or better, compared with 35 per cent in 1980.

Ask anyone in the old-boy network. The road to leadership begins with education. In 1975 women received 11.7 per cent of the MBA degrees granted; today they receive 33 per cent. Women now earn thirteen times more engineering degrees than in 1975, says the American Association of Engineering Societies in Washington, DC.

Today women represent about 20 per cent of all physicians and lawyers, an impressive proportion, though not as high as other professions cited here. That is because men so dominated these professions, women had had to build from a base close to zero.

More dramatic is the remarkable increase in the percentage of women graduating from law and medical school. In 1966 fewer than 7 per cent of MD's were granted to women. By 1987 it had reached 32.3 per cent, nearly one-third. In 1966 women were awarded an even tinier proportion of law degrees (LLB and JD)—a mere 3.5 per cent. But by 1987 women were taking home 40 per cent of all law degrees.

In the 1990's the ranks of women doctors and lawyers will increase substantially as will their influence.

Women have reached a critical mass in the professions. No longer are they a token minority. Their values, their management styles are closer to the norm, while all around them, male colleagues, their age and younger, identify with the new management rather than the old.

Women missed out on the industrial age, but in America they have already established themselves in the industries of the future.

Women advance fastest in 'cutting-edge industries,' says Michigan State Professor Eugene Jennings. Either there was no time to establish the old rules or they didn't apply because the game has changed so much.

At Apple Computer, 30 per cent of managers are women, as are 40 per cent of professionals.

'Many computer companies don't bother with affirmative action programmes. The attitude is, "Let's just get the best talent. Period",' says Phyllis Swersky, executive vice-president and chief financial officer at Artificial Intelligence Corporation, a software maker for IBM mainframes. 'Both as an employee and an employer, I've found that gender is irrelevant.'

'When a company is rushing into the future as we have been, management uses talent, any available talent, much more eagerly,' says Marilyn Laurie, an AT&T senior vice-president in New York.

When the overwhelming majority of the work force was male, there was uneasiness about women's ability to lead men. But even in the 1950s no one thought much about a woman's heading up the typing pool. Today the majority of the information/service sector is female. Women hold supervisory positions earlier and progress into management, preparing the way for the most talented to become leaders.

Women are already leading their own businesses, which they are now starting in the US at twice the rate of men.

Although women will reach the top in the 1990s, they were too often barred from the boardroom during the 1970s and 1980s. No wonder so many talented, successful women said, 'The heck with this' and started their own businesses.

The Small Business Association (SBA) reports that 30 per cent of small businesses are owned by women.

Each decade the percentage of female-owned small businesses has increased and it will continue to do so, the SBA projects. In 1986, the most recent year available, women in America owned 4.1 million businesses, compared with 2.5 million in 1980.

However, the National Association of Women Business Owners (NAWBO) reports that government statistics like the above overlook up to two-thirds of women business owners. Incredibly government statistics count only sole proprietorships, probably the smallest firms, not partnerships or corporations, NAWBO charges. Plus, it says, government figures are three to six years out of date. NAWBO argues that an additional four to five million women business owners have entered the economy in the last fifteen years.

The New Leadership: Winning Commitment

Male or female, the effective leader wins commitment by setting an example of excellence: being ethical, open, empowering, and inspiring.

The most straightforward way to earn loyalty is through honest, ethical management. A 1988 Lou Harris poll sponsored by Steelcase Inc asked office workers what they most valued at work. Most important was, 'management that is honest, upright, and ethical' in its dealing with employees and the community. It was considered 'very important' by 81 per cent of those polled, but only 41 per cent said it was 'very true' of their own employer.

It is your 'management' that counts toward your being a good manager. It is you who matters as a leader. You are always leading by example.

People want to know what is going on in their company. In the same Steelcase poll, 76 per cent rated 'free exchange of information among employees and departments' as very important; only 35 per cent said it described their office.

Jan Carlzon built SAS (Scandinavian Airline Systems) into a $5 billion carrier. After losing $30 million in 1979 and 1980, SAS earned nearly $300 million in 1988. He firmly believes that the leader who expects results must first give people free access to information. 'An employee without the information cannot take responsibility. With information, he cannot avoid taking it.'

Everett Suters, chairman of three Atlanta companies, began getting the message that his employees sent. 'We're doing the work and you're getting most of the credit and all of the money,' he writes in *INC*. He had them guess how much profit the company was earning and how much he personally was earning. After everyone had guessed too much, he told them the truth.

'As time went on, my managers became almost as interested in all facets of the company as I was,' he says. People who are kept posted and feel they have a stake in the company, 'work even harder when all is not going well'.

Leader as Teacher, Facilitator, Coach

Today we are replacing the manager as order giver with the manager as teacher, facilitator, and coach. The order giver has all the answers and tells everyone what to do; the facilitator knows how to draw the answers out of those who know them best—the people doing the job. The leader as facilitator asks questions, guides a group to consensus, uses information to demonstrate the need for action.

Terry Armstrong, an associate management professor at the University of West Florida, has been studying the character traits of successful CEOs, presumably leaders whom managers would seek to emulate. 'They are more like coaches than quarterbacks,' says Armstrong. 'They are really very conscious about their organization winning and not necessarily their own success.'

At the manufacturing and distributions operations of Domino's Pizza, Inc, in East Granby, Connecticut, people are never called employees; they are team members, team leaders, and coaches. 'If somebody says "employee", they jump all over you,' says Jeff De Graff, a member of Domino's coaching staff.

Averitt Express, a Tennessee trucking firm, divided its 1400-member work force into productivity improvement groups of 3 to 10 people; sales shot up 38 per cent, earnings by 48 per cent.

'We just take the coach approach. Lots of feedback, lots of encouragement; our people do the rest,' says Averitt CEO Gary Sasser.

The primary challenge of leadership in the 1990s is to encourage the new, better-educated worker to be more entrepreneurial, self-managing, and oriented toward lifelong learning.

The company most committed to the task of lifelong learning is arguably Motorola, Inc, which has undertaken the immense task of training all its 99,000 employees—one-third each year.

'Just as when you buy a piece of capital equipment, you put aside money to maintain that equipment, we require that 1.5 per cent of pay-roll be put aside to maintain the competency level of the employees,' says Bill Wiggenhorn, head of Motorola's training.

Over the course of seven to ten years every Motorola employee will be retrained. In 1987 Motorola invested $44 million in employee training—$100 million if you count salaries paid during training—and another $3.5 million to finance associate, bachelor, or master's degrees.

Small businesses have as much to gain as giants like Motorola, maybe more.

Metal Forming & Coining of Maumee, Ohio, which employs only seventy people, has offered education benefits to its salaried and hourly employees for the past seven years. Chairman and President Mike Czerniak credits the education investment with half the company's sales increases. Today it grosses $12 million a year.

American business is spending $210 billion for on-the-job training and education, a system about the same size at the nation's public elementary, secondary, and higher education institutions combined, according to Anthony Patrick Carnevale, chief economist for the American Society for Training and Development in Washington, DC. Some Japanese corporations say they spend even more.

Is it a Leader's Job to Motivate People?

Any successful leader will tell you it is a lot easier to hire people who are already motivated. 'Leaders who believe they must continuously scurry about *motivating* everyone are destined to a fatiguing, ulcerating career,' says Robert Wright, a professor of organization theory at California's Pepperdine University.

'I don't look for either youth *or* experience,' says J. William Grimes, head of ESPN, the all-sports cable network. 'I want intelligence and, primarily, motivation. I want people who are very eager to accomplish a task, who can't wait to get something done and will always look to do it in new ways.'

A good product or a brilliant founder alone does not make a company, says Michael Cooper, president of the Hay Group's Research for Management. Success comes when leaders have 'managed their people in ways that *keep* their involvement and sense of partnership high'.

Keeping people excited *is* the leader's job.

In this regard, small business has a great competitive advantage over large companies. People in smaller companies are able to maintain a more positive attitude, says Cooper. 'If I were a Fortune 500 CEO, I'd be worried.'

RECRUITING THE LABOUR FORCE OF THE 1990s

The cigar-chomping executive who barks, 'I just *feel* better when I can see my people all around me here', is expressing the control pattern of the management model. 'Nobody works part time around here either' are probably his next words. 'It's full time or nothing—and no temporaries.'

To attract and keep good people, flexibility must become the watchword of leadership. 'We survey all of our employees, and there's a message that comes in loud and clear,' says Mike Shore, a spokesman for IBM. 'And that's flexibility.'

In the 1990s, however, growing labour shortages will require corporations to stretch a whole lot more.

In the next decade, 14 or 15 million new jobs will be created in America, not as many as the 20 million created in the 1980s. Its a good thing, because there are not enough people to fill the anticipated new jobs. America's labour supply will increase less than 1 per cent a year, the slowest growth since the 1930s. The 1990s will be the tightest labour market in decades.

Corporations will have to recruit people who did not work in the 1980s: 'undiscovered' sources of people, like the estimated 3.3 million people who have taken early retirement, those handicapped people who are now unemployed, and new immigrants who will inevitably enter the United States when labour shortages get so bad that Congress will be required to liberalize immigration quotas, perhaps even child labour laws. What's so terrible about a fourteen-year-old working limited hours after school?

But the largest potential source of all is the estimated 14 million non-working women caring for their families at home. The only chance of coaxing millions of these women back into the work force is company-subsidized day care and flexible work arrangements in the whole range of professional, technical, clerical, manufacturing jobs—part-time, job-sharing, contract work, and home-work arrangements.

That is why flexibility should become the motto for personnel policies in the 1990s. Such arrangements will also help your company keep or recruit women—already in the work force or expected to enter—and retirees.

'More and more potential employees are asking about day care, maternity leave, and flexible time,' says Art Strohmer, director of human resources and staffing development at Merck, the pharmaceutical company with pioneering policies in these areas. 'We are increasingly seeing that employees are shopping around.'

Women will take two-thirds of the new jobs created in the 1990s. They will be the key work force for the booming service and information sector. Along with their productivity, women introduce a somewhat unpredictable factor to corporate life that was conveniently absent during the later part of the industrial society—children.

Day Care

The majority of mothers with children work outside the home. More than 75 per cent of working women are in prime child-bearing years, and most women either have children already or will have them at some point in their career life.

In the 1990s day care will become a common employee benefit.

In the past year, as labour shortages have worsened there has been a surge in the number of American companies providing day care—3500, up 40 per cent since 1984. About 200 of these added the benefit during a six-month period of 1988. Most do not have on-site facilities but offer some financial help or referral services. Some companies issue vouchers or pay a proportion of costs. There are 750 on-site corporate day-care centres in the United States.

Even so, 90 per cent of establishments with ten or more employees *do not* provide direct benefits such as day care or financial assistance, according to the Survey of Employer-Provided Child Care Benefits.

This is not just a way to keep and attract good people. There are substantial cost savings as well. A 1988 study by the Dominion Bankshares Corporation reported a 31 per cent drop in absenteeism among parents who used day-care centres. And a 10 per cent drop in the turnover rate. At Nyloncraft, Inc, of Mishawaka, Indiana, where 85 per cent of the employees are women, there was a 57 per cent turnover rate in 1979. After the company spent $250,000 on a day-care centre, turnover immediately dropped to 31 per cent and then fell to only 3 per cent in 1988.

But you need not be a big company or build an expensive

centre to provide leadership in day care. Your small business can become a community hero by cooperating with local schools.

Independence, Missouri, schools provide affordable, quality child care for three-year-olds and up. Grade school children can attend before and after school programmes. Because they are held in school buildings, the programme saves on utilities, rent, and transportation. Parents pay only $45 a week for day care, and $18 a week to extend the day of a grade school child from 7:00 A.M. to 6:00 P.M.

'Instead of closing up, locking the gates and sending everyone home at 3 o'clock, we are modifying the schools so they more clearly meet the needs of the family today,' says Bill Ewing, director of a similar effort in Pomona, California, where twelve different programmes serve some 900 children aged six weeks to thirteen years old. In addition to a centre for sick children, there is a centre that stays open until midnight—seven days a week and on holidays.

Eldercare

If business and society can master the challenge of day care, we will be one step closer to confronting the next great care-giving task of the 1990s—eldercare.

Eldercare will affect a wider segment of employees than child care, from CEOs to secretaries, according to 'Employers and Eldercare: A New Benefit Coming of Age', a report by the Bureau of National Affairs, a private research group in Washington, DC. Almost one-third of all working adults are responsible for providing some care for an elderly person. Three-quarters of those who care for the elderly in a family are women.

The Transamerica Life Insurance and Annuity Company, in Los Angeles, loses at least $250,000 a year because employees have missed work to care for their parents, according to Andrew E. Scharlach, a senior research associate in gerontology at the University of Southern California, which surveyed Transamerica employees. That survey also discovered that at least half the workers involved in eldercare are still raising their own children.

In the United States there are more than 1500 adult-day-care centres caring for some 60,000 people. Some 300 companies have started programmes to help employees care for the elderly up from zero five years ago, reports the National Council on Ageing. But the results of the Transamerica survey cited above suggest an intriguing model already anticipated by one company.

In 1990 Stride Rite, the Cambridge, Massachusetts, shoe company will open a joint centre for 55 children and 24 older folks.

Later in the 1990s, as the parents of the baby boom generation require increased help, more pioneering companies will build on the precedent of day care and begin offering partial reimbursement for eldercare costs as part of the overall trend toward cafeteria plans in which employees select from a menu of different benefits according to their needs.

'We're trying to deal with the whole concept of the balance between work and family life,' says Mike Shore of IBM, which grants unpaid leave with benefits of up to three years to give people time to care for children or sick relatives or to pursue 'once-in-a-lifetime' personal opportunities.

When Maternity Leave Policies = Recruitment

The opportunities of the information age, the demands of an established career, or the simple need to make money are luring women back into the work force almost immediately after giving birth.

Most women return to work within six months after giving birth, according to Catalyst, a research organization specializing in women's careers. The shortest leave is at the top and bottom of the pay scale, where women take only six to eight weeks. In just eleven years the proportion of women back at work within a year of giving birth jumped from 31 per cent in 1976 to 51 per cent in 1987, the study says.

Colgate-Palmolive offers twelve weeks of unpaid leave to both women and men for birth, adoption, family illness, or eldercare.

Aetna Life & Casualty offers unpaid 'family leaves' of up to six months. Aetna says it's cheaper to 'manage' absences than replace employees.

Merck & Company, in Rahway, New Jersey, has had a maternity leave policy for more than thirty years. New mothers are entitled to six-week leaves with pay and up to eighteen months of unpaid leaves with benefits. 'With all the benefits you have here, it makes you think twice about going anywhere else,' says Diane Dalinsky, a Merck employee.

Merck's maternity leave policy is cost-effective. Even after deducting the cost of leave, the programme saves an average of $12,000 an employee since the company saves the expense of training new workers, says J. Douglas Phillips, senior director of corporate planning. The cost of losing a worker and retraining a successor costs one and a half times the employee's salary, he adds.

In the labour market of the early 1990s creative leave policies will help employers keep seasoned employees, who would otherwise have to be replaced from a dwindling labour supply.

Full Time/Part Time

Retirees and mothers, the two untapped groups where new workers of the 1990s will be found, are known to favour part-time employment. In Denmark, Norway, Sweden, the Netherlands, and Britain, part-time workers now represent more than 20 per cent of the workforce. Part-timers represent 17.4 per cent of the US work force, according to the National Planning Association.

Labour shortages will actually increase productivity, by forcing corporations to deploy existing labour in more creative, efficient ways.

Job-sharing programmes are offered by about 16 per cent of US companies, including Quaker Oats and Levi Strauss, according to the American Society for Personnel Administration. These programmes will increase, along with other part-time arrangements, as employers are compelled to restructure empty, full-time positions into part-time jobs. In addition, the reverse, making part-timers permanent, is an other effective approach.

In Sarasota, Florida, where unemployment is 4 per cent, Lechmere, Inc, a discount retailer, has enriched and upgraded part-time jobs into attractive career opportunities.

At the Sarasota store 60 per cent of the work force is full time, compared with only 30 per cent for the rest of the twenty-seven-store chain. Retailers, the store discovered, can no longer rely on part-timers as a source of good, cheap labour. There were just not enough people out there, and the few available could command $8 to $10 an hour. So Lechmere gave raises to employees who would learn to perform a variety of jobs so the store could move them around to adjust to different shifts.

Lechmere, which will try the system out in several other stores, has tapped into the secret strategy that most employers (and all retailers) will have to discover one way or another: how to increase wages enough to attract good people yet up productivity enough to pay for them and consequently preserve profits.

MANAGING THE EXTERNAL ENVIRONMENT

After this rousing cheer on behalf of women in the information economy, it is important to note the one factor holding them back—themselves. Women over thirty today formulated their career goals in a world where women *were* a minority. Many set their goals too low.

A generation of women has reached the age where senior management jobs are in its sight. The average age of senior executives is about fifty-one according to a study by Korn/Ferry International and the Graduate School of Management at the University of California. Women who were twenty-five in 1975 —when larger numbers of women started getting MBAs—will be fifty in 2000.

At the dawn of the 1990s, the decade when women's leadership comes of age, it is time that women start re-examining those goals. For many it is time to revise them upward. To reach top positions around the year 2000, women in their late thirties and forties must begin *now* to think like the CEOs they never planned or dreamed they could be. As Regina Herzlinger of the Harvard Business School points out, it takes thirty-five years of business experience to sit in the CEO's chair.

For most women that requires a new set of skills. The people skills of middle management, where women may possess a slight advantage over men, are not enough at the top. Those skills must be coupled with extensive knowledge about the external environment in which a business exists.

The major themes of the 1990s—technological change,

compressed product cycles, and global competition—require a leader to scan the global environment and organize the internal tasks, while remaining market-sensitive.

Following are examples of companies and leaders that demonstrate the ability to tune into external trends and adjust the company accordingly.

1992

Sweden's business hero Jan Carlzon has entered a global mode to meet the challenges of the 1990s. SAS will be ready for 1992 even though two out of its three consortium countries do not belong to the Common Market. No chance that other big European airlines will put SAS out of business. In fact, Carlzon, not his European competitors, seems to be trying to put together the first global airline. SAS bought 8 per cent of Continental Airlines and will link up with the US airline with flights to Newark. He has also set up a venture with Thai Airlines and has offered to buy 40 per cent of Argentina's Aerolineas Argentinas.

Could SAS improve service on Continental flights? we asked a SAS flight attendant who had just flown from Newark to Denver. She laughed and said 'Are you kidding?'

The Global Economy

US companies should be studying Swedish firms, rather than Japanese, says Thomas R. Horton, president and CEO of the American Management Association. Sweden is similar to the United States in terms of 'free markets, global scope, and technological diversity', he says. The Swedes are committed to creativity and action on the global level. A skilled work force, a high level of literacy, and innovation explain Sweden's success, in spite of an enormous tax rate that would have destroyed the incentives of most Americans.

Global Environmental Concern

With more than 350 boutiques in Europe, Canada, Australia, the Middle East and most recently in the United States, the Body Shop ranks among the largest cosmetic retailers in the world. Its all-natural products—such as camomile eye make-up remover and cucumber cleansing milk—are based on healing rituals

214

owner Anita Roddick experienced in Africa and Polynesia as a young United Nations employee. Without advertisements anywhere, 1988 sales hit $83.2 million, a 62 per cent increase over 1987.

It wins customers with an awareness of the earth and its creatures. None of the products has been tested on animals, and all suppliers must certify that none of their products have either. Staff members must study natural cosmetics and the environment. The company is also engaged in programmes to help children in poor areas of Britain, India, and Mexico.

Young women customers connect body care with the environment and animal life. Shares of company stock, fought over in the London market, have soared 600 per cent, baffling the financial community. 'I keep telling them that it's investing in people,' Roddick says.

Labour Shortages

Middlesex Truck and Coach, a $4.2 million one-stop truck repair service in Roxbury, Massachusetts, has increased sales fourfold since 1981. 'I believe in management by commitment rather than authority,' says founder and president Brian Maloney, winner of the Small Business of the Year Award from the Greater Boston Chamber of Commerce.

Maloney's success is noteworthy because it has won him the loyalty of a work force consisting almost exclusively of minorities and handicapped people. These workers—along with women—will make up most of the new members of the US labour force until the year 2000. Along with a little French and Spanish, Maloney has learned lipreading and sign language to communicate with his workforce.

At Middlesex Truck formal job titles and descriptions are shunned; people learn a variety of tasks. 'Many of my sheet metal men are also painters,' says Maloney. He says his greatest role is helping employees reach their potential. 'I want them to look back and say they have learned something.' He lives that goal by constantly challenging people to learn new skills.

Pacific Rim

The business life of Abraham Krasnoff reads like an adventure in globalism. For sixteen years he has been the CEO of the Pall

Corporation, which produces filters that screen contaminants in a multitude of industries from beverages to surgical products.

Twenty-six years ago the company took its first global step, buying a company in Great Britain. Today more than 55 per cent of its annual $385 million in sales will come from overseas. After that first step into the UK the company entered Germany, France, Italy, then Japan and Singapore.

'Start small' was the motto. First would be a small sales unit, then technical support. Krasnoff's advice to others: 'Hire competent locals, use competent locals, and listen to competent locals.'

What are the company's plans for the decade of the Pacific Rim? Today the company is working with China's nascent oil industry and buying Chinese-made hydraulic filters to sell in third markets. 'India and China are edging toward consumer societies,' says Krasnoff. 'Any business person who doesn't have a global perspective is either dead or dumb.'

Accelerating Change

Is there such a thing as a base rate of change? Like a desired rate of interest, inflation, unemployment? Is it 5 per cent or 15 per cent? Does it change with time and circumstances? Although it is impossible to calculate, we must somehow build room for it in our lives, allowing the time for renewal and innovation.

The accelerating pace of change, especially in technology, has brought corporations face-to-face with the competitive advantage of speed—getting products to customers faster and thereby increasing market share while reducing inventory costs.

General Electric now makes custom industrial circuits in three days instead of three weeks. Motorola used to make electronic pagers in three weeks. Now it takes two hours, and Motorola pagers beat Asian competition in the marketplace.

High-tech products that come to market six months late but on budget will earn 33 per cent less profit over five years, while products that come out on time and 50 per cent over budget will cut profits only 4 per cent, according to a scenario developed by McKinsey & Company, the international management consulting firm.

Leaders committed to the credo of speed are known to impose 'impossible' product development schedules to force people to reconceptualize the approach to a problem. Simply doing things faster will not work. The leadership of constant change requires people who are comfortable with ambiguity, although most of us prefer order.

Charles Exley, chairman and CEO of NCR, has built the company into a $6 billion business with record share earnings. He has no fear of accelerating change. 'When there are relatively few changes, you don't find dramatic opportunities,' says Exley. His plan was to double the increase in NCR's development spending in 1988 but to make certain the money is going into the areas—finding both the right market opportunity *and* the right technology.

In the decade of the 1990s we are moving from managing control to leadership of accelerated change.

Most of these examples, not surprisingly, concern men. Female role models at the top are still hard to find. Ten years from now it will be a different story. The important point, for women, as well as their male colleagues, is to begin preparing for the future today.

The challenge for individual managers in the 1990s is to evolve their own personal leadership styles. The first step is to study the strategies of business heroes like the Bill Gore and Jan Carlzon. Next it is important to synthesize those pioneering efforts with experience of the managers and environments that brought out the best in people.

Women and the information society—which celebrates brain over brawn—are a partnership made in heaven. And wherever the information society is flourishing, women are entering the labour force. Wherever the information revolution has spread, women have flocked into the work force.

Even in Japan, a culture so traditional that the word 'wife' means 'inside the house', 40 per cent of the work force is female and 48.6 per cent of women work. The number of women in administrative positions has doubled in ten years—about 50,000 of the more than 16 million working women. In Japan more than half of married women work, and in a recent survey, 80 per cent of the women polled said they wanted to develop lifetime careers. In Japan all this change necessitated the invention of a new word, *soto san*, to describe a wife who is active outside the house.

This decade of women in business leadership is dawning at a

time when women are achieving unprecedented prominence in politics. As legislators, cabinet ministers, governors and mayors, women politicians throughout the world have won elections and appointments they would have lost only a decade or two ago.

Today's most visible women leaders, those who serve as prime ministers or heads of state, have carved out their own identities. None are male imitations, cardboard party stereotypes or 'charismatic' pieces of fluff. Each is her 'own woman', with a highly personal leadership style.

In the Philippines, former housewife and political widow Corazon Aquino democratically ousted Ferdinand Marcos, tackled the immense problems of a country in chaos and has held onto power longer than anyone predicted.

Patrician, Harvard-educated Benazair Bhutto became the first female head of state in a Moslem country, vowing to improve the lot of women and initiating a massive privatization effort.

Commanding, conservative Margaret Thatcher came from a solidly middle-class background to become the first British prime minister in this century successfully to contest three general elections.

Forthright and positive Norwegian Prime Minister Gro Harlem Bruntland has assumed global leadership in issues of the environment and the Third World. Her government boasts the world's highest proportion of women in top government jobs.

In male-dominated Japan, Takako Doi, a dynamic and confident woman, heads the leading opposition party, the Socialists, and would become prime minister should her party ever win a majority. In 1989, the ruling Liberal party named Mayumi Moriyama Japan's first female chief cabinet officer.

Women who wish there were more female role models in business can perhaps draw strength from women leaders whose domain spans the complex affairs of entire countries, rather than single corporations.

In the first decades of the third millennium we and our children will look back at the later half of the 20th century and remark on how quaint were the days when women were excluded from the top echelons of business and political leadership, much as we today recall when women could not vote. How naive were the men and women of the 1980s, we will say, those people who believed in something called a 'glass ceiling' and thought it would forever exclude women from the top.

8

The Age of Biology

We are shifting from the models and metaphors of physics to the models and metaphors of biology to help us understand today's dilemmas and opportunities.

Physics furnished the metaphors and models for the mechanistic industrial age. *Physics* as metaphor suggests: energy-intensive, linear, macro, mechanistic, deterministic, outer-directed.

Today, however, we are in the process of creating a society that is an elaborate array of information feedback systems, the very structure of the biological organism. Furthermore, we are poised on the threshold of a great era of biotechnology.

Biology as metaphor suggests: information-intensive, micro, inner-directed, adaptive, holistic.

In the information era we borrow from the vocabulary of biology. Even the 'new physics' is advancing by thinking in biological metaphors.

We speak of a computer 'virus'. The computer screen on which this chapter is being composed has a picture of a hypodermic needle when the computer is first turned on, meaning that there is a programme in the computer called Vaccine that is constantly scanning for aberrations in the behaviour of the computer. Similar programmes have names like Interferon and Virus Rx. The selection device used by this computer is called a mouse. The whole thing was put together by a company named Apple.

Information feedback systems, biological and electronic, are mutually reinforcing. Computers are being used to help unlock

219

the secrets of life; biology instructs new information software and systems.

Technical jargon in the information age draws on the words and phrases of biology: 'feedback'; 'in the loop'; 'seminal'; 'reprogrammed'; 'symbiosis'. In business we hear of 'seed capital', 'hothouses' for entrepreneurial projects, organizational 'growth' and 'evolution'. The metaphor of transformation from caterpillar to butterfly is almost universal.

Biology rather than electronics may hold the key to a new generation of 'thinking computers'.

Isao Karube, of the Tokyo Institute of Technology, has developed a 'freshness chip', a device consisting entirely of artificially engineered proteins and organic polymers that will be built into packets of fish sold in supermarkets. When a fish begins to decay, it produces aromatic chemicals that the freshness chip detects long before it would be apparent to the average nose. When a patch on the fish changes colour, customers (and management) know that the fish's best days are over. (Freshness chips for other foods will follow.)

This biomolecular device is a living computer. The next step —expected within a decade—is an artificial nose, a chip that could detect a wide variety of odours. During evolution the earliest brain structures were devoted to the sense of smell. Biology is perhaps a better route to an artificial nervous system than the electronics road to 'artificial intelligence'.

BIOTECHNOLOGISTS AND BIO-FUNDAMENTALISTS

Biotechnology is becoming a powerful presence in our lives, yet most of us know very little about this massive scientific phenomenon and even less about its social and ethical implications. Most of us are somewhat put off by technology, and the confusing ethical component of biotechnology reinforces the temptation to avoid the subject entirely. That would be a mistake. The issues of biotechnology will not go away. And it is too important to delegate to the experts.

The purpose of this chapter is to identify in lay language the major directions in biotechnology today.

The first thrust of biotechnology occurred in health care when scientists altered mice and goats to produce proteins and chemicals useful for humans—a drug to aid haemophiliacs and TPA to dissolve blood clots. We will soon be able to identify specific-disease-prone persons, and a new generation of vaccines is on its way.

Today the genetic manipulation of crops and farm animals is expanding rapidly. Fertilizers and insect resisters are being placed in seeds.

Biotechnology can end hunger through a new green revolution. Advances are being made in genetic techniques to grow fish and beef faster and put more protein in potatoes and rice. Endangered species can be kept from extinction through the transplanting of embryos into surrogate mothers.

Biotechnology will eventually make it possible to identify and manipulate inherited characteristics. And that's the scary part. While biotechnology suggests awesome contributions to the improvement of life, it also raises questions that make people very uneasy.

Opposition

Periodic attempts to field-test genetically engineered organisms have brought a hailstorm of criticism.

Environmentalists, animal rights activists, farmers, and clergy, and articulate people are concerned: Is it ethical to manipulate nature? Will new species harm the environment? Are animals being mistreated? Are the pharmaceutical and agricultural industries in it only for the money? In general, what are the ethical, legal, and social implications of biotechnology?

Scientists at the University of California at Berkeley wanted to spray a strain of bacteria on a small patch of potatoes in a plot near the Oregon border to see if it would inhibit frost formation. Local citizens objected vigorously.

'The residents of this community feel that they are being used as guinea pigs for the rest of the world,' protested Glenn Church of the Action League for Ecologically Responsible Technology. Under the threat of lawsuits, the university cancelled the test.

Environmentalists fear that biotechnology could transform nature itself—according to a blue-print designed by humans instead of nature. Already fish like the carp have been genetically altered to grow faster. Theoretically scientists could make an implant into salmon genes that would alter their migration patterns, making it easier to catch the species in the oceans. Rivers, lakes, and even oceans might become aquatic corrals in which once-wild species are spawned, raised, and harvested like cattle—moving from the hunting of fish to the artificial breeding of them.

Will the intrusion of technology into nature transform people's perception of life itself? Will future generations see life as just another manipulable computer program?

The most common questions raised about biotechnology are:

How can we be sure that a genetically altered organism—even potentially beneficial to humans—won't have a disastrous consequence when released in the environment?

What should be the trade-offs between ensuring public safety and continuing scientific progress?

There are many questions, few answers.

Legislation

'We are at the present time woefully unprepared to grapple with the serious ethical choices with which the new technology will confront us,' said US Senator Albert Gore, Jr. 'The very power to bring about so much good will also open the door to serious potential problems. If we are not careful, we may well cross the line separating the two.' Gore has proposed a national commission to monitor biotechnology developments that affect human genetic engineering.

Lacking answers, legislators may impose controls over biotechnology research. The New Jersey Assembly introduced a bill in 1987 to tighten the regulations controlling the release of genetically engineered microbes. Texas, Wisconsin, and North Carolina have considered bills regulating biotechnology.

Internationally neither Italy nor Japan permits the release of genetically engineered organisms into the environment. West Germany's genetic commission has called for a five-year moratorium on such experiments. The Green party in West Germany views biotechnology as it does nuclear energy: something to be resisted at all costs.

The Rifkin Factor

No critic anywhere has spoken louder than Jeremy Rifkin, a Washington attorney and biotechnological gadfly. Rifkin opposes any manipulation of human genes on the ground that it will lead to a policy of creating 'perfect people', raising the emotional issue of eugenics. He is against the release into the atmosphere of altered organisms because, he says, eventually one may interact with the ecology with dire consequences.

For five years Rifkin helped delay field trials of Frostban, the recombinant microbe that protects plants against frost. When tests eventually were carried out in a strawberry patch, the California Department of Food and Agriculture ordered the scientists to wear fully sealed space-suitlike outfits, complete with helmets, gloves, and breathing packs. Just a few feet away a crowd of reporters and onlookers munched doughnuts and sipped coffee without any kind of protective gear. In a subsequent field test the need for spacesuits was reconsidered and deemed overly cautious. Spraying proceeded without the outfits.

Rifkin wants a five-year moratorium on the free release of genetically engineered materials of any kind into the environment and a ban on the patenting of transgenic animals (animals carrying genes from other species). A genetic accident could be more disastrous than a nuclear mishap, he warns. He believes that 'the future of civilization is at stake'. Not every environmentalist agrees.

Environmental activist Barry Commoner, who is also a scientist, views Rifkin's comments as 'hokum'.

David Baltimore, a Nobel laureate molecular biologist, answers Rifkin's concerns equally bluntly. 'He doesn't know what he's talking about. . . . I think Rifkin is trying to stop everything that's going on in biotechnology . . . As far as I'm concerned, Rifkin is in the same pot with religious fundamentalists who believe certain things shouldn't be done. In his own way, Rifkin is a biological fundamentalist.' The *Economist* regularly refers to Rifkin as a biofundamentalist.

While many think that Rifkin is an extremist, they admire his energy in raising the issues. 'I think genetic engineering in general is something people should be concerned about because molecular biology is extremely potent in what it can do,' Baltimore acknowledges. 'People ought to be aware of what's going on.'

Baltimore argues that today's genetic manipulations are no greater than what dog breeders and nectarine growers have engaged in for decades. Growth hormones change a species more than do today's laboratory interventions, he maintains.

'The difference between a domestic dog and a wild dog is much greater than the differences we're creating in the laboratory—and that difference was created artificially by breeding dogs over generations. How about the nectarine? That's a hybrid between two existing fruits. We've been fooling around with genetics for a long time.'

That is the general opinion of the experts: that genetic engineering is simply a better way of doing what breeders have done for millennia in trying to improve agriculture.

But it that true? Is the nuclear bomb just another development along a continuum that started with clubs and axes and bows and arrows? Is genetic engineering a quantum leap that requires a whole new set of rules and considerations—just as the nuclear bomb did?

Five Main Assumptions

The rapidity of scientific advances has certainly outpaced public assimilation—or interest. But it is too important—and moving fast. If you are not informed on this topic, you are letting other forces play God.

This chapter will deal with the recent developments and discuss the ethical and moral issues. By presenting the principal ideas and arguments, we hope to help you decide for yourself.

Here are our assumptions:

1. Although biotechnology is technical and sometimes frightening, we can't keep ignoring it.

2. It is later than you think. Even at this point it would be difficult to put the genie (gene?) back in the bottle. It's out.

3. The responsibility for what is happening has already been thrust upon us.

4. Technology is not inherently evil. It is neutral. How we use it is key. There is a lot more positive than negative that will be coming out of biotechnology, but we need to know what we are getting into.

5. We must evolve spiritually if we are to handle the re-

sponsibility of manipulating life itself. Perhaps we do need safeguards and time slowdowns to handle this responsibility.

PLANTS, ANIMALS, AND HUMANS

As we move through the next millennium, biotechnology will be as important as the computer. We all sense that. We know we *ought* to know about biotechnology and where it is leading.

Although some of us are as dead set against biotechnology as Jeremy Rifkin, others have worked through to a middle ground. They think that manipulating the genes of plant cells seems all right but that playing around with human genes is definitely not. Animals are somewhere in between; it depends on whether what is being done is humane or not.

Plants

Jesse Jaynes, a Louisiana State University biochemist, is working in collaboration with John Dodds of the International Potato Centre in Lima, Peru. He hopes he can engineer the lowly potato so that it will have the protein value of meat.

'The genes that I synthesized encode proteins that are much better than beef as far as the essential amino-acid content goes,' Jaynes says. Jaynes hopes that he can similarly improve other widely eaten plants like rice and cassava (a tropical plant with starchy roots). As many as 2 billion people in the world rely on cassava, which is a very poor source of protein, as is rice.

'It may take another four or five years,' says Jaynes. 'But we will have plants including potatoes, cassava, and rice—those are the three that we're focussing on—that are going to be more nutritious and, hopefully, prevent the protein malnutrition that one sees.'

Jaynes and his colleagues have already found a possible way to help these food plants resist the attacks of bacteria and fungi that account for the annual loss of 40 per cent of the world's crops.

Jaynes is very optimistic. 'I really think that biotechnology and genetic engineering can do some great things to help people in the developing world. I know a lot of people talk about all the great things that are going to happen in the United States. And certainly we will be beneficiaries of that. But I think, overall, the prospects for improving the lot of those people are much brighter in the developing world through this technology.'

Supertomato

A biotech breakthrough from Monsanto has developed a tomato with a built-in resistance to parasites, viruses, and herbicides. The supertomatoes are the grandchildren of tomatoes genetically engineered for endurance.

More good news for those who want to increase productivity down on the farm: it should be possible to transfer the supertomatoes' properties to potatoes, sugar beets, and every other member of the broad-leafed dicot plant group. Farmers will then become technicians whose main job to decide which characteristics they want their crops to exhibit.

Other companies are trying to develop tomatoes with higher solids content, so that soup, tomato paste, or ketchup can be produced with fewer tomatoes.

New discoveries and new techniques will allow growers to leave tomatoes on the vine longer, for better taste, without risking spoilage.

'Right now everything you buy in the store was picked green,' says microbiologist William Hiatt, of Calgene, a Davis, California, company that is working with Campbell Soup to improve tomatoes.

Consumers look for nice red tomatoes. At present therefore, shippers use ethylene gas to darken the firm skins that haven't had a chance to soften, or fully ripen.

Alan Bennett, a plant geneticist at the University of California at Davis, explains that tomatoes are picked when they are 'a nice hard green baseball' and resistant to rough handling.

Genetically Buttered Popcorn—and Without All the Calories

Biotechnology will be a boon to millions of weight watchers around the world. Not only will it slash the fat content of 'forbidden foods' like pork, but it will enhance the natural taste of popcorn with butter flavour while adding no calories.

Buttered popcorn is even easier to create than supertomatoes. DNA Plant Technology, in Cinnaminson, New Jersey, uses a technique called somoclonal variation to select naturally occurring strains of popcorn that have their own butterlike flavour. Their approach involves cutting up parts of the whole corn plant and growing individual cells in a special mix of hormones and nutrients. With this technique 'you can quickly come up with an enormous variability in a crop', says Richard Lester, president of DNA Plant Technology. 'In effect, you're speeding up natural selection.'

At Cornell University, scientists are breeding new types of apples that will not brown when the inside is exposed to the air. The Japanese have developed a seedless watermelon.

Plants have long been the source of flavourings and fragrances. Now scientists envision growing cells from the plants in laboratories to produce the chemicals that create the flavours and fragrances. The laboratories will offer you chocolate, vanilla, or chili pepper flavourings.

Most of the world's top-quality natural vanilla, from the vanilla orchid, is grown in Madagascar; it is expensive and in short supply. Cheap artificial vanilla contains only 1 of the more than 150 components of natural vanilla. The new vanilla from laboratory cells will be almost as rich as natural vanilla at a far lower price.

A New Type of Seed Capital

Pest-resistant and frost-resistant crops and fertilizers are now available or nearing the marketplace. They promise to improve farm yields by 20 per cent or more. Genetic engineering can fortify seeds so that:

- The resulting plants are resistant to pests and viral disease.
- The crops are more nutritious.
- The plants can grow in arid and even polluted soils.

Genetic engineering will conquer farm diseases for which there are now no cures.

In America's great Corn Belt there are currently no chemical defences against at least thirty insect pests and fifty crop diseases. In 1989 field trials were under way on genetically engineered seeds for alfalfa plants that hold more protein, need less fertilizer, and grow more rapidly. Alfalfa provides most of the fodder for America's cows and is the country's fourth-largest crop.

At the University of California at Davis, biologists are trying to insert other species genes into seeds of walnuts, apples, oranges, and other fruits to create hardy, disease-resistant trees.

In coming years these biologists hope to add genes that will protect walnut trees from major pests like the codling moth, navel orange worm, and a virus infection called black-line disease, which together cost the industry $10 to $20 million annually. During the next decade or so, scientists will start on apples, oranges, peaches, and cherries.

Farmers will be shifting their spending priorities from fertilizers and pesticides to genetically altered seeds that do the same job. Robert Fleming, a British securities firm, estimates that genetic engineering will make seeds a profitable and growing business in the next few years. Having seen this shift coming, large chemical companies (England's ICI, the Anglo-Dutch Shell group, Monsanto of the United States, Switzerland's Sandoz, and France's Rhône-Poulenc) have in the past decade spent more than $10 billion buying up seed companies.

Eventually plants could be given desirable traits from animals. A gene from bacteria that kill insects can be put into a tobacco plant. Insects will then avoid it.

Biotechnology researchers realized early that if the genetic instructions for the manufacture of a desirable protein are inserted into a living cell's DNA, that cell not only manufactures the protein but also passes it on to future generations. To create an insect-repellent tobacco, the appropriate gene need be injected only into the parent plant, which subsequently hands down the characteristic to its off-spring.

Biotechnology has Already Made Its Mark on Agriculture

Over the past half century, crop yields in America have risen 1 to 2 per cent a year. Dr David Paisley of the University of Illinois examined the rise in corn yields from 1930 to 1980 and concluded that 70 per cent of this increase was attributable to genetic improvements resulting from selective breeding.

These improvements in selective breeding took decades. Similar or bigger ones may in future be accomplished in a matter of months by using genetic engineering techniques. And improvements that previously could not be done at all or only in a limited fashion—such as controlling the ripening of vegetables and reducing postharvest spoilage—will be the focus of laboratory studies.

In September 1988 Epitope, Inc, a small biotechnology company in Beaverton, Oregon, entered a research agreement with the Sakata Seed Corporation of Japan to determine whether it can learn how to control the ripening of vegetables, fruits, and flowers through genetic engineering. Sakata produces 80 per cent of the world's broccoli seeds.

'Any time you can control ripening and bring products to the marketplace when you want, you've hit it big,' says Richard A. Bock, senior vice-president of Sutro & Company's bioscience group in Los Angeles. 'You're talking about the potential ability to bring strawberries to market in January, or tomatoes to the market two weeks before they become seasonal.'

Gene engineering may be the epitome of high technology, but it won't always be that way. With each new discovery it becomes easier to manipulate genes.

'What we are doing now is going to look mindless and simple five years from now,' says Tom St John, a molecular biologist at the Fred Hutchinson Cancer Research Centre in Seattle. 'You can pick up any recent issue of *Science* magazine, flip through it, and find ads for kit after kit of biotechnology techniques. These techniques have basically been put into Styrofoam boxes . . . this month's hard project is next month's kit.'

Monsanto Company senior vice-president and chief scientist Howard Schneiderman, a biotech pioneer, says, 'It's easy to picture a high-school class in the early to middle 1990s using biotechnology to produce insulin, especially if a Genentech sponsored a few high-school labs.'

Animals

In January 1988, on a farm in Wheelock, Texas, seven genetically identical pure-bred bull calves were produced from man-made embryos.

Identically copied embryos of prize bulls (ie, clones of them) can be created for gestation in ordinary cattle. Future breeders will be able to clone large numbers of cattle, pigs, and sheep

229

from a single embryo, with a uniform quality and a high standard never possible before.

'Theoretically thousands of identical [animals] could be produced through cloning,' says Dr Steen M. Willadsen, a Danish physiologist at the University of Calgary who developed the cloning technology.

Those Texas calves represent the state of the art for technology. They also portend revolutionary changes in the $30 billion-a-year beef industry and the $18 billion-a-year dairy business.

The combination of genetic engineering, surrogate motherhood, and artificial insemination can make things happen very fast. A genetic engineer can put new genes into a cell knowing that the resulting embryo can be transferred to a foster mother and brought to term. If this results in an improvement that can be transmitted through the male, artificial insemination can quickly spread the advantage. A single superior bull may service 100,000 cows a year through artificial insemination. In the United States alone, there are about 150,000 embryo transfers in cows each year.

More Milk from Fewer Cows

A mass-produced hormone found in cows can boost milk production 30 per cent, even 40 per cent in cows injected daily.

It is called BST (for bovine somatotropin), and its effect on farms and farmers will be impressive. BST will increase milk production by 522 pounds per cow per year. By the year 2000 the use of BST will sharply reduce the number of cows needed to meet milk requirements in the United States, from 10.8 million to 7.5 million; the number of commercial dairy farms could be cut in half. The US Food and Drug Administration is expected to approve BST in 1990.

Small family dairy farmers are fighting it, trying to persuade state and provincial legislatures in the United States and Canada to ban the use of BST. They don't contend that shooting up cows with chemicals is unsafe, but that it would harm milk's wholesome *reputation*. Their main objection is on economic grounds. It would, they say, increase milk supplies and lower milk prices. Three Canadian provinces have banned the testing and sale of bovine somatotropin. The Netherlands barred research on BST in 1988; Sweden banned it earlier, and the European Parliament recommended in 1988 that milk and meat from animals given the drug should not be fed to people or other animals.

Five of the United States' largest supermarket chains, including Safeway and Kroger, announced in August of 1989 that they would not carry milk from cows treated with BST. In September of 1989 the European Commission proposed a 15-month delay in the use of BST in the EC. The European Community has produced an absurd surplus of milk and butter through its previous policies of subsidy, and its politicians are fearful of a drug that will increase milk production by 522 pounds per cow per year. But it is doubtful if politicians can forever keep milk expensive to housewives and babies by standing in progress's way.

Four American companies are developing BST: Monsanto, American Cyanamid, Eli Lilly, and Upjohn. When it is put into use in 1990, BST could, they say, generate sales of more than $500 million annually in the United States alone.

It seems to be shaping up as a classic economic struggle between big business and family farmers, with some consumers feeling a little squeamish about milk from drugged cows.

New Drug Factories

In 1987 US and British scientists found a way to introduce human genes into the mammary glands of sheep, thereby producing a blood-clotting chemical, Factor 9. The sheep then produce milk containing Factor 9, which can be extracted and sold as a drug for haemophilia. Rorer, the US drug firm involved, is also working on developing a process whereby a cow will produce milk containing human albumen, used in surgery.

Milk-producing animals can serve as virtual drug factories. TPA, the substance that dissolves blood clots and has saved many heart attack patients, has been produced in the milk of altered mice. Katherine Gordon, a research leader at Integrated Genetics, says goats will produce TPA in their milk starting in 1990. She says a herd of 100 to 200 goats could produce enough TPA annually to supply the United States' entire demand. As few as 300 goats could supply the world.

Animals will produce valuable biological products for humans, almost like factories—which some people think very wrong, but they will thereby save many human lives.

Cows as Surrogate Mothers for Bison

Ranchers and scientists in Wyoming are looking for a way to use cows as surrogate mothers for bison, a source of low-cholesterol meat. They hope to raise large numbers of bison for the US market by implanting bison embryos into cows and milk-feed the calves until they reach the age of slaughter. With the help of University of Wyoming researchers, the ranchers inseminate female bisons treated with hormones. The fertilized embryos are then implanted into cows, so that the bison can produce more embryos instead of going through pregnancy.

Biotechnology can be used to mass-produce special breeds and perpetuate endangered species. Using the embryo transfer process, farmers can produce Charolais beef, which makes a tastier steak, and Angora sheep, which grow softer wool. The Cincinnati Zoo has bred bongos, rare antelopes that originate in central Africa, by transfering bongo embryos into ordinary antelopes. Biotechnology could prevent the disappearance of scores of endangered species around the world.

Researchers at many American universities, including Johns Hopkins, Purdue, Oregon State, Washington State, Louisiana State, and the University of Minnesota, are looking for ways to speed up the growth of fish through genetic manipulations.

Nothing to Carp About

In May 1988 a genetically altered carp made its debut at the Chesapeake Bay Institute in Shady Side, Maryland. The fish grew 20 per cent faster than normal carp. By isolating and duplicating a single gene from rainbow trout, the scientists produced a hormone which could be injected into carp eggs. Once injected, it revolutionized fish growth.

The year before, Chinese researchers had demonstrated how genes from other animals could alter the inherent characteristics of fish. They introduced the gene that produces human growth hormones into goldfish, which is similar to carp and an important food in Asia. The fish promptly grew up to four times faster than normal.

Gene-splicing technology is evident throughout the aquaculture industry. Catfish will be produced in twelve months instead of eighteen months. Americans spend $6 billion a year on fish imported into America like pike and striped bass. But biotechnology will make it easier to domesticate and reproduce these fish.

In Britain, fish and chips are a popular fast food for ordinary families, but quality fish grew more and more expensive in restaurants. Both should come down in price and increase in supply.

Transgenesis

Transgenesis means introducing genes from one species into another. A lot of people are becoming worried about this, and are particularly bothered by such symbols of 'progress' as Mighty Mouse and the geep.

Dr Richard Palmiter, Dr Ralph Brinster, and their colleagues at the University of Washington and the University of Pennsylvania pioneered transgenesis when they injected genes from a rat growth hormone into fertilized mouse eggs. The very large result became known as Mighty Mouse. An even odder creature, the geep, owes its heritage to a goat, a sheep, and the work of scientists in England's Cambridge. Created in 1983, the geep was born with goatlike horns and a partly sheeplike coat. The geep is sterile, like the mule.

In the years since the birth of Mighty Mouse and the geep, hundreds of different genes have been inserted into mice, rabbits, pigs, and sheep. Most look and behave just like natural animals, except for their newly introduced individualized traits. Less than a decade old, gene transplant techniques have produced more than 1000 strains of altered mice and more than 12 varieties of transgenic pigs.

In Australia, Robert Seamark and colleagues at the University of Adelaide are nurturing the seventh generation of pigs descended from animals with an extra growth hormone gene. These pigs convert feed into meat 30 per cent more efficiently and reach market weight seven weeks earlier than normal pigs. The Australian researchers expect the pigs will be available to farmers within five years.

The world's first test-tube chickens were born in 1988 at the Institute of Animal Physiology and Genetics in Edinburgh, where Margaret Perry is the primary researcher. An embryo began its growth in a jar, was transferred to an eggshell, and was sealed up in a container where the chick developed normally. Now scientists can micro-inject new genes directly into chicken embryos at the single-cell stage, as they already do with many other animals.

Why pursue this strange practice of transgenesis?

'Our view of what life is—and the boundary lines between species—are going to change, perhaps blur, and it's hard to say what form those changes will take,' says BioTechnica International's Lynn Klotz. 'One can transfer genes from species to species—and it always goes a hell of a lot faster than we think it's going to go. I don't envision centaurs or mythical half-animals coming to life. But the possibilities in transferring genes between species—somehow that has to impress on one's psyche what a species is.'

Despite the fears about them genetic engineers are still limited in what they can do. They can't add more than a few genes to an animal, for example. A cow has tens of thousands of genes. Science can't turn a cow into a kangaroo.

Scientific capability will expand, however. In a few decades it may be possible to insert genes that change an animal's fertility, size, and behaviour—altering salmon migration patterns for example. It's just a matter of time—and not much of that.

'Will beaming children, ten to fifteen years from now, be presenting their genetically engineered sheep at the 4H Club?' asks genetic engineer Brian Seed, assistant professor of molecular biology at Massachusetts General Hospital. 'No doubt about it.'

In the Rocky Mountains, people are now skiing on genetically produced powder snow.

Snowmax is a tapioca-like natural protein that can be genetically produced in very large amounts. When water touches the protein, it produces huge quantities of a dry, powdery snow. It is a big improvement over traditional artificial snow. With ordinary fake snow production, a lot of water used is wasted. Not with Snowmax. About $650 worth of Snowmax used in 1 million gallons of water covers an acre with five feet of snow.

The Eastman Kodak Company bought the production and marketing rights to Snowmax, developed by Advanced Genetic Sciencies of Berkeley, California, and expects to produce ten tons of it annually in a $30 million plant in Rochester, New York. That will make enough powder to cover several thousand acres of ski slopes.

Human

Genetic engineering represents biotechnology's most important technique because it gives us the key to cracking life's code. The question is: are we ready for such an advance?

Genes are the instructions by which a parent's characteristics are passed on to offspring. They are like the directions for assembling a computer or a car; there is a list of parts and instructions about the order in which they are to be put together. But genes are descriptions of proteins, not of circuits or bearings, and the instructions are written in a code not on paper but on molecules of DNA (deoxyribonucleic acid), which provides plenty of space to record detailed instructions; the DNA in a single cell would stretch six to seven feet long if its long double strands were unfolded.

The DNA in one human body would reach to the moon and back 8000 times.

The deciphering of the genetic code—with its instructions for building, running, and reproducing bodies—may well prove to be the greatest scientific achievement in this century. 'Genetics is a great engine driving the advancement of knowledge in a whole host of fields in biology,' says Dr Philip Leder of the Harvard Medical School.

A human's genome (all the genes taken together) contains from 50,000 to 100,000 genes, all stored on twenty-three pairs of chromosomes. To find one of these genes on its chromosome, you need a map. We don't have one yet. The crude maps we do have are very sketchy, but they are improving.

In 1977 researchers from Collaborative Research and scientists from the Whitehead Institute in Cambridge, England, published the first rough map of the human genome. It cost $11 million, took five years, and barely scratched the surface of the genome.

Once a gene is located, it can be copied—that is, cloned. Cloned genes are loaded with information. They can tell scientists how to spot carriers of genetic diseases, diagnose genetic abnormalities, and even identify a person's predisposition for some diseases.

Mapping of the human genome will come. It was given a boost in October 1988, when Dr James D. Watson agreed to help organize a US-funded project to do just that. Dr Watson was the young American who was awarded the Nobel Prize for co-discovering DNA, together with Britain's Francis Crick at Cambridge University in 1953. The two young men then made one of the greatest discoveries of our time through one of its cheapest research projects—they just fitted pieces of plastic together until they made a plausible pattern. Now Dr Watson will lend his great prestige and vigour to what will be the largest biological research project ever contemplated. The objective of the genome project is to map and chemically to define all human genes. This enormous task will take about fifteen years and cost billions of dollars. Dr Watson wants 3 per cent of the projects budget to be devoted to ethical issues.

Eugenics Revisited

Eventually it will be possible to identify and pick out genes for virtually any inherited characteristic.

This is the prospect that frightens most people.

Parents could arrange to have their embryos—or their children's—programmed with customized packages that correct genetic defects. In theory, parents might ensure that their children (and their children's children) all are six feet tall, with hazel eyes. For many of us even the prospect of such a choice recalls Adolf Hitler's Aryan genetics programme. This would be a Darth Vader future that few sensible people will want anything to do with.

But this technology possesses an equally compelling positive side. As the first decade of the new century unfolds, adults and children will be routinely screened for genes that make them susceptible to killer diseases like cancer. To prevent and treat scores of other diseases, defective genes will be replaced with normal ones.

Scientists have many of the tools they will need. They can already identify defective genes and determine from the DNA of a weeks-old foetus if sickle-cell anemia, thalassemia, and other disorders are present.

Biotechnology will help solve the mysteries of multigene disorders, like heart attacks where many genes interact and combine with environment and life-style to produce disease. About a dozen genetic aberrations linked to mental disorders and cancer have already been found; many more will be added.

Gene probes—short stretches of single-stranded DNA that

help researchers detect diseases—will be a major focus of research. About seven gene probes for diagnostic kits have been approved by the US Food and Drug Administration since 1985, including probes to detect herpes virus and *Legionella*. At present twenty companies are designing probes for diagnosing susceptibility to heart disease or other genetic diseases. Geneticists at the University of Indiana have compiled family genetic trees in search of markers for such inherited illnesses as Huntington's chorea.

Collaborative Research, in Bedford, Massachusetts, whose chief scientific adviser is Nobel laureate David Baltimore, was among the first biotechnology companies to recognize the importance of gene probes. Investing more than $11 million on probes since 1984, the company has produced DNA tests for cystic fibrosis, for monitoring bone-marrow transplants, for diagnostic tests for lymphoma, a cancer of the white blood cell, and DNA tests for paternity determination. Now the company is looking for markers for disorders linked to defects in single genes, such as adult polycystic kidney disease and Duchenne muscular dystrophy (a fatal muscle disease).

The New Age of Vaccines

By the first decade of the new century, biotechnology could pave the way to a new era in health care. Through genetic engineering, it may be possible to vaccinate fully against many diseases, with a single jab in the arm.

'Genetic engineering will lead to the creation of a new age of vaccines,' says Dr Kenneth Warren, a member of the Rockefeller Foundation. 'It is almost inevitable that over the next twenty years it will become possible to produce vaccines through biotechnology for most infectious and parasitic causes of death.' Genetic engineering has already helped create vaccines against hepatitis B, and tests are being conducted for the first malaria vaccine synthetically created in a laboratory.

In 1980 the first biotechnology patent was awarded to Dr Ananda Chakrabarty, a researcher at General Electric, for a microbe genetically engineered to improve its capacity to break down crude oil. With the award the US Patent Office established a historic and controversial principle. Life can be patented. Plants altered genetically were extended protection beginning in 1985.

On 13 April 1988, the US Patent and Trademark Office issued to Harvard University Patent No. 4,736,866, the world's first patent for a higher form of life, a mouse created through genetic manipulation. Dr Philip Leder, a geneticist, and Dr Timothy A. Stewart, a senior scientist at Genentech, Inc, had succeeded in isolating a gene that causes cancer in humans and other mammals and had injected it into fertilized mouse eggs. This new mouse is now being supplied to laboratories around the country for experimentation.

A big problem for the US Patent Office is a horrendous back-log, because the government doesn't understand biotechnology. Going into the 1990s, the logjam stood at about 8000 biotech patent applications. Its 100 underexperienced biotech patent examiners are taking from two and a half to four years to process an application, by which time some of the small start-up applicants could be out of business. In mid-1989 the Patent Office launched a '13-point biotechnology catchup plan'. All fingers crossed.

BUSINESS AND BIOTECHNOLOGY

The development and commercialization of biotechnology have been compared with the unfolding history of the computer (a somewhat simplistic comparison since computers do not involve life).

'The parallels to the microprocessor industry are there,' says Lynn Klotz, formerly on the faculty of Biochemistry International, a Cambridge, Massachusetts, recombinant DNA firm.

'As a body, the biotechnology industry is not unlike where the computer industry was in 1975,' says sociologist Everett Rogers, a University of Southern California professor famous for his book *Diffusion of Innovation*. 'There's a lot of uncertainty, a lot of rapid innovation, and no single main consumer product.'

The *Economist* compares where we are now with genetic engineering with the auto industry in about 1900 and computers in about 1960, the 'stage where it was comfortable to suppose that such science-fiction notions would never really replace the horse and the assembly-line welder,' says the *Economist*, 'but changes were afoot that were soon to change our lives.'

From the commercial perspective it is possible to compare biotechnology with cars and computers. But the comparison risks trivializing the enormous life-or-death ethical consequences of biotechnology.

The sixteenth International Congress of Genetics held in Toronto in 1988 was the largest by far. More than 4000 scientists from eighty countries attended, twice the number of people and four times the number of countries represented three decades ago.

'Today genes can be identified, weighed, measured, counted, manipulated, replicated, and mutated in test tubes,' said Congress President Dr Robert Haynes of Toronto's York University upon opening the meeting, 'and shuttled from cell to cell, even across species barriers.'

Biotechnology Spending and Research

In the decade or so since scientists discovered how to inject foreign genes into bacteria, investors have poured more than $3 billion into biotechnology. More than 600 biotechnology companies have been founded, nearly all in the United States. Fewer than ten have gone bankrupt or disappeared because of takeovers or mergers, even though nearly every one has consistently lost money. Thanks to the apparently unquenchable faith of persistent investors, biotech companies survive.

Research costs are breathtaking. It takes around ten years and about $100 million to bring a new drug to market. And that may be cheap. California's Genentech, considered the most successful biotechnology company (though it did take a dip in 1988), spent nearly $400 million to bring just two products to market.

Investor hopes remain high because any biotechnology company that comes up with a blockbuster drug will make a fortune. In 1988 alpha interferon (used to treat leukemia); a human growth hormone; human insulin; and TPA (the anticlotting drug) each grossed $100 million or more in the United States alone. Sales may expand even more in other countries because different governments have different traditions of expanding health care by subsidizing it (sometimes making it virtually free to the customer as in Britain's National Health Service), different ageing patterns, different access to medicines.

Major companies in this business include several pharmaceutical and chemical multi-nationals, whose involvement was inevitable, since biotech products are mostly drugs and farm chemicals.

The research arms of Monsanto and Schering-Plough, a drug firm, are essentially biotech companies. Eastman Kodak will consolidate links with biotech companies and universities through its recent acquisition of Sterling Drug. Along with Union Carbide and Corning, Kodak helped establish a $7.5 million biotechnology institute at Cornell University. Two giant US drug firms, Eli Lilly and Bristol-Myers, have acquired biotechnology firms.

European chemical companies such as ICI, Sandoz, and Ciba-Geigy spend up to one-third of their research budgets on biotechnology.

Big pharmaceutical companies are strengthening their ties to promising biotech firms. In 1988, Pfizer, SmithKline Beckman, and Hoffmann-La Roche, anticipating blockbuster products, all made deals with small biotechnology companies, tacitly acknowledging that small entrepreneurial companies are ahead of the giants. For their part, many small companies are badly in need of capital and are looking for deals.

United States in the Lead

Some 403 US biotechnology companies and 77 other US corporations have 'significant investments' in biotechnology, according to a study released in 1988 by the Congressional Office of Technology. During 1987 the US private sector spent about $2 billion on biotechnology research and development, mostly for health care applications. Federal and private spending exceeded $4.5 billion. Biotech sales exceeded $1 billion for the first time.

These figures put the United States ahead of the rest of the world.

In Western Europe, by comparison, government spending on biotech research and development was only $800 million in 1987. But that was double the $400 million spent in 1986. The US government's investment rose by only 19 per cent.

The Japanese government spends an estimated $500 million a year on biotechnology research; private industry invests another $1 billion.

After stock prices plunged in October 1987, private investment in biotechnology dropped sharply. But local governments (in the US, state governments) and universities are increasingly interested in it.

'Investing in this technology is a natural for North Carolina,' said Lieutenant Governor Robert B. Jordan, who has been instrumental in developing the state's Biotechnology Centre. 'So much of our economy comes from the water and the soil. We also have a huge stake in medical research and in health care. All of these industries are going to be affected by developments in biotechnology.'

At universities across the world, as the *Economist* noted, 'Biotech is the first business with enough glamour to persuade eminent scientists that the entrepreneurial spirit and academic respectability are not mutually exclusive.'

Japan

In Japan the biotechnology players tend to be large, wealthy, and patient.

'Biotechnology is a magic word in Japan,' says Wataru Yamaya, managing director of Mitsubishi Chemical Industries, Ltd, which had a $233 million research and development budget in 1987; 40 per cent was devoted to biotechnology.

Japan has begun to go after the commanding US lead in biotechnology. Japan's government, universities, and big corporations are all joining the effort. Japan is thought to be ahead in research in biochips, the making of complex semi-conductors using biotechnology.

Japanese scientists are trying to automate the job of reading the human genetic blue-print. Since launching the project to do so in 1981, Japan's Science and Technology Agency has given 766 million yen ($5.8 million) to five companies—including Seiko, the watch manufacturer, and Fuji, the film company—to design machines that automatically decipher DNA. 'We want to use all the technologies available: computers, material science, electronics, robots, and biology,' explained Akiyoshi Wada, a professor of molecular biophysics at the University of Tokyo, who conceived the effort.

Japan wasn't the first to automate the process. The European Molecular Biology Laboratory in Heidelberg, West Germany, and California's Lawrence Livermore National Laboratory have pioneered methods of automating DNA sequencing. Several American companies, including the Du Pont Company and Applied Biosystems, Inc, have built DNA-sequencing machines.

Today's DNA-sequencing laboratories resemble the first auto

factories, where cars were built by hand, one by one. Most of the lab steps are tediously low tech, as scientists manually break DNA into sections, reproduce it into bacteria, separate it, purify it, separate it again, and make film images that can be analyzed visually.

Automation could help in several ways, says Wada of Tokyo University. 'It's just like with cars and semi-conductors. If you mass-produce, costs come down and quality control goes up.'

Nanotechnology

No one has pushed the direction of technology and science farther than K. Eric Drexler, whose life has been devoted to the concept of creating nanomachines.

A nanometre is one-billionth of a metre. The theory is that we will someday be able to build smaller and smaller machines of only several nanometres, which would be capable of building virtually anything, atom by atom.

Drexler, the author of *Engines of Creation: The Coming Era of Nanotechnology*, has been a visiting scholar at Stanford University. He says that with nanomachines we can fabricate steaks from hay just as cows do. A house could be built in a matter of days, atom by atom, in the same way an oak grows from an acorn. These futuristic machines would possess the ability to remake the whole physical universe.

The possibility was first suggested by the late Richard P. Feynman, one of the world's greatest theoretical physicists and Nobel Prizewinner, whose surprising best-seller *'Surely You're Joking, Mr Feynman!'* made him known to the general public. Certainly Eric Drexler is not joking about his nanomachines, and he is taken seriously by his scientific colleagues.

ETHICS

On 18 August 1987, the National Academy of Sciences, the United States' most prestigious organization of scientists and engineers, reported that genetic engineering poses no greater risk than selective breeding or other methods of altering organisms.

Genetic engineering techniques 'constitute a powerful and

safe new means for modification of organisms', the report said.

Are scientists so close to their work that they don't see the larger questions? Are some of the rest of us overly concerned as a result of our limited technical knowledge?

If scientists can genetically programme a mouse for cancer, could a scientist in the employ of an evil dictator programme humans for disease? Will parents abort children whose eyes turn out to be brown instead of blue?

Animal scientist Neal First of the University of Wisconsin says: 'I think the potential is very high in terms of tailor-making livestock to what the consumer market situation and the economic situation is at a particular time.' This confirms the worst fears of those who think the biotechs are manipulating genes for profit with little concern about ethics or ecology.

We are moving to 'the day when geneticists can custom-design chickens to resist disease, lay bigger eggs, or have other traits valued by producers', says Dr Lyman B. Crittenden at the US Department of Agriculture's East Lansing, Michigan, research station.

Suppose it hurts or injures the chicken to lay bigger eggs. What if milk production *is* up 30 per cent, but the cow's udder becomes so huge it can barely walk?

Dr Sheldon Krimsky of Tufts University says he knows of no religious or philosophical principle that forbids transplanting genes from one animal to another. But he sees potential problems of several kinds, economic, environmental, and humane.

Jeremy Rifkin says his biggest objections to genetic engineering are ethical. He believes the building blocks of life are too precious to be tampered with in laboratories. Rifkin sees his mission as protecting the planet from biotechnologists. In 1987, when the US Patent Office announced that genetically engineered animals could be patented, he said, 'With that one decision by a couple of guys in the patent office, the Government handed the entire animal kingdom over to the multi-nationals, the pharmaceutical and biotech companies.'

Sometimes he gets carried away. The *Economist* says Rifkin 'is as dangerous to biotechnology as he believes the industry could be to man'.

Hyperbole—on both sides—aside, Rifkin's point about the decision making's taking place almost by default is well taken.

Who is going to decide? Who is going to make the decisions about the manipulation of human genes?

Biotechnology brings us face-to-face with the most negative and terrifying stereotypes: Mary Shelley's Frankenstein, the Dr Strangelove of biology.

Does it not take incredible hubris to interfere with the life process?

Humanity has not evolved sufficiently to be beyond the abuse of power. Yet here is a technology where the potential for abuse is extraordinary. We all know there are enough (political and psychological) nuts around who would willingly misuse the power of biotechnology. Madmen and terrorists. How are we going to deal with these critical questions?

One possible solution is to reinvent the first phase of the age of biology to be more about *learning* how nature works than about how to manipulate it. There is a big difference between a Dr Watson who wants to spend the next decade of his life mapping the human genome so he can have a greater *understanding* of how life works and someone who wants that same knowledge so he can *manipulate* life.

As the *New York Times* put it, 'The science of genetics is fast becoming what geneticists always knew it was: the central and most provocative science of life.'

The Ethics Debate of the 1990s

The ethical considerations of biotechnology will be played out on a larger field. In the United States and other rich countries there is a new concern for ethics in general. Insider trading, bribery of foreign officials, and outright fraud, even in religion, have prompted a search for new moral standards.

Biomedical problems including organ transplants, and surrogacy have already prompted fierce ethical debates in the 1980s. These have laid the theoretical groundwork on which we will consider the far trickier ethics of biotechnology in the 1990s.

Philosophers and theologians, chronically underemployed for centuries, will be pursued by headhunters as though they were computer scientists.

Hospitals in New York employ philosophers to advise doctors on life-or-death decisions. The New Hampshire legislature, prison authorities in Connecticut, and even the US Congress have hired philosophers. Bolt Beranek and Newman, an artificial intelligence firm in Massachusetts, employs several philosophers. How many are employed in the United States' 403 biotech firms?

Philosophy and Values in the Schools

All countries will have to allow an increasing place for values and ethics in the school curriculum. Some 5000 US schools now teach the philosophy-for-children syllabus developed by Matthew Lipman with the Institute for the Advancement of Philosophy for Children. Chicago, Los Angeles, and St Louis, along with dozens of other school districts throughout the US, have created 'values training' or 'character instruction' courses as a part of the school curriculum. At Gahr High School in Cerritos, California, values have been integrated into course work for more than 15 years.

'It is impossible to teach knowledge without values,' says Nathan Quinones, retired New York City school chancellor.

During the 1970s, 322 courses in business ethics were started at American universities and colleges. The University of Chicago's Pritzker School of Medicine offers a fellowship in ethics.

'The resurgence is due to people realizing the world is not either religious or atheistic. There is some middle ground for values,' says Patrick McCarthy, president of the Thomas Jefferson Research Centre in Pasadena, California, which develops values training programmes. Initially, most of the ethical questions of biotechnology will fall on the shoulders of the leaders of biotech companies. They will have to employ some graduates of those value-training programmes.

Medical Ethics: Precursor of Biotechnology

In 1983 only 4 per cent of the America's large hospitals had 'ethics committees' to review treatment decisions, according to the President's Commission for the Study of Ethical Problems in Medicine. By 1987 more than 60 per cent of the American Hospital Association's members had ethics committees. These are not simply a precaution in America's expensive medical malpractice lawsuits, which will spread to Europe anyway.

245

Between living wills and foetal surgery—and with the age of biotechnology fast approaching—these committees are very busy.

In 1986 the American Medical Association's (AMA) Council on Ethical and Judicial Conduct declared a doctor could ethically discontinue 'all means of life-supporting medical treatment', including food and fluids, in a terminally ill or irreversible comatose patient. But the AMA itself says a doctor 'should not intentionally cause death'.

For most physicians, that is a very thin line.

Thirty-nine American states and the District of Columbia allow living wills—instructions, written before people become ill—which say that doctors should remove life-support machines in the event of a terminal or debilitating illness. A 1987 Harvard Community Health Plan survey found that 84 per cent of Americans favoured following a patient's living will.

Should a patient be kept alive so his or her organs can be used to help others?

'The kernel of the ethical controversy is whether or not it is appropriate to modify the treatment of a patient for the sake of some other patient,' says Dr David Larson, director of Loma Linda University's Centre for Christian Bioethics.

When Brenda Winners found out that her unborn child had anencephaly—it lacked most of the brain's cerebral cortex—she could have decided to have an abortion or to have the child and let it die. Instead, she and her husband chose to have the baby, keep it alive, and let its organs be used as transplants.

'God brings these babies into the world and they should be able to do some good, even if they can't live,' said Brenda Winners.

Surrogate Parenthood

By the beginning of 1989 more than 1000 children had been born in the United States to surrogate mothers, women paid to be inseminated with a man's sperm—and then, according to contract, hand the baby over to the father and his wife.

Now, every state has at least one bill up for consideration to ban or regulate surrogacy. The New Jersey Supreme Court ruled, in 1988, after the Baby M case, that commercial surrogate motherhood contracts were illegal. Seven states have now banned surrogacy: Utah, Louisiana, Kentucky, Indiana,

Nebraska, Florida, and Michigan. In Europe there is a strong political movement to ban surrogacy, labelling it a commercial import from America.

'The problem is how to enjoy the benefits of the technology —especially for infertile couples—while minimizing the risk of abuse,' New Jersey Chief Justice Robert N. Wilentz wrote.

The ethical problems of surrogacy, biotechnology, and other biomedical issues will only increase as we approach the millennium. We must try to anticipate the future of biotechnology to prepare us for the spiritual dilemmas we will face.

These ethical questions are related to our need to understand what it means to be human, especially as we reject the notion that science and technology have all the answers.

In the 1990s we will witness a decade of debate about what scientists are doing. Some will call it a showdown with science.

It will be like the furore that followed the publication of Charles Darwin's *The Origin of Species* 130 years ago. Darwin was talking about 'natural selection'. The subject here is unnatural selection.

The age of information will also be the age of biology.

9

Religious Revival of the Third Millennium

At the dawn of the third millennium there are unmistakable signs of a worldwide multidenominational religious revival.

American baby boomers who rejected organized religion in the 1970s are returning to church with their children in tow; but they are not coming to the mainline churches. They are setting a fundamentalist or mystical trend that intellectuals in other rich countries are preferring not to notice:

- With 15 million members, the fundamentalist Southern Baptists are now the largest Protestant denomination in the US. Smaller and more fundamentalist denominations have been growing even faster. Many of these congregations are being taught to prepare for a literal Second Coming of Christ at the millenniun.
- About one-fifth, or 10 million, of America's 53.5 million Catholics now call themselves Charismatics, emphasizing a personal relationship with Jesus Christ. The worldwide Charismatic movement has tripled in the past decade, to nearly 300 million.
- Mormons celebrated the 'best year' in their 158-year history in 1987, when they gained a record 247,000 new adherents. This raised Mormons (a devout group of Christians, who believe a man should have several wives), to 6.2 million worldwide of which one-third are outside the United States.
- Between 5 per cent and 10 per cent of Americans are now associated with the New Age movement . It has ties to

Eastern yoga, meditation—and sometimes to a belief in reincarnation and to talking through mediums to people who have been dead for thousands of years. The New Age movement is spreading fast in the cities of Europe.

- Youth for Christ operates teenage centres throughout Europe. It drew young people from thirty-seven countries to a 1988 conference, and attracted 12,000 to a rally in Africa's Burkina Faso (formerly Upper Volta).
- Across the world reconstructivist Jews, who edited the supernatural out of prayer books forty years ago, are restoring references to miracles, mythology, and the Messiah.
- Shinto neighbourhood festivals have been revived in Japan, along with life-cycle rituals and returning to the local pagoda.
- A Shinto priest known as 'the miracle man of Japan' has won 5 million followers in Japan, the United States, and Brazil, where 80 per cent of converts are non-Japanese.
- There are 3 million followers of Islam in the US, half of them Black Muslims. That means there are now more American Moslems than Episcopalians.
- As well as being a powerful political force in Iran and Afghanistan and throughout the Arab world, fundamentalist Islam is undergoing a revival among the Westernized middle class of countries like Turkey and Egypt.
- Chinese and Soviet young people are fascinated by religions and enjoy attending church, to the dismay of some of their communist-trained parents, but to the delight of their grandparents. Despite more than seventy years of discouragement, about 30 million Soviet citizens seem to be Christian believers. They included once former general secretary of the Communist party (Malenkov) at the time of his death.
- Churches which have been a political force against the Left (such as the Catholic Church in Poland, the fundamentalist churches in the US) seem to have gained members. Churches which have been a political force against 'hard-heartedness' on the Right seem to have lost members (such as the Church of England whose bishops spoke out against Thatcherism in 1979–87, while popular

opinion was swinging towards it). But the main movement of congregations has been into churches that strike spiritual chords rather than twang political ones.
- Theologian Harvey Cox, who has taught as many as 1000 students in his course 'Jesus and the Moral Life' (one of the biggest classes at Harvard University), describes a revival in Islam, Shinto, Buddhism, and Judaism. This trend, he says, was 'unforeseen by forecasters twenty-five years ago, who predicted that religion would wither away because of modernity'.

TOWARD THE MILLENNIUM

Religious belief is intensifying worldwide under some gravitational pull from the year 2000, the millennium. Described first in the Old Testament Book of Daniel and then in the New Testament Book of Revelation 20: 1–7, the millennium is the 1000-year period, when Christ and his saints will reign supreme on earth in peace and joy. It marks the beginning of a golden age in human history. But it can come only after Christ's Second Coming and apocalyptic victory over his final enemy, the Antichrist.

One thousand years ago, in the 990s before the last millennium, the Christians of Europe's Dark Ages believed the end of the world was at hand. In ancient times the early Christians believed the millennium would rescue them from Roman persecution. During the Middle Ages bands of peasants led by Charismatic preachers expected the millennium at any moment, argues Norman Cohn, author of *The Pursuit of the Millennium*. The fourteenth-century English peasant revolt and the German peasant revolts of the fifteenth and sixteenth centuries were fuelled by millennial expectations.

As we approach the year 2000, it is happening again.

When people believe 'the time is at hand', they typically cluster into small groups around colourful, eccentric leaders. Because they feel they are living in a time of enormous change, millions of Americans and Europeans are being attracted to the unorthodox ends of the religious spectrum: from New Age channellers to 'speaking in tongues' charismatics, to scandal-prone and hell-fire-promising American TV preachers.

The last time the United States experienced such an unorthodox religious period was during the nineteenth century, when the country's economy changed from agriculture to industry. That century witnessed the creation of several major made-in-America religions—Mormon, Adventist, Jehovah's Witness and Christian Scientist, along with the rise of the Transcendentalists and the popularity of spiritualism.

When people are buffeted by change, the need for spiritual belief intensifies. Most seek reassurance in one of two ways: either through inner-directed, 'trust the feeling inside' movements or through outer-directed, 'this is the way it is' authoritarian religions. Both are now flourishing. There is a yearning that escape out of history into the peace and plenty of the millennium might be the best prospect for a better life.

The symbolism of the millennium is not confined to the Judeo-Christian religions. Anthropologists, historians, and theologians have discovered parallel concepts in Islam, where millennial hopes fuelled a string of nineteenth-century movements, including revolt in Sudan in 1881; in Buddhism, where the third Buddha is to appear at the height of catastrophes 1000 years after the nirvana of the second Buddha; in the Persian religion Zoroasterism, as well as in Third World cultures of Brazil and Africa.

The Religion of Science

Scientists once thought that the search to find 'truth' would bring a megatrend to worship of science instead of religion. This culminated in the secular 'God is dead' philosophy articulated by radical theologian Thomas J J Altizer in the 1960s and 1970s. Today, with the millennium in sight, the powerful countertrend of the religious revival is repudiating blind faith in science and technology.

Science and technology do not tell us what life means. We learn that through literature, the arts, and spirituality.

'As reason and science and the idea of progress prospered, it was said, the old gods would go, leaving in their trail free and happy people,' explains the University of Chicago theologian Martin Marty. Now, he believes, the limits of science have been recognized. 'Thus, technological medicine is welcomed for what it can do but is not worshipped because such medicine cannot do everything.'

Instead, we are rediscovering the emotional side of ourselves. Both channelling and speaking in tongues assert the validity of the irrational. Americans responded astonishingly to Bill Moyer's *Power of Myth* television series, in which Joseph Campbell re-introduced Public TV audiences to the spiritual symbolism of mythology, catapulting a book based on the series and another two Campbell book (previously known only to the cognoscenti) on to the best-seller list.

With the rejection of science as religion has come the rise of the feminine in the most patriarchal of institutions, churches. Today eighty-four denominations ordain women, and there are 21,000 female ministers in US churches. Although 1989 saw the ordination of the first female Episcopal bishop, many Christian feminists, including both Catholic nuns and Protestant women theologians, say they seek not to ascend through the male-dominated power structure.

Instead, they want to expose the very depth of sexism in traditional religion by challenging all language, symbols, rituals, and texts that dismiss or minimize the power of the feminine. Why, they ask, speak of God the Father without acknowledging the Godhead as Mother, too?

DECLINES IN MAINLINE RELIGION

Mainline churches fare well in stable eras but decline in times of great change.

Mainline religion is uncomfortable with a literal definition of millennarianism; Catholicism brands it a heresy. In the 1960s the mainstream's previously healthy growth rates in North America began to decline precipitously.

The figures below compare membership in 1965 with the latest numbers cited in the *Yearbook of American and Canadian Churches 1988*:

- The United Methodist Church dropped from a high of 11 million members in 1965 to 9.2 million.

- The Presbyterian Church, USA, has lost nearly 1 million members. Membership now stands at 3 million.
- The Disciples of Christ have lost almost 1 million, with a membership of 1.1 million.
- Episcopal Church membership declined from 3.4 million to 2.5 million.
- The three largest Lutheran denominations lost more than half a million members.

There were 53.5 million Catholics in the United States, according to the 1988 *Official Catholic Directory*, 1.1 per cent more than in 1987. There were no gains among priests and nuns, however; the census of 53,500 priests reflects a loss of more than 6000 since 1968.

The number of Catholic nuns in the US declined from 176,000 in 1968 to 107,000 in 1988. In 1987 alone 5577 nuns left religious life.

A 1988 study by the National Council of Churches of Christ in New York City counted 143 million church members, 59 per cent of the US population. The 1988 *Yearbook of American and Canadian Churches* counts 220 denominations. For two years in a row, the yearbook reported, church membership has remained flat.

'Those of us known as "mainline" denominations are now called "old line", and we are in trouble,' says United Methodist Bishop Richard Wilke of Little Rock, Arkansas. 'Now the numbers aren't increasing any more than the population is,' says Constant H. Jacquet, Jr, editor of the *Yearbook of American and Canadian Churches 1988*.

Indeed. Christian and Jewish congregations gained 4.1 per cent in the 1970s, while America's population grew 10.9 per cent.

Overall membership would have declined a lot more without huge increases among fundamentalists and evangelicals.

Southerners are the most faithful churchgoers in the US: 43 per cent attend services weekly. Midwesterners, with 42 per cent, run a close second. In the East 39 per cent attend weekly, and in California and the irreverent West only 35 per cent. In non-Catholic countries of Europe, attendances are much lower.

Spirituality, yes. Organized Religion, no

A 1987 Gallup poll found 94 per cent of Americans believe in God. 'India, Poland, and the USA have the most religious people,' says William D'Antonio, of the American Sociological Association.

Other American commentators deny this. They say that the right description of their fellow citizens is not religious but 'spiritual'.

Nearly 70 per cent of America's baby boomers believe in God or 'a positive, active spiritual force'. Half have become more spiritual in the past five years, according to the Centre for the Vietnam Generation. Three-quarters of Americans feel spiritually fulfilled, and 61 per cent say religion is 'very important in their lives', according to a 1987 *USA Today* poll. People said they turn to religion for peace and well-being.

But there is evidence that they are not finding it at church. A 1988 Gallup poll showed that 59 per cent complain their churches or synagogues are too concerned with 'organizational as opposed to theological or spiritual issues'. College-educated people are particularly critical of their churches' lack of spiritual nurturing. In Britain the main complaint of dwindling congregations is that the churches have become too political: rendering speeches against Caesar, rather than tending to feelings about God.

While mainline religion declines, the Gallup poll in America confirms that faith and belief grow. Overall, 84 per cent of Americans said they believed in the divinity of Christ, an increase from 78 per cent in 1978. In 1988, 44 per cent of Americans said they didn't go to church or synagogue—up from 41 per cent in 1978. Among these 'unchurched', as Gallup calls them, 30 per cent said religion was very important to their lives and 77 per cent occasionally prayed.

'The unchurched today are, by many measures, more religious than they were a decade ago,' concludes Gallup, who conducted the study for Congress 88, a conference including thirty-five denominations held in Chicago in August 1988. Alarmed by losses from the centre, mainline religion is organizing conferences and commissioning studies like this to focus attention on a return to religion's evangelical roots.

In periods of massive social change, the depth of religious experience exceeds organized religion's capacity to invoke it.

FROM MAINLINE TO THE FRINGES

In North America an array of new religions outside the Judeo-Christian framework is taking root.

While the centre—mainline Catholic, Protestant, and Jewish groups—has shrunk, hundreds of smaller, more decentralized 'made-in-America' churches, both fundamentalist and alternative, have flourished.

Typically scores of new religious bodies—from denominations to cults—are created each year. But recently their numbers multiplied into the hundreds and then doubled. When *The Encyclopedia of American Religions*' Second Edition Supplement was published in 1987, 206 new groups were listed. Greatest gains were outside the mainstream: 28 new Eastern religious groups, 19 Pentecostals, 11 Adventists, 11 Mormons, and 11 'Spiritual, Psychic or New Age' groups. Yet Dr J. Gordon Melton, editor of *The Encyclopedia of American Religions*, estimates that between 1987 and 1989 alone 400 new groups were formed.

Four per cent of the US population is Moslem, Buddhist, or Hindu. Though many adherents are immigrants, there is no doubt that these groups are gaining US-born converts as well:

- There are 4 million followers of Islam in the United States, about one-quarter Black Muslims. But the faithful are not all in big cities. The Moslem community in Colorado numbers more than 6000 and may be as high as 10,000, says the *Rocky Mountain News*. There are mosques in Denver, Boulder, Fort Collins-Greeley, and Pueblo.
- There are at least 600,000 US Buddhists from the two main Japanese sects; thousands more from Southeast Asia. But the total number of Buddhists in North America is between three and five million according to the American Buddhist Congress in Los Angeles.
- Buddhist chaplains are recognized in the US armed forces.

- In the United States there are more than 40 Hindu temples and more than 500 Hindu religious organizations. It is difficult to estimate their number because many American Hindus worship in their homes, says Diane Eck, a professor of comparative religion at Harvard University.
- In 1965 there were only 30 Korean churches in the United States, says Il Sik Sam Choe, of the Korean World Mission Council. Now there are 2000.

In turbulent times, in times of great change, people head for the two extremes: fundamentalism and personal, spiritual experience.

Millions of Americans have studied yoga, meditation, or other disciplines adopted from the Eastern religions.

Both those who meditate and those whose Christianity has turned more fundamentalist seek the same thing: a link between their everyday lives and the transcendent. This vital connection has not been found either in the traditional churches or in the secular worship of science and technology.

Fundamentalism offers a return to simpler times, when values were more clear-cut. New Age adherents take a different tack, rejecting outside authority, turning inward to seek guidance, perhaps through Eastern religion, meditation, or the human potential movement.

As one New Ager put it, 'The way religion is presented traditionally has spoken to our inner selves less and less. People want a living, feeling experience of spirituality. They learn to get in touch with the soul.'

Word for word, that very quote could just as easily have come from a fundamentalist Christian.

WHERE THE GROWTH IS

Though most of the growth is among fundamentalist and alternative religions, a certain percentage of America's baby boom generation is giving the churches a second try.

The Centre for Social and Religious Research in Hartford, Connecticut, found that 43 per cent of those baby boomers born between 1945 and 1954 attend church or synagogue three or more times a month, up from 34 per cent in the 1970s.

There is a Jewish renaissance in the San Francisco area, home of 223,000 Jews, America's eighth-largest community—many of them baby boomers. The religious revival there has a distinctly California flavour. There are a Jewish film festival, two Jewish theatre groups, five community centres, New Age-style Friday night Sabbath services at one temple, and a synagogue 'without walls' which holds outdoor services.

Sunday school attendance is on the increase. Some 69 per cent of parents are seeing to it that their children get religious educations, according to a 1988 Gallup poll.

By far the fastest-growing American churches, however, are those which are authoritarian and conservative.

Evangelical churches have gained 10 million Americans in the past ten years. Every five years since 1965 the evangelicals have grown 8 per cent, while mainline Protestants have lost 5 per cent. There are nearly 40 million evangelicals in the US, according to the National Association of Evangelicals in Washington, DC. Nearly 60 million Americans from all denominations call themselves born-again Christians.

Many conservative denominations have doubled since 1965. Jehovah's Witnesses rose from 330,000 to 752,000, and Seventh-Day Adventists from 365,000 to 666,000. But Assemblies of God have quadrupled from 572,000 to 2.1 million people, and there is now a 16-million-strong congregation for the Assemblies of God worldwide. These are one group among the 100 million people across the world who call themselves Pentecostals. Even more dramatically, in just ten years the charismatic movement has tripled to 277 million. The expressive, emotional Pentecostals and Charismatics profess some fundamentalist beliefs. They are known for openness to the Holy Spirit, faith healing, and speaking in tongues.

More evangelical than the evangelicals, and more authoritarian, the Mormons have grown from about three quarters of a million in 1940 to 6.2 million today—4 million in the United States, the rest abroad. By the year 2000 membership abroad will exceed that in the United States. There are 30,000 college-age missionaries—more than any other US denomination—in ninety-five countries and twenty territories. In 1987 they gained more adherents than any other year in their history.

In this decade before the millennium, energetic proselytizing clearly reaps its own rewards.

Mississippi's nearly 2000 Baptist churches, which already claim more than 650,000 members, have joined together in Bold New Growth Mississippi, which will reach out to inactive members, singles, the elderly, ethnic groups, and the handicapped.

Fundamentalism and the High-Tech Church

A recent article in *America*, an unofficial Jesuit publication, offered this description of fundamentalism: 'a reactionary emotional movement that develops within cultures experiencing social crisis'.

Humanist magazine was even harsher: 'authoritarian, intolerant, and compulsive about imposing itself upon the rest of society. It is a mindset which sees everything in black and white and for which compromise is alien'.

If these characterizations are accurate, why is fundamentalism so popular?

In times of great social change, the same times when millennial movements spring up, fundamentalist religion spells out the answers for people—so they need not make decisions alone.

Fundamentalism's most visible strength has been its effective use of television—an outlandish, incongruous, perfect balance. The hard edge of technology in service to the high touch of religion.

These Charismatic American television preachers attracted extraordinary publicity across the world, which was all the more unfortunate for some of them when scandal struck:

- Before falling from grace, Jimmy Swaggart had broadcast in 140 countries weekly and in fifteen different languages. He claimed to reach one-third of the planet. Jim and Tammy Baker's PTL's cable TV network reached 12 million households.
- Jerry Falwell's TV shows reached 610,000 households in 169 markets across the US; his 1987 TV income: $91 million.
- Robert Schuller has remained untarnished and upbeat.

But the hard times that have hit his competitors have reduced his own audiences from 2 million to 1.2 million.

A 1987 Gallup poll showed 63 per cent of Americans called TV evangelists 'untrustworthy', while 23 per cent voted them 'trustworthy'. Since the PTL, Swaggart, and Oral Roberts scandals, TV evangelists have lost a staggering amount of support. From February 1986 to July 1988 Jimmy Swaggart's viewers in the United States went from 2.3 million to 836,000, according to the Arbitron Ratings Company, while Jerry Falwell's dropped from 700,000 to 284,000.

You may dislike their morals and methods, but evangelical preachers have recognized the opportunities of the high-tech information age and applied them to their field—whether making money or saving souls.

Considering television's potential service to education, the preachers are way ahead of the teachers.

NEW AGE MOVEMENT

With no membership lists or even a coherent philosophy or dogma, it is more difficult to define or measure the unorganized New Age movement. But in every major US and European city thousands who seek insight and personal growth cluster around a metaphysical bookstore, a spiritual teacher, or an educational centre.

Though hard to pin down, researchers estimate New Agers represent 5 to 10 per cent of the population. According to Maryland Poll, a semi-annual study conducted by the University of Maryland, 6 per cent of Marylanders identify with the movement. Those numbers compete with any Protestant denomination. Though rare in the Bible Belt, concentrations of New Agers in East or West Coast cities or in the affluent Southwest could easily total 12 to 15 per cent.

Most agree that the New Age has its roots in the human potential movement and that it has to do with a complex awareness—of the oneness of creation, the limitless potential of humanity, and the possibility of transforming the self and today's world into a better one. Some would differ from that last point.

The true goal, says Ken Eyer, head of the Northwest Foundation, which conducts 'A Course in Miracles', 'is not to change the world, but to change yourself'.

New Age groups share no orthodox theology, but many adopt the East's belief in reincarnation. Unlike the Judeo-Christian God pictured far above humankind, there is a strong sense that humanity partakes of the divine.

This drives fundamentalists mad. 'This notion that man is somehow God is just blasphemous,' most would say. Yet even the most orthodox catechism states that man is made in the image and likeness of God.

Is there room for any theological common ground?

Channels

Fundamentalists may dominate the cable channels, but New Agers have sewn up the market in channel mediums—individuals who say they permit their bodies and voices to be used as vehicles for teachers and messages from the great beyond—and sometimes grab a lot of the headlines.

Charlene Pittman, in Tampa, channels for a spirit named Boyaed, a teacher born in India AD 324.

Jack Pursel of San Francisco grosses more than $1 million a year on seminars, counselling, and videocassettes as the channel for 'Lazaris, the consummate friend'.

J. Z. Knight, a woman, channels Ramtha, a 35,000-year-old man. Some reportedly pay $1500 to attend her seminars.

To your average fundamentalist, this is the devil in action. Some New Agers criticize channelling, too. Even believers frown on people growing so dependent on their favourite medium that they miss the whole point of spiritual development: cultivating one's own inner guidance. A responsible channel might encourage you to seek guidance but would also urge you to measure it against your own inner voice.

Dr J. Gordon Melton, editor of *The Encyclopedia of American Religions*, estimates that nationwide there are perhaps 400 to 500 channels. 'Centred in New York, Los Angeles, and San Francisco, there aren't many in between,' he says.

Dr Melton's research has apparently not led him to Colorado, New Mexico, Arizona, Florida, or Virginia—all hotbeds of New Age activity, each claiming numerous channels or other psychics. As early as 1987 the number of channels in the Los Angeles area alone was estimated at more than 1000.

New Age: a Whole System

Religion is only one aspect of a holistic belief system for the New Age. Holism means 'the tendency in nature to produce wholes from the ordered grouping of units'.

'We see this movement as a different perspective on life, a holistic view of life,' says Ralph White, who teaches philosophy at one of the most successful New Age organizations, New York's Open Centre.

The movement, he says, encompasses 'an enormous spectrum involving the body, mind and spirit, including an increased awareness of nutrition, the rise in ecological thinking, a change in business perspectives . . . greater emphasis on the individual's intuition.'

New Age classes are taught on a wide variety of subjects:

- New Age Ministries in Clearwater, Florida, offers a course called 'Metaphysical and Spiritual Approach to Business Success'.
- Rainbow Reflection Light Centre in Chicago teaches channelling classes at $35. For $75, you can take a five-session class in how to become a healer.
- A recent issue of *Yoga Journal* listed eighty-six New Age seminars in its vacation/retreat guide.

New York's Open Centre offers 2500 people a month courses in holistic health, body work, spiritual inquiry, psychological insights, and inner creativity. Walter Beebe, a partner in a Wall Street law firm, founded the centre in 1984 and describes the students as 'primarily well-educated people like me who found their life in the midst of Western culture less than fully satisfying.

'They are seeking a deeper spiritual involvement in the world without getting hooked by a guru, channeller, or other substitute for their own individual creativity,' he says.

The original American centre concerned with personal and social transformation is Esalen Institute, in Big Sur, California. For more than twenty-five years, it has served as a facility for ethical and spiritual growth, awareness training and disciplines, creativity, peak performance, massage, and social action groups. After a stay in India, Michael Murphy created Esalen as a centre for initiating the philosophical and religious dialogue between East and West, and later it became involved in US-Soviet relations.

The Findhorn community in Scotland, founded in 1962, initially gained renown for its success in growing spectacular produce in barren soil. Today it hosts international conferences on subjects including business and entrepreneurship and is internationally famous as a New Age centre.

Seattle is another hive of New-Age activity, and staged a debate with fundamentalists. 'New Agers are tired of the tyranny of fundamental religion trying to take away the right of freedom of religion and the press,' stated Elizabeth Burrows, who calls herself a Christian mystic. Burrows debated with Constance Cumbey, an orthodox Christian, before 700 people. Outside the centre, 200 more lined up who could not fit in the building.

Seattle's Unity Church, which emphasizes inner spiritual peace and flexible theology, has doubled membership in four years. 'The church is not really a New Age church,' says Unity spokesperson Edward Eiffler, 'but a very liberal church that allows its members to investigate other religions.' The Puget Sound chapters have nearly 25,000 families on their mailing list.

New Age Church?

The national Unity Church is about the closest thing to organized religion in which the eclectic modern New Ager could feel comfortable. It is probably the largest nondenominational church outside mainstream religion. The church, which celebrated its centennial anniversary in 1989, has 500 ministries. Its inspiring pamphlet *Daily Word* and *Unity* magazine have a combined circulation of 3 million.

The Unity Church avoids the New Age label, while embracing both Jesus as the Christ and reincarnation. Its basic textbook is the Bible.

The Unity Church is as close to common ground as New Ages and fundamentalists could reach. Nothing in its publications could possibly offend even Jerry Falwell.

The Avery Fisher Hall in New York's Lincoln Centre has been the sanctuary for a Unity Church service for more than ten years. Almost all of the nearly 3000 seats are full each service.

CONCURRENCE OF NEW AGE, FUNDAMENTALIST, AND ANCIENT PROPHECIES

Today amid lasers and robot technology, videotaped channelling sessions, and fundamentalist preachers on satellite television, the ancient symbol of the millennium is stirring our religious imaginations again. Popular prophecies from both ends of the spectrum are filled with similar millennial images and are read by millions.

Though New Agers and fundamentalists commonly dislike each other, they share more than either cares to acknowledge.

Today's fundamentalists expect a literal millennium—hellfire, brimstone, and all—right out of the Bible. The New Age millennium is more high tech; some groups predict spaceships will rescue the chosen few before the final cataclysm.

Author Ruth Montgomery, the former White House journalist who is now a writer of spiritual and occult books, is said to 'channel' a group of spirit guides who have advance knowledge of the future. They predict the earth will 'shift on its axis' around the year 2000. Then a period of peace will last 1000 years. An Antichrist who has already been born, they foresee, will be a powerful world leader.

The end of the world theme will re-emerge again and again as we approach the millennium.

Preacher Hal Lindsey's *The Late Great Planet Earth*, with 25 million copies in print worldwide, connects the fulfillment of biblical prophecies of the end of the world to present-day events.

World War III will begin, Lindsey predicts, when Russia and an alliance of Arab states invade Israel. 'As the battle of Armageddon reaches its awful climax,' he writes, 'and it appears that all life will be destroyed on earth—in this very moment Jesus Christ will return and save man from self-extinction.'

Hillel Schwartz, a Yale University PhD, and former teacher at the University of California at Berkeley, is a serious scholar and author of the definitive article on 'Millennarianism' in *The Encyclopedia of Religion*. He concludes, **'It seems to many that 2000 will be truly millennial.'**

From Rome to the Dark Ages: Millennium revisited

Millennarians like Mrs Montgomery and the Reverend Lindsey have their roots in religious history. From the early Christians to the millennial movements of the Middle Ages and Reformation, to the Jehovah's Witnesses of the 20th century, people have been trying to figure out when the millennium would arrive, how it could be predicted, how much time they had left, and what they should do to prepare.

Around AD 200 the learned Roman Hippolytus, an early convert to Christianity, tried to persuade his contemporaries that the end would come about the year 500. By then Rome had fallen to the barbarians and the Western Roman Empire had collapsed. To the few who read him, he must have seemed right on target.

Over the course of history, in addition to the years 500 and 1000, the millennium has been set at 1260, 1420, 1533 (the fifteenth centennial of Christ's death), 1843, 1844, 1845, 1847, 1851, and 1914.

But the power of the year 2000 is almost unique. The only other date like it was the year 1000.

The Last Millennium: The Year 1000

Just before the last millennium, in the 990s, most sources report a popular belief that the world would come to an end in the year 1000.

Recently, however, some historians have debated whether this fear was indeed widespread. Only a handful of records authored by monks remain from AD 1000.

Such a writer was the Abbot of Fleury, a monastic reformer, who lived from 945 until 1004. He writes, 'When I was a young man I heard a sermon about the end of the world preached before the people in the cathedral of Paris. According to this, as soon as the number of a thousand years was completed, the Antichrist would come and the Last Judgment would follow in a brief time.'

The learned abbot would have none of this, however, 'I opposed this sermon with what force I could from passages in the Gospels, Revelation and the Book of Daniel'.

Though some historians have invoked the abbot to discredit this end-of-the-world fear, the opposite conclusion should be drawn. Unlike the abbot, most folk were poor and illiterate. Christianity and pagan superstition reigned side by side. When the priests preached about the coming millennium, the people would probably have accepted it without question. According to the Christian calendar, the magical number of years since the coming of Christ—1000—was about to elapse.

Considering the beliefs of New Agers and New Right fundamentalists in today's era of modern technology, is there any doubt that our less sophisticated ancestors faced tremendous fear as the year 1000 approached?

The Vision of the Year 1000

At the same time the year 1000 was a historical milestone—the first time since ancient Rome that Europe had been united under a single banner, the cornerstone of modern Europe. The founder of this primitive European community was Otto I. Through marriage and military victory, he was crowned Holy Roman Emperor in 962 and considered 'the ruler of other kings'.

This new Holy Roman Empire saw itself as a more spiritually evolved Christian version of the Roman Empire at its height around the first century AD. Like Rome, this new empire was supposed to last forever.

Otto's grandson, Otto III, who was crowned in the year 1000, probably did not accept the popular superstition about the world's end. Nevertheless, he behaved like a monarch of great spiritual principle, living in an auspicious moment, who just might be meeting his Maker.

He was guided by the ideal of reforming the world in a genuine Christian spirit and sought to embrace the newly converted Slavic world through friendship with a Polish leader rather than through conquest. This hope, this vision for the year 1000, remained unrealized when Otto died in 1002 at only twenty-two.

In the face of a common superstition that the world was coming to an end, the greatest leader of the time was building the foundations for 1000 years of European dominance.

'. . . The problems which Otto III so passionately wanted to solve are the same ones which even in our own time exercise their impact upon the destinies of the countries and peoples of central Europe,' writes Oscar Halecki, author of *The Millennium of Europe*, who speaks of the 'vision of the year 1000' and believes that although it failed, it influenced future generations.

As the Soviet Union in 1987 celebrated the millennium of the introduction of Christianity into Russia, there were signs that in the *glasnost* era the official stand against religion was becoming increasingly liberalized. In 1988 the Soviet Union permitted the Russian Orthodox Church to print 100,000 Bibles in the USSR and also allowed the importation of more than 1 million Bibles, including 150,000 sets of a three-volume study Bible and 5000 copies each of a fifteen-volume Bible commentary. At least 30 per cent of the USSR's 280 million people are believers, estimates Sovietologist Paul Lucey. In 1989 Mikhail Gorbachev told a surprised world that he had been baptized, and many people began to speak of the reunification of Eastern and Western Europe.

THE MAINLINE: CATCHING ON AND REACHING OUT

The way that unorthodox churches are thriving in this millennial era has impressed some of America's mainline churches. Catholic, Protestant, and Jewish congregations are trying to put themselves back on the religious map. Their methods include: getting back to the basics of conversion, opening up to Charismatics, appearing on TV, creating prayer or Bible study groups and spiritual retreats, as well as experimenting with alternative services.

Every mainline Protestant religion has set up an office to study census-based demographic research, says *American Demographics* senior editor Brad Edmondson. Presbyterians have called for a return to their evangelical roots. The United Presbyterian General Assembly in Louisville, Kentucky has developed a five-year evangelical programme, 'Overture 95', to be launched in 1990. Twenty-two of the thirty-five Christian denominations that participated in Congress 88 funded the mid-1988 Gallup poll; all called their meeting an evangelical festival demonstrating the shifting focus back to conversions.

266

Charismatic Catholics; Spirit-filled Episcopalians

The Catholic Church is reflecting the evangelical influence by tolerating a full-fledged Charismatic movement that makes some Southern Baptists look tame.

Ten million US Catholics, about one-fifth, call themselves Charismatic or Pentecostal. Perhaps eager for more Catholics (even if they are a bit unorthodox), the church has embraced them—fainting and all. The Charismatics emphasize a personal relationship with Jesus Christ.

The Charismatic Prayer Groups in Philadelphia sponsor special conferences for Charismatic priests and parishioners. The June 1988 retreat brought in 130 priests, and the 1988 annual Charismatic Rally attracted 5000 people. In Philadelphia alone there are 166 Catholic Charismatic prayer groups.

Another centre of the charismatic movement is Darien, Connecticut, the site of St Paul's Church, which inspired the book *Miracle in Darien*, describing the Charismatic experiences there. About 1000 people attend the church's four services, and the congregation is considering expanding its facilities. There are forty Bible study groups.

The Charismatic movement satisfies the deep need for a more emotional religion.

Truro Episcopal Church in Fairfax, Virginia, is a 'spirit-filled' church with nearly 3000 members. It sponsors prayer, healing, and Bible study groups and believes in 'the gifts of the Spirit and their free expression'.

Faith Alive, in York, Pennsylvania, holds 100 'renewal weekends' yearly. Associated with the Episcopal Church, it is open to other denominations. At 'renewal weekends' people are expected to share what God has done in their lives.

The Mainline High-Tech Church

Mainline churches are joining the electronic fold.

The National Christian Network in Cocoa, Florida, is on the air twenty-four hours a day and reaches 2 million homes via satellite and 5 to 6 million on cable. It is open to Catholic, Protestant, and Jewish denominations. Programming is mostly commentary and Bible teaching; there is very little fundraising.

Fort Lauderdale, Florida, is the home of Vision Interfaith Satellite Network, a religious cable network whose format includes preaching, music, interfaith films, and programmes on social issues. Participants include: Seventh-Day Adventists, Episcopals, Greek Orthodox, Mennonites, Roman Catholics, Presbyterians (USA), as well as the Reformed Church and the Evangelical Lutheran Church in America.

'The Faith Channel' is a twenty-four-hour-a-day interfaith cable channel based in Louisville, Kentucky, offering a mainline alternative to typical religious television. It represents 75 per cent of the city's religious bodies, including Southern Baptists, Roman Catholics, and Jews.

The interfaith model could work in other cities, too, says the Reverend Ben Armstrong, executive director of National Religious Broadcasters, with 1300 member stations, though he concedes, 'Baptists and Catholics tend not to coexist—at least not on the same project.'

Mother Mary Angelica's the Eternal Word Television Network (EWTN) in Birmingham, Alabama, is the world's only Catholic satellite and cable network.

'Right in the middle of the Baptist Belt behind a Catholic cloister! Can you beat it? Does God have a sense of humour?' quips Mother Mary.

Started in 1981 with $200, EWTN programmes are now broadcast to forty-five states and seen in 12 million homes. Only twice a week, for about three minutes, does Mother Mary Angelica solicit contributions.

Mainline Marketing

Evangelical consultants are preaching the gospel of target marketing.

'Churches must adapt and have a marketing orientation if they are going to attract baby boomers,' says Jack Sims, a former pastor and religious consultant in Placentia, California. 'I think that if the churches adopt three simple changes, 5 to 10 million baby boomers would be back in the fold within one month.'

Sim's big three are: (1) advertise, so people know where the churches are; (2) emphasize product benefits, such as social club or nursery school; (3) be nice to new people—good customer relations.

'God may not be dead, but the mass market is,' exclaimed a recent article in *American Demographics*. 'American religious institutions are adjusting to a new marketplace, just like other service industries.'

That message is dogma at Willow Creek Community Church in Illinois, the second-largest Protestant church in the United States. Each week 12,000 attend services in the $15 million complex featuring Christian rock music and a multi-media show. Pastor Bill Hybels canvassed the neighbourhood in 1975 to see what people really wanted at church. Now they are getting it.

'We decided to defer to the customer except where it conflicted with Scripture,' he says.

The hottest new form of marketing is telemarketing—marketing through telephone for churches, that is. Incredible though it may seem, between 1986 and spring 1989, 2000 new churches in over ninety denominations have been 'assembled' through telemarketing, according to Norman Whan, a telemarketing specialist, founder of Church Growth Development International and creator of 'The Phone's for You', a guide to religious telemarketing. A Huntington Beach, California, church under Whan's guidance welcomed 502 people to its first service. A Dallas, Texas, church had 400.

His work basically follows the classic 1 per cent rule of direct mail marketing. It takes 20,000 phone calls, follow-up mailings, and calls to bring 200 people to the first service of a new church. An average of 125 shows up the next week.

But a congregation of 100 can support a small church and pastor. About half of US Protestant churches have 75 people or fewer in attendance, says the Dr C. Peter Wagner of Fuller Theological Seminary, which has introduced marketer Whan to fifty denominations.

Dr Wagner was only teaching the theory of church growth, 'until Norman Whan came over the horizon,' he says. 'This guy's a winner. We broke our precedent and now highly recommend this technique for planting churches.'

In his former job as director of church planning for Friends Church Southwest, an evangelical branch of Quakerism in

Whittier, California, Norman Whan and associates started six churches in Southern California and Arizona, including Desert View Friends Church in Hesperia, California.

Aboite United Methodist Church in Fort Wayne, Indiana was one of the first telemarketing successes outside the Quaker denomination. Its inaugural service on 6 December 1987 attracted 264 people. More than 200 now attend and there are two Sunday services.

Whan is making overtures to other mainline groups with some initial success. 'If only the mainline churches would just listen, we could help them,' he adds. 'We believe the way this is exploding that by the year 2000, we can achieve our goal of starting 100,000 churches,' says Whan.

One reason large mainline churches have lost so many since the mid-1960s is that small, independent churches can adapt their services to the needs of churchgoers, can remain closer to the 'consumer'.

'The real story of American religion today isn't about Baker or Swaggert or Roberts or Robertson,' says religious consultant Jack Sims. 'It's about ageing donors, declining revenues, declining market share and a changing market.'

THE MILLENNIAL CONSUMER: ECONOMIC IMPLICATIONS OF THE RELIGIOUS REVIVAL

Theology aside, fundamentalists and New Agers concur as consumers. Books, music, and videotapes are big sellers for both.

The 60 million adults who describe themselves as born-again Christians, constitute such a huge market that it is almost too large to target. But that doesn't seem to hurt books sales. In 1975 the Christian Booksellers Association had fewer than 2000 members. Today there are 3000, and the association estimates another 2000 religious bookstores are non-members. Business is booming; total 1987 sales were nearly $1.5 billion. Average store sales rose from $155,000 in 1980 to $257,000 in 1987. The total market for Christian 'products'—videos, music, gifts, along with books—is nearly $3 billion.

'Sacred Melody Centre' of Syracuse, New York, is hardly an average store. It is a 12,000-square-foot converted drugstore that new sells Christian products—books, Bibles, marriage manuals, sheet music, compact discs, coffee cups, videotapes, and dolls that quote the Word. Annual sales have reached $1.6 million.

It seems there is no end to this market. More than 1 million Hanna-Barbera home videos of a cartoon Bible series for children were sold the first year they were released, earning $20 million.

Bellwether Building Boom—Central Florida

In the bellwether state of Florida the religious revival is spurring an extraordinary church building boom. Central Florida's more than 450 churches are not enough. 'We're growing so rapidly that we're growing out of our churches,' says Edward Thomas, an Orlando architect, whose firm has designed more than 200 Florida churches.

'We had been forced to put people into separate rooms, where they had to watch our service on closed-circuit TV. This just wasn't what worship is all about,' says Pastor Bill Marr of First Baptist of Oviedo, which recently built a $1.8 million 800-seat sanctuary.

Today's mega-churches are nothing like the simple structures of the past.

First Baptist Church of Orlando's $14 million complex seats 6100. Carpenter's Home Church, formerly the Lakeland Assembly of God, recently opened a 10,000-seat sanctuary.

Calvary Assembly's $20 million complex in Orlando seats 5000 and comes complete with twenty-two nursery rooms, twenty-five classrooms, a television studio, choir and orchestra rehearsal rooms, a wedding chapel, a bookstore, a prayer room, and two escalators. In five years membership went from 2000 to 6000.

New Age Marketing

By head count, the New Agers are a good, substantial lot, maybe 10 or 12 million Americans. Say they are even 20 million. They are still completely outnumbered by the fundamentalists, at around 60 million. If you are out to sell your product, why even bother with the New Agers? To begin with they are rich.

271

Ninety-five per cent of the readers of *New Age Journal* are college-educated, with average household incomes of $47,500.

New Agers represent the most affluent, well-educated, successful segment of the baby boom.

Furthermore, the influence on the culture as a whole extends beyond their numbers. This group, says John Garrett of SRI International's Values and Lifestyle (VALS) Programme, tends 'to set the trends in America'.

What were once considered New Age ideas are increasingly mainstream. A full two-thirds of Americans say they have had an ESP experience and 42 per cent say they have had 'contact with the dead', according to the National Opinion Research Council of the University of Chicago. In 1973 those percentages were only 58 per cent and 27 per cent respectively.

The older half of the baby boom people around forty are what the VALS programme categorizes as 'inner-directeds'. 'They don't care for existing religions, so they've come out with a new kind of religion—a New Age one, a kind of attunement,' says SRI's Garrett.

New Age thinking has spawned a publishing phenomenon. Books and magazines exploring the themes of this non-religion have exploded. *New Realities*, *Yoga Journal*, *East West Journal*, and *New Age Journal* link readers nationwide.

New Age Journal describes itself as 'a magazine that brings readers the latest in leading-edge trends and ideas, including the best thinking of the East and the West . . . chronicles the way thousands are trying to create a more harmonious world by seeking spiritual fulfillment, by demanding the best of themselves and others, by using their talents to help others, by looking for new ways to improve and protect their health, and by developing more satisfying relationships at home and at work.'

Circulation was 50,000 in 1983. In 1989 it was 165,000.

The first *National New Age Yellow Pages* has more than 450 listings, ranging from 'A Course in Miracles' to 'Zen Studies'. Now in its second edition, it has expanded from 200 to 260 pages and is sold out.

Sophia Tarila's *New Age Marketing Opportunities* lists 456 New Age publications and a total of 7000 listings, including publishers, distributors, electronic media, and retailers.

Most metropolitan areas have a local New Age publication: *Pathways* (Washington, DC), *Free Spirit* (New York City), *L.A. Alive* (Los Angeles) and *New Texas* (Austin).

- Bodhi Tree in West Los Angeles stocks 30,000 New Age books.
- Bantam Books has increased its list of New Age books tenfold in the past ten years.
- The New Age Publishing and Retailing Alliance, officially created in June 1987 with just 30 members, now has grown to nearly 400.
- Between 1985 and 1989 the number of New Age bookstores doubled to 4000, according to the New Age Publishing and Retailing Alliance.
- The Ingram Book Company, a huge distributor, created a 'New Age' catalogue with 2000 titles in late 1987 and watched its sales increase 20 per cent six months later.

Total sales of New Age titles now exceed $100 million a year. New Age records sell $50 million a year. Audio and videotapes for mind expansion and the like are a $300 million-a-year business.

A New Age for Corporations?

Corporations spend an estimated $4 billion per year on New Age consultants. A *California Business* survey of 500 companies found that more than 50 per cent had used 'consciousness-raising' techniques. Procter & Gamble, TRW, Ford Motor Company, AT&T, IBM, and General Motors all have signed on New Age trainers.

Krone training, a New Age-type of training, was required for all Pacific Bell of California's 67,000 employees. It has led to an enormous controversy and a court case.

When programmes concerning the private sphere of religion and values are introduced into the more public sphere of the corporation, people are likely to experience an enormous intrusion. But if you doubt that New Age thinking has permeated the highest bastions of American's business institutions, consider this—the syllabus of Stanford University Graduate School of Business's 'Creativity in Business' course taught by Michael Ray lists meditation, chanting, and dream work. Yoga, Zen, and tarot cards are also part of the class.

MILLENNIUM AS METAPHOR FOR THE FUTURE

The religious revival is 'a global phenomenon that has to do with the unravelling of modernity,' says theologian Harvey Cox, who believes it also marks the end of 'a kind of faith that science would master all of our problems.

That faith was born of the Industrial Revolution, which introduced the power of technology. When used for benevolent purposes, science and technology endowed humanity with almost godlike powers. With Industrialization came the 'Ideal of Progress', the notion that scientific advances would always make life progressively better.

'From Voltaire to Marx every Enlightenment thinker thought that religion would disappear in the 20th century because religion was fetishism, animistic superstition,' says Harvard's Professor Emeritus Daniel Bell.

Instead, in this century we have watched the ideal of progress give way to the return of faith. The worship of science and the rational to a great extent has been thrown over for a religious revival that specifically values the emotional and the non-rational.

It did not happen, however, without our first hitting bottom spiritually. The underlying assumption of the ideal of progress was that humanity would use technological power to serve life, not destroy it. The 20th century watched that supposition crumble. The wholesale slaughter in the trenches of World War I brought people face-to-face with the human capacity for self-destruction. The ideal of progress was shattered as it became clear that technology could create hell as well as heaven.

The way things looked for much of the 20th century, hell had a far better chance of winning out. The years after World War I offered little to alleviate a growing sense of pessimism. Despotism and repression accompanied the rise of Nazism and the growth of communism. World War II and the creation of nuclear weapons confirmed the worst fears. The tools for self-destruction would be readily available. Given the track record, who could doubt humanity would use them?

A new literary genre, dystopia, the opposite of utopia, emerged to warn of the negative future if present trends continued. Examples included Aldous Huxley's *Brave New World* (1932) and George Orwell's *1984* (1949). The dystopic films

Metropolis (1926) and *Modern Times* (1936) portray humanity overcome by technology and political oppression.

Shattering of the myth of progress occasioned a major rewrite of history: Oswald Spengler's *The Decline of the West*, a two-volume, 1000-page gloomy analysis of history.

As we approach the millennium, visions of dystopia re-emerge.

For within the symbolism of the millennium *is* the apocalyptic battle between good and evil. Will we face the demise of civilization as we know it by nuclear accident or the greenhouse effect? Chemical warfare or the ultimate tear in the ozone layer? A hellfire-and-brimstone millennium or a spaceship rescue? Will the end come from a gene gone mad from the age of biotechnology?

The millennium is a two-sided metaphor of choice. On the one side, a man-made apocalypse represents the possibility that godlike technology in human hands could destroy the environment, create nuclear annihilation.

But what if, in the language of symbolism, the Antichrist has already appeared in the form of the 'God is dead' philosophy, in the worship of only science, culminating in the creation of weapons of mass destruction and untold other ways to destroy ourselves and the earth?

Then the turning away from the religion of technology and the re-emergence of spirituality as manifested in the religious revival are signs of great hope. Having vowed to make war and weapons of mass destruction obsolete, a renewed humanity begins the task of healing the environment.

The dawn of this new epoch in history, this return to faith is the sign that we are prepared to embrace both sides of human nature. If the zeal of both religious fundamentalism and the New Age movement is at times extreme, perhaps they can be interpreted as part of a larger overall process that is very positive—the refusal to define life only in terms of science and technology.

As the symbolic year 2000 approaches, humanity is not abandoning science. But, through this religious revival, we are re-affirming the spiritual in what is now a more balanced quest to improve our lives and those of our neighbours.

10

Triumph of the Individual

The great unifying theme at the conclusion of the 20th century is the triumph of the individual. Threatened by totalitarianism for much of this century, individuals are meeting the millennium more powerful than ever before.

It is an individual who creates a work of art, embraces a political philosophy, bets a life savings on a new business, inspires a colleague or family member to succeed, emigrates to a new country, has a transcendent spiritual experience. It is an individual who changes him or herself first before attempting to change society. Individuals today can lever change far more effectively than most institutions.

The 1990s are characterized by a new respect for the individual as the foundation of society and the basic unit of change. 'Mass' movements are a misnomer. The environmental movement, the women's movement, the anti-nuclear movement were built one consciousness at a time, by an individual persuaded of the possibility of a new reality.

INDIVIDUAL RESPONSIBILITY

The first principle of the New Age movement is the doctrine of individual responsibility. It is a Westernized version of the ancient Eastern dogma of karma—that every action generates consequences the actor will eventually face. As the Bible puts it, 'As you sow, so shall you reap'. Individual responsibility, however, stresses the present; each individual is responsible for everything he or she does.

This is not an 'every man for himself' type of individualism, gratifying one's desires for their own sake and to hell with everyone else. It is an ethical philosophy that elevates the individual to the global level; we all are responsible for preserving the environment, preventing nuclear warfare, eliminating poverty. Individualism, however, *does* recognize that individual energy matters. When people satisfy genuine achievement needs—in art, business, or science—society gains.

Globalization and Individualization

This new era of the individual is happening simultaneously with the new era of globalization. The 1990s will be largely devoted to the full realization of one, single global economy. As we globalize, individuals, paradoxically, become more important, more powerful. This change is reflected in the media. In this, the age of global television—2 to 3 billion people watched the Olympic Games in Seoul—individuals, through audio and video cassette technology, can customize their own entertainment and cultural nourishment. Both enhance the individual's power.

The Demise of the Collective

The triumph of the individual signals the demise of the collective. Even Communists are persuaded that only the individual creates wealth. President Gorbachev has said that what was required for the Soviet Union was a new 'individual-based socialism'. Unions concede that people must be rewarded for their individual efforts. It is the triumph of individual responsibility as against the anonymity of the collective. Within all collective structures—organized religion, unions, the Communist party, big business, political parties, cities, government —there is the possibility of hiding from one's individual responsibility. At the level of the individual that possibility does not exist. There is no place to hide.

From Individualism to Community

Yet it does not mean the individual is condemned to face the world alone. Stripped down to the individual, one can build community, the free association of individuals. In community there is no place to hide either. Everyone knows who is contributing, who is not.

Individuals seek community; avoiders of responsibility too often hide in the collective.

The old British trade union philosophy was to treat everyone the same: equal salaries for maths teachers in areas where they are desperately wanted as for English teachers in areas where they are in surplus, the rate for the job whether employment is coming up or down. This is completely out of sync with today's sentiment that individual differences, especially those reflecting contributions to enterprise, must be noted and rewarded.

ENTREPRENEURS IN A GLOBAL ECONOMY

Small-time entrepreneurs have seized multi-billion-dollar markets from well-heeled businesses. Individual entrepreneurs are playing larger roles in the world economy. For years more than 85 per cent of US exports used to come from 250 of the top American multi-national corporations, according to a study by BDO Seidman, an international accounting firm. Now more than 80,000 American companies export, including many very small businesses. In just one year—1988—total US exports increased more than 26 per cent.

Americans are surprised at such facts as that:

- Old Jefferson Tile, a Texas company with seven employees and about $500,000 in 1988 sales, now exports to Europe.
- Superior Technical Ceramics Corp. of St Albans, Vermont, had eighty-five employees and $5 million a year in 1988 sales. The company plans to increase exports to 20 per cent of sales.

Western Eye Press of Telluride, Colorado, has only two employees (who are also the owners), Lito Tejada-Flores and Linde Waidhofer. In their home-office this couple creates an electric range of books—from travel guidebooks to photographic art books—that compete successfully with those produced by the traditional New York-based publishing establishment. They edit and design their books on a Macintosh computer, create camera-ready art on their own laser printer, have the books printed in

Seoul, Korea, and in Hong Kong, and sell to the world. Often Linde and Lito create a book—from conception to finished product—in two months, a time-frame not remotely possible for big, conventional publishers (where the time from finished manuscript to final book averages about nine months). So here are two people competing globally from a remote mountain village where they have chosen to live for aesthetic reasons, not out of economic constraint or pressure.

New technologies have changed the importance of scale and location and extended the power of individuals.

Europeans are less surprised. Many very small British businesses in the information age (consultants etc.) expect to make far more money from foreign markets than the British one.

Entrepreneurship is playing a stronger role in the arts, where individuals of every stripe explore their visions for something better. Artists like Robert Rauschenberg and Christo create huge international projects that cost millions of dollars. These entrepreneurial artists not only create the works of art but raise all the necessary funds. Entrepreneurial musician Bob Geldof creates multi-million-dollar planetary events.

Entrepreneurial Politics

Citizen diplomacy has become an extraordinary arena where individuals can take personal responsibility for international relations—not only Jesse Jackson as a private citizen negotiating with a foreign power for the release of prisoners and Britain's Terry Waite acting as a gallant intermediary in Lebanon, but eleven-year-old Samantha Smith creating her own détente with the Soviet Union.

At the dawn of the new millennium individuals everywhere feel empowered, freer to determine their own political fate. The Soviet elections in early 1989 showed the public's outcry against the 'party' politics in place for seventy years. Voters went to great lengths to express themselves. In some districts, although only one name appeared on the ballot, so many crossed it out that the official lost power. Five top Communist leaders lost in Leningrad alone. Almost all of the Communist party candidates lost in the June 1989 election in Poland.

In the United States, hardly anyone runs as a Democrat or Republican anymore. Candidates run as individuals.

In the primaries in the presidential race in the United States, each candidate runs as an individual. At the summer conventions the party's imprimatur is bestowed on the entrepreneurial politician who has already won the race. In state and local elections—before the 1960s—people used to petition one of the political parties to be its candidate. Now individuals vie in primaries, and parties endorse the candidates who win.

Turned off by traditional big-party politics, fewer and fewer Americans are even voting for President. In 1988 only 57.4 per cent of those registered voted, down from 59.9 per cent in 1984 and 67.8 per cent in 1968. The percentage of the *eligible* who actually voted was much lower.

Look at 1984. Nationally two-thirds of the people elected to office were Democrats. But the same people who elected them voted 59 per cent to 41 per cent for Ronald Reagan. In 1988, the same thing. Two-thirds of those elected were Democrats, but George Bush beat Michael Dukakis 53 to 46 per cent in the presidential race.

The shift is from party politics to entrepreneurial politics.

'The new breed of politicians have shaped a Congress [into] an institution that encourages entrepreneurial activity and large personal enterprises,' writes University of Kansas Professor Burdett Loomis in *The New American Politician: Ambition, Entrepreneurship and the Changing Face of Political Life*.

On Capital Hill individualism is rampant. There are now 535 political parties in Congress, the same number as members.

TECHNOLOGY IS EMPOWERING THE INDIVIDUAL

When the great dystopian George Orwell wrote *1984*, Stalin was still alive and Hitler had recently died. No wonder Orwell believed the dictator of the future would use technological advances to hold people in subjugation. This was also the premise of Aldous Huxley's *Brave New World*. Dictators *do* need to control information to maintain control, since knowledge *is* power.

But it did not work out the way Orwell and Huxley feared. Global television and video cassettes have curbed the power of dictators.

There are fewer dictators on the planet today because they can no longer control information; look at all East Europe in 1989. In the age of global television it is pretty difficult for a government to hold 'free elections', then go back on its word, as an exiled Ferdinand Marcos learned. The old men in China did decide to shoot down the student demonstrators in the full glare of television, but ten years earlier the students would never have reached the square in the first place. With individuals' power extended by most modern technology, citizens can keep tab on governments a lot more efficiently than governments can keep tabs on people.

At a time of global broadcasting, we also have the phenomenon of audio and video cassettes, the ultimate in narrowcasting, where the individual is the broadcaster. In past revolutions or coups d'état, the first action of the new government was to seize the radio or television station. The overthrow of the Shah of Iran and the ultimate revolutionary success of Poland's Solidarity movement occurred after their proponents had circulated outlawed cassettes underground.

Global television and video cassettes are the ultimate in broadcasting and the ultimate in narrowcasting.

'Rather than pushing [sic] control to Big Brother at the top, as the pundits predicted, the technology by its very nature pulled power back down to the people,' writes George Gilder. 'All the world will benefit from the increasing impotence of imperialism, mercantilism, and statism.' Individuals today possess 'powers of creation and communication far beyond those of the kings of old,' he says.

Computers, cellular phones, and fax machines empower individuals, rather than oppress them, as previously feared.

Meanwhile, governments are scrambling to figure out how to get technology to work for them.

FROM THE INDIVIDUAL TO A GLOBAL NETWORK

Now we are beginning the process of linking PCs globally, creating powerful networks of individuals. Just as a truly global system of 1 billion *stationary* telephones—with direct dialling among them—is getting in place, we have begun a process of mobile cellular telephone technology that will link *individuals* directly—without going through national systems.

Within a few years people, no matter where they are, will be able to call anyone with a portable phone anywhere in the world—directly—and without knowing where they are (thankfully we shall also be able to shut these things off).

Fax Machines

Facsimile machines empower people everywhere to operate at the individual level. 'Why pay $14 and absolutely, positively wait until tomorrow when you can fax it in seconds?' asks Bill McCue of Public Fax Inc. The line that once formed at the copier is now forming in front of the fax machine.

This low-tech phenomenon is growing faster than any high-tech competitor. By 1990, 5 million fax machines will operate across the United States—in cars, restaurants, hotels, airport terminals, and private homes. There are public fax stations. The IRS will accept your income tax filing by fax.

There will be 9 million faxes by 1992, says CAP BIS International, a fax consultant.

Ever wonder why fax machines have become so popular while high-tech electronic mail is such a slow poke?

It is the principle of high-tech/high-touch described in *Megatrends*.

Through the technology of the telephone you receive a fax, which you then rip off the machine and proceed to cut up, photocopy, mark up, and otherwise be physically engaged with—high touch. Also, you can write (or draw) something long-hand and send it over the wires. With electronic mail there is no high-touch, just high-tech.

NEW ELECTRONIC HEARTLAND

Linked by telephones, fax machines, Federal Express, and computers, a new breed of information worker is re-organizing the landshape of America today, and Europe tomorrow. Free to live almost anywhere, more and more individuals are deciding to live in small cities and towns and rural areas. A new electronic heartland is spreading throughout developed countries around the globe, especially in the United States. Quality-of-life rural areas are as technologically linked to urban centres as are other cities. This megatrend of the *next* millennium is laying the groundwork for the decline of cities.

The Industrial Revolution created the great cities of Europe, America, and Japan. The physical infrastructure of the world's cities, John P. Eberhard, Professor and head of the Department of Architecture at Carnegie Mellon University, points out, are based on inventions made 100 years ago: indoor plumbing; the light bulb; the electric trolley; steel frame buildings and elevators; the automobile; the subway; the telephone. Extraordinarily, all of these basic elements were invented in the seventeen years between 1876 and 1893.

With 19th-century technology you could move goods cheaply by railway and canal over long distances, but it was very expensive to move people even short distances. Workers lived next to their work, aggregating into places that became larger and larger cities.

Automobiles changed that somewhat, suburbanizing much of America and Europe. Now individual-empowering electronics will change it even more, dispersing us away from cities toward rural areas. For the first time in history, the link between a person's place of work and his or her home is being broken.

In the United States, for the first time in 200 years, more people are moving to rural areas than urban—many more. In the Northeast, West, Great Plains, and Southwest, everywhere, people are moving from cities and suburbs to rural areas. They are abandoning cities for quality-of-life reasons: low crime rates, comparatively low housing costs, recreational opportunities, and, perhaps most of all, a return to community values.

Five years ago we moved to Telluride, Colorado, a tiny mountain village in the southwest corner of the state. Our house and our town (population 1200) are at 9000 feet in a box canyon where the mountains all around us soar to 13,000 and 14,000 feet. It looks a little like the Swiss Alps.

Although we are six hours from Denver, with our computers, telephones, fax machine, and Federal Express we are as in touch with the rest of the world as if we were in downtown London or

Tokyo. Indeed, Telluride has the world's highest concentration of Apple and Macintosh computer users, says Judi Kiernan, founding director of the local Macintosh User Group.

This move to a quality-of-life rural area is being duplicated by hundreds of thousands of Americans. It is one of the great untold stories of the 1980s and 1990s. Between one-third and one-half of the American and Canadian middle class will live outside metropolitan and suburban areas by 2010, according to Jack Lessinger, Professor Emeritus at the University of Washington.

'Population growth in suburbia stopped accelerating about 1970. The dream is now elsewhere,' he says. He names that elsewhere Penturbia, the fifth big historical US migration.

The first migration, says Professor Lessinger, was north and south from the first colonies, between 1735 and 1846; the second was west to the Mississippi-Ohio River valley towns, between 1789 and 1900; the third was from the country to the cities, between 1846 and 1958; the fourth, beginning around 1900, was from the cities to the post-World War II suburbs, overlapping somewhat with the third.

The new electronic heartland is not the same as the 'electronic cottage', where people stay home, working on their computers, instead of going to nearby offices. But once companies get used to their people not being around all the time, it will pave the way for more contract work to be awarded to self-employed people, who can live almost anywhere. People working in 'electronic cottages' today might be among the first settlers in the new heartland, before the end of the decade.

People who operate businesses at home are also prime candidates. There were 14.6 million full-time home-based businesses in 1989, according to the American Home Business Association. It predicts there will be 20.7 million by 1995. 'Quality of life is the prize they're chasing,' says Thomas Miller, director of the 1988 National Work-at-Home Survey conducted by LINK Resources.

The very nature of the information economy makes it easier to be part of this trend. As many as 5 million Americans could be working at home in computer-related jobs alone by 1993, according to the Center for Futures Research at the University of Southern California.

The new electronic heartland will be peopled by individuals who are not location-dependent, not location-bound. They will be software writers and engineers, stock and bond traders, transcribers and translators, artists, composers, writers of every stripe who can do what they do anywhere and look for agreeable places to do it. Technology and information-knowledge work make it possible. People who travel a lot—performers and airline crews—will flock to the heartland for quiet downtime. We do not have to cluster together in cities or suburbs to get our work done as we did during the industrial era.

In many ways, if cities did not exist, it now would not be necessary to invent them.

In the developed world, that is. In developing countries, cities are growing to sizes unprecedented in human history. In the North people are moving out of cities; in the South people are moving to the cities.

By the year 2000 there will be twenty-two cities of over 10 million people. In 1950 five of the ten largest cities in the world were in Europe and the United States. By the year 2000 there will be only one: New York City. By the year 2000 the two largest cities in the world will be Mexico City and São Paulo, Brazil.

In the year 2000, however, the truly global cities will not be the largest; they will be the 'smartest'.

Computers are turning buildings into 'smart' buildings that monitor and run themselves—and connect occupants with the rest of the world.

The second state is to create networks of smart buildings. In an ambitious scheme to do just that, Mitsubishi Real Estate recently connected thirty-two buildings in Tokyo's Marunouchi district with a network of optic fibres. If you connect enough smart buildings, pretty soon you have a 'smart city', which will eventually be connected to others. These will be the global cities of the future.

THE PRIMACY OF THE CONSUMER

When the focus was on the institution, individuals got what suited the institution; everyone got the same thing. No more. With the rise of the individual has come the primacy of the consumer. It has been *said* for many years that the customer is king. Now it is true.

The history of the auto industry advanced with no options —Henry Ford's notion of exactly the same black cars for everyone. Today with the aid of computer has come the (almost) unique automobile, the customized car order. A Volvo customer can select from more than 20,000 possible combinations to create his individual preference. Today's computerized 'assembly lines' individualize products, creating many different versions that each respond to a unique customer's taste.

TRIUMPH OF THE INDIVIDUAL AND THE MEGATRENDS OF THE 1990s

Recognition of the individual is the thread connecting every trend described in this book.

The new golden era where humankind earns its daily bread through the creativity of the individual instead of as a beast of burden already exists in the developed world which is now entering the global economic boom of the 1990s. In a high-wage information economy, people are paid for what is unique to them—their intelligence and creativity, not their collective brawn. Individual contributions to enterprise are rewarded with a customized compensation package of bonuses and stock ownership, rather than a uniform system that treats everyone the same.

Any well-trained person could be a manager. A leader is an individual who builds followership by ethical conduct and by creating an environment where the unique potential of one individual can be actualized. Today's workplace democracy is guided by enlightened entrepreneurs willing to share ownership.

Behind the renaissance in the arts is the individual artist creating a work that might be enjoyed by many but that is ultimately experienced and evaluated by an individual.

Communists, socialists, and welfare statesmen are trying to jump-start their economies by encouraging and rewarding individual effort and entrepreneurship. The emergence of free-market socialism frees countries to experiment, to adjust, to do better by their individual citizens. Ideas about society's responsibility to citizens change with the advent of the age of the individual.

The new responsibility of society is to reward the initiative of the individual.

The challenge behind the global lifestyle trend and the counter-trend of cultural nationalism is the question: how can individuality be preserved when so many forces promote uniformity, universality, sameness?

Unique individual genes are the basic building block in the age of biology. The ethical decisions of individuals will determine when this new age of biotechnology takes hold and whether humankind is spiritually prepared to undertake it. When that happens, breakthroughs never before thought possible, such as identifying and correcting inherited detrimental genes, will celebrate the value of an individual's life.

The religious revival reflects a shift from the collective of organized religion to the individuality of faith, whether that is a faith in a healing ministry, a spiritual teacher, or the word of the Bible. Only individuals can experience the transcendent.

This new primacy of individual power will only slowly be acknowledged.

Throughout history, power has been associated with institutions, with physical and military power. Kings, governments, and God were powerful. Individuals were not. People felt powerless against their social context. The only way they could assert themselves was by opposing tradition, by tearing down what was no longer useful, by rebelling.

Today there is a new possibility. The individual can influence reality by identifying the directions in which society is headed. Knowledge is power, it has often been said. Even if you do not endorse the direction of a trend, as in Jeremy Rifkin's opposition to biotechnology, you are empowered by your knowledge about it. You may choose to challenge the trends, but first you must know where they are headed.

By identifying the forces pushing the future, rather than those that have contained the past, you possess the power to engage with your reality.

Conclusion

These, then, are the ten most important new trends of the decade leading to the year 2000. On the threshold of the millennium, long the symbol of humanity's golden age, we possess the tools and the capacity to build utopia here and now.

Yes, there are major obstacles to overcome—from the economic development of the Third World to healing the environment and finding a cure for cancer and AIDS. To a large extent, however, the direction of today's megatrends strengthens society to confront its worst social ills throughout this great deadline decade.

The developed world's economic boom will be the foundation for higher evolution and global affluence.

Wealth has not led to increased greed, as conventional cynicism would have us believe. The 'hierarchy of needs' theory of humanist psychologist Abraham Maslow expressed it simply and well. As basic needs, such as shelter and safety, are met, high needs, such as those for belonging, achievement, and self-actualization—that is, transcendence—rise in their place. It is as valid for societies as for individuals. The satisfaction of basic needs has stimulated the search for meaning exemplified by the renaissance in the arts and the revival of spirituality.

As more countries grow prosperous, they must identify new areas for investment. Less-developed countries, where labour is cheaper, become more attractive areas for that profitable investment. Once the Four Tigers achieved developed status, investment in Thailand (from Japan, the Tigers, and others) soared. It also increased in Malaysia, while some observers argued the better-educated Philippines would have been a better target. Now Hong Kong and Taiwan are pumping capital into China.

The Pacific Rim has rewritten the history of economic development, jumping right over the industrial period and into the information economy, where the most important resources do come not from the ground but from people.

Throughout the Third World there is a growing consensus that small enterprise, not central planning, is the road to real prosperity. The spectacle of the Soviet Union and China reaching for market mechanisms will only accelerate the Third World's shift from a Marxist model of economic development to an entrepreneurial model sanctioned—indeed copied— by the Communist superpowers. That will invigorate the quest for economic self-sufficiency.

Prosperity and democracy are what will finally end deadly regional conflicts. As Bob Dylan put it, 'when you got nothing, you got nothing to lose'. Wealth is a great peacemaker. The forty-four richest nations have been at peace for more than forty-five years. When developing countries make peace with their neighbours, a greater proportion of their resources can be invested in economic development.

The scourge of AIDS and the suffering it has wrought symbolize our ignorance of our bodies and their priceless immune systems. Yet today, as we learn more about the role of positive visualization and imaging in health, we are on the brink of being able to see into the very nature of the human cell, even the DNA code itself.

'We have just begun to use a wide array of new imaging technologies such as nuclear resonance to peer into living tissue. We have just begun to apply biophysics to the relationships inside the cell, as in DNA,' writes T. George Harris, editor-in-chief of *American Health*. 'We will soon be able to fight viruses and bacteria even before we identify them.'

The rapprochement between the superpowers reduces the chance of a regional conflict escalating into a world war. Furthermore, the United States and the USSR have less of an incentive to inflame their client states in order to gain political or military advantage. That creates a more fertile climate for resolving conflicts, which in turn blunts the effectiveness of terrorism. Developing countries that succeed in preserving their cultures remain stronger and find it more difficult to justify striking out against the West.

The end of the cold war has shifted the world's attention to the environment. Though some would argue it is too little too late, never before has there been *competition* among heads of state for global leadership in the environment. George Bush wants to be an 'environmental' President. Mikhail Gorbachev mentioned the environment many times in his historic United Nations speech. Margaret Thatcher at times sounds like an environmentalist 'Green'. All of Britain's increasing number of other political parties try to be greener than her.

The post-cold-war era will see the United States and the Soviet Union collaborate on the environment and on new non-ideological approaches to ending poverty.

The meaning of that great symbol the millennium depends entirely on how it is interpreted. It can mark the end of time or the beginning of the new. We believe the decision has already been made to embrace its positive side. Within the hearts and minds of humanity, there has been a commitment to life, to the utopian quest for peace and prosperity for all, which today we can clearly visualize. Humanity is entering a decade-long race to confront the great challenges remaining in the hope of making a fresh start in the year 2000.

The 1990s will be an extraordinary time. The countdown —1992, 1993, 1994—is just about to begin. Get ready. You possess a front-row seat to the most challenging, yet most exciting, decade in the history of civilization.

Endnotes

1. THE GLOBAL ECONOMIC BOOM OF THE 1990s

16 The photovoltaic energy information is from 'A Commercial Breakthrough for the Sun', *Financial Times*, 15 December 1988.

17 The *Financial Times* quote is from an editorial about how the tax revolution has finally reached Sweden, 25 November 1988.

17 The Sven-Olof Lodin quote is from 'Supply-Side Sweden', *Wall Street Journal*, 30 November 1988.

18 Alan Greenspan's article 'Goods Shrink and Trade Grows' appeared in the *Wall Street Journal*, 24 October 1988.

24 Charles Wolf's article 'America's Decline: Illusion and Reality' appeared in the *Wall Street Journal*, 12 May 1988.

28 The source of the number of companies bought by foreign buyers is W T Grimm & Company, Chicago, Illinois.

29 The Milton Friedman quote is from his article 'Why the Twin Deficits Are a Blessing', *Wall Street Journal*, 14 December 1988.

32 The Bluestone-Harrison study, *The Great American Job Machine: The Proliferation of Low-Wage Employment in the US Economy*, December 1986, was prepared for the Joint Economic Committee. The later revisions are reported by Warren Brookes in 'The Myth That Won't Quit', Washington *Times*, 7 September 1987.

32 The March 1985 to March 1989 percentage is calculated from *Employment and Earnings*, April 1985, and April 1989, Bureau of the Labour Statistics US Department of Labour.

32–3 The percentage of new professional and managerial jobs, from 'The Employment Situation: March 1989', news release, 7 April 1989, Bureau of Labour Statistics, US Department of Labour.

33 The 1977 to 1981 statistic is from Brookes, 'The Myth That Won't Quit', loc. cit.

33 Anne McLaughlin quote from 'How a Bush or Dukakis Victory will Affect Jobs', Washington Post, 16 October 1988.

33 Retail sales for 1987 reported in 'Hiding a Boom in a Statistical Bust', *Wall Street Journal*, 6 August 1987.

33   'Prosperity Index' is from fact sheet, 12 July 1988, Economic Policy Division, US Chamber of Commerce; update from interview with Orawin Velz, US Chamber of Commerce, 31 August 1989.

33   The annual *Changing Times* 'Prosperity Index' appeared in the March 1989 issue, p. 27.

34   The 'Misery Index' in 1980, from *Changing Times*, January 1987, p. 67, in 1988, from the US Department of Labour.

34   Massachusetts loss of manufacturing jobs and increase in income are reported in Brookes, 'The Myth That Won't Quit', loc. cit.

34   David Gordon's story appeared in 'The New Class War', Washington *Post*, 26 October 1986.

34   Barbara Ehrenreich's story was in the 7 September 1986 issue of the *New York Times Magazine*, p. 42.

34   The faulted Joint Economic Committee Democratic Staff Study was released July 1986; that it was pulled from publication is reported in *Insight* (22 September 1986), p. 49.

35   Robert Avery's comments from *Fortune*, 14 September 1987, p. 32.

35   The *Monthly Labour Review* report appeared May 1988, p. 3.

35   Increased earnings of black and white families over $50,000, from *Money Income and Poverty Status in the United States: 1987*, Current Population Reports, Consumer Income, Series P-60, No. 161, Bureau of the Census, US Department of Commerce, August 1988.

35   The number of households earning over $50,000 computed with figures from *Money Income of Households, Families and Persons in the United States: 1987*, Current Population Reports, Series P-60, No. 162, February 1989, Bureau of the Census, US Department of Commerce. Description of well-to-do households, from 'Growing Middle Incomes', Washington *Times*, 15 August 1986.

35   The *Wall Street Journal* quote appeared in 'US Rich and Poor Increase in Numbers; Middle Loses Ground', 22 September 1986.

36   The *Economist* quote from the 9 April 1988 issue, p. 13.

36   Increases in family income, black family income from *Money Income of Households, Families and Persons in the United States: 1987* loc. cit. Percentage of various categories of people employed are from *Labour Statistics Derived from the Current Population Survey 1948–1987*, Bulletin 2307, Bureau of Labour Statistics, US Department of Labour.

36   James Smith's figure on the black middle class, from the 14 September 1987 issue of *Fortune*, p. 32. Data on elderly, from same story.

37   All poverty figures, from Ellie Baugher, Bureau of the Census, Poverty Division, US Department of Commerce, 28 August 1989.

37   Robert Samuelson's comments appear in his article 'The Two-tiered Nation', Washington *Post*, 19 August 1987.

37   Poverty of female-headed households, tendency to escape poverty via marriage, figures on families headed by women and of poor families with children, cited in various Bureau of the Census reports and findings, including interviews with Ellie Baugher, Poverty Division, 18 April and 28 August 1989, and *Poverty in the United States 1987*, Current Population Reports, Consumer Income, Series P-60, No. 163, Bureau of the Census, US Department of Commerce.

37   Robert Samuelson quote is from 'The Two-Tiered Nation', loc. cit.

38   Median income figures for 1973 and 1985 are from *Changing Times*, January 1987, p. 67, as are women's income figures.

38–9 Incomes by education level, from *Money, Income and Poverty Status in the United States: 1987*, loc. cit.

38   Unemployment by education, from 'Education Level of US Labour Force Continues to Rise', news Release, 29 August 1989, Bureau of Labour Statistics, US Department of Labour.

42   The quote about de-regulation is from 'Europe's Internal Market', the *Economist*, 9 July 1988.

46   The Green party quote is from 'Europe Looks to 1992 as Year Dreams of Union Come True', The *New York Times*, 16 July 1988.

49   The Juan Luis Cebrián quote is from 'Europe Looks to 1992', loc. cit.

2. RENAISSANCE IN THE ARTS

53   More information on each item here appears later in chapter.

54–5 Numbers on the Alabama Shakespeare Festival, from interview with Richard Norris of the Festival, 20 July 1989.

55   Broadway Theater ticket sales, from The League of American Theaters and Producers. New York football ticket sales in 1989, from Giants' PR Dept., and Jets' President's office.

55   Ticket sales for British musicals, from *Variety*, reported in 'Record Regards for Broadway's 1987–88 Season', the *New York Times*, 2 June 1988.

55   Advance sales figures, from *ADWEEK'S Marketing Week*, 11 July 1988, p. 4, and 'It's Not Open Yet, But "Les Mis" Has Already Set a Record', San Diego *Union*, 8 March 1987.

56   Data on theatre outside New York, from *Town & Country* (November 1987), p. 207.

56 Theatre Communications Group data, from 'Theatre Facts 88', *American Theatre* (April 1989).

56 Gary Sinise is quoted in 'Directors Point Out Theatre's Changing Patterns', *Christian Science Monitor*, 26 February 1987.

56 Information on Old Globe Theatre, from interviews with Mark Hiss and Tom Hall of the theatre, 26 January 1989.

56 Number of professional companies, from *Profile 1988*, a publication of Opera America, Washington, DC.

56–7 Number of season premiéres and number of companies with budgets under $100,000 from Central Opera Service, New York City.

57 Deficit figures for 1986, from 'Background Information on Recent Trends in National Endowment for the Arts Funding and the Current Conditions of the Five Major Disciplines', 27 March 1987, American Arts Alliance, Washington, DC.

57 Symphony attendance figures, from American Symphony Orchestra League, Washington, DC.

57 Growth of regional orchestras, from 'A Cacophony of Troubles', Denver *Post*, 25 January 1987, and the American Symphony Orchestra League.

57 Growth of chamber music groups, from Chamber Music America, New York City.

57 Hollywood Bowl numbers are from the Los Angeles Philharmonic.

57 Chicago and Boston Symphony numbers, from 'The Sounds of Summer', The *New York Times*, 5 July 1987.

57 Caribana attendance numbers, from Caribbean Cultural Committee, Toronto, Canada.

58 Cleveland-San Jose Ballet, reported in 'In the Ballet, a Second Home Helps the Budget', The *New York Times*, 27 January 1988, and 'E. F. Hutton Gives Ballet Co-Venture Record $250,000', San Jose *Mercury-News*, 7 March 1987.

58 Coventures in dance, from Dance/USA, Washington, DC.

59 Dara Tyson is quoted in 'Arts Are No Longer Only for Urbanites', The *New York Times*, 30 August 1987.

59 Growth of small publishers appears in *Publishers Weekly*, 24 June 1988, p. 18.

59 Data on writing degree programmes, from 'The Strange Case of Modern Poetry', Washington *Post*, 26 July 1987.

59 Don Austin of Chicago, Illinois, interviewed 10 March 1989.

59 Leslie Singer is quoted in 'Boom in Art Market Lifts Prices Sharply, Stirs Fears of a Bust', *Wall Street Journal*, 24 November 1986.

60 Museum attendance figures are from American Association of Museums, Washington, DC.

60 National Gallery numbers, from interviews with Anne Dia-

monstein and Joanne Prunell of the National Gallery of Art, Washington, DC, 3 April 1989.

60 Twin Cities data, from *Winter Cities Newsletter*, 1987.

60 Joel Wachs is quoted in 'Eyeing the Gallery Scene', Los Angeles *Times*, 4 April 1987.

60 Arnold Glimcher is quoted in 'Artwork Orange', Los Angeles *Times*, 20 April 1986.

60 Earl Powell is quoted in 'Museum Mania Grips the Globe', Los Angeles *Times*, 23 May 1986.

60 Getty Museum's budget in *Art and Antiques* (December 1986), p. 53.

60 Thomas Hoving quote from the June 1987 issue of *Connoisseur*, p. 25.

61 Sotheby's and Christie's 1987 sales from *Newsweek* (18 April 1988), p. 60, 1988–1989 sales from Southeby's, New York.

61 Sotheby's Art Index and comparison with S&P 500, from a report in 'Investing', *Wall Street Journal*, 23 March 1989.

61 Seattle tax figures, noted in 'Voting for Downtown Museum Could Pay Good Return', Seattle *Post-Intelligencer*, 7 September 1986, and 'Museum Breathes Sigh of Relief', Seattle *Times*, 2 September 1986.

61 German cities with new museums, from the *Economist* (27 September 1986), p. 100.

61 Information on Cologne and Frankfurt, from the *Economist*, 27 September 1986, (p. 100), and *Art in America* (September 1987), p. 152.

61–2 Musée d'Orsay attendance figure, from '4 Million Pack Orsay Art Museum in Year', *Rocky Mountain News*, 11 January 1988.

62 Les Disharoon's fund-raising efforts and quote from 'Orchestras Face The Music', *Christian Science Monitor*, 7 July 1988.

62–3 Financial impact of Cleveland Playhouse Square and Centre, arts in LA and Great Britain, from *Horizon* (December 1986), p. 9; 'Cities Finding That Art Often Beautifies Budgets', the *New York Times*, 27 March 1986; and the *Economist* (30 July 1988), p. 59.

63 David Birch on the arts, from 'Broward Puts Money on Culture to Attract and Keep Business', Miami *Herald*, 27 October 1986.

63 Importance of the arts to Americans, from *Americans and the Arts 1984 Highlights*, Louis Harris poll.

63 Van Gogh in New York study, reported in *Art and Antiques* (May 1986), p. 116.

63 Edinburgh, from the *Economist* (8 August 1987), p. 82. Spoleto USA in Charleston, from the *Economist* (31 May 1986), p. 24.

64 Mass MoCA, described in various sources, including 'A Mega-museum', the *New York Times Magazine*, 5 March 1989, and 'Thinking Big at the Guggenheim', The *New York Times*, 29 May 1988.

64   The Goodland Carnegie Arts Centre is described in *Connections Quarterly*, a publication of the National Assembly of Local Arts Agencies, Washington, DC (January 1987), p. 3.

64   The Bakehouse Art Complex from various sources, including 'Bakery Gives Rise to Artists' Studios', Miami *Herald*, 2 February 1987, and 'Art Rises at Bakehouse', Miami *Herald*, 6 February 1987.

65   John Robinson writes in *American Demographics*, September 1987, p. 42.

65   Data on work force and artistic occupation increases 1960–1980, from *American Demographics* (April 1988), p. 28.

65   Data for new jobs created and artistic careers in 1980s, from the US Department of Labour.

65   The Census Bureau data are reported in 'Research Division Note No. 31—17 April 1989, Artist Employment in 1988', and 'Research Division Note No. 29—17 February 1988, Artist Employment in 1987', National Endowment for the Arts, Washington, DC.

65   Judith Jedlicka is quoted in 'Corporations' Growing Taste for Visual Art', San Jose *Mercury-News*, 30 July 1985.

66   The US government's arts spending represents the sum contributed by the federal government to the National Endowment for the Arts.

66   Per capita spending figures calculated by dividing US population into annual budgets of US Departments of Defence and Education (provided by the US Office of Management and Budget) and of the National Endowment for the Arts.

66   That corporations contribute $1 billion a year to the arts is a figure from the Business Committee for the Arts, New York City.

67   Government funding of the arts in European countries cited are from 'In Britain, Many in the Arts Say Profit and Loss Has Replaced Beauty and Truth', the *New York Times*, 21 February 1988.

67   Membership in San Francisco and Boston museums, from various sources, including 'The Art Boom Sets Off Spree', the *New York Times*, 23 June 1985; interview with membership spokesperson at San Francisco Museum, 21 July 1989; 'Museums Seen Catering to Their Visitors', *Christian Science Monitor*, 11 January 1988; and interview with spokesperson, Boston Museum of Fine Arts, 21 July 1989.

67   Arata Isozaki is quoted in 'Museum Mania Grips the Globe', Los Angeles *Times*, 23 May 1986.

67–8 Financial data on the Met's museum shop, from 'A Non-profit Institution', the *New York Times*, 27 May 1988, and the museum's *Annual Report*.

68   Smithsonian figures appeared in 'Shopping the Mall', Washington *Post*, 12 December 1988.

68   Sales data from Boston's Renoir show appeared in 'Renoir Exhibit Brought $30 Million', Boston *Globe*, 30 May 1986, and 'The MFA's Selling of Renoir', Boston *Globe*, 22 December 1985.

68   Symphony fund-raising tactics, from 'Symphonies Go "Light"', Orlando *Sentinel*, 7 January 1987 (Buffalo, St Louis, and Phoenix), and 'Marketing Symphony', St Petersburg *Times*, 4 December 1985 (Boston and Pittsburgh).

68   Louis Spisto was quoted in 'Marketing Symphony As If It Were Soap', St Petersburg *Times*, 4 December 1985.

68–9   Robert Schlosser is quoted in 'Theatre Facts 85', *American Theatre* (April 1986).

69   Arena Stage's new marketing approach was described in 'Cultural Institutions Join Money Hunt', Washington *Post*, 26 November 1985.

69   The National Endowment for the Arts study is 'Research Division Note No. 30—30 November 1988, The Arts in the GNP Revisited and Revised: For the Third Consecutive Year Consumer Expenditures for Performing Arts Events Exceed Spectator Sports', National Endowment for the Arts, Washington, DC.

70   Boston's leisure activities are measured in *The Economic Impact of the Arts on the City of Boston*, a study conducted by ARTS/Boston and Boston's Office of the Arts and Humanities. Washington's are cited in 'Museum Going the Most Popular Leisure Activity', Washington *Post*, 5 January 1989.

70   The $1 billion figures is cited by Business Committee for the Arts, New York City.

70–1   John Robinson writes in the September 1987 issue of *American Demographics*, p. 42. Alvin Reiss's comments appear in *Advertising Age* (18 January 1988), p. 18.

71   Carol Palm interview was 31 July 1989.

71   Numbers on women as consumers appear in a special report, 'Marketing to Women', *Advertising Age* (7 March 1988).

71   Robinson's study on male and female participation in the arts appeared in *American Demographics* (September 1987), p. 42.

71   Public TV viewership data, from Public Broadcasting Service, Alexandria, Virginia.

71   Viewership of *Live from Lincoln Centre* and *Live from the Met*, from *A Report for Business Leaders from the Consolidated Corporate Fund 1988–1989*, Lincoln Centre.

71   Corporation for Public Broadcasting contributions, from *Giving USA, The Annual Report on Philanthropy for the Year 1987*, American Association of Fund-Raising Counsel Trust for Philanthropy.

71   Sources for opera radio listeners as follows: *Opera Profile 1988*, a publication of Opera America, Washington, DC (Metropolitan);

Opera Pro: :e :986 and *Opera Profile 1988* (Chicago and Louisville).

72 The Saatchi & Saatchi survey is described in 'Cable Transition on Way, Says Agency Study', *Variety* (3 August 1988).

72 Cable penetration and projected 1993 figure are from the US Department of Commerce, reported in 'BO Outlook Flat—Music, Cable Rising', *Variety* (4–10 January 1989).

72 Steven Ross's quote is reported in 'WCI's Ross Says Future Is in Cable, Foreign Biz', *Variety* (10 August 1988).

72 Data on A&E network, from various sources, including interviews with Chris Haselfeld, A&E Public Relations Department, 20 and 21 March 1989, and 'Cable TV Showcase for the Arts', *Christian Science Monitor*, 27 July 1988. Nicholas Davatzes's quote and description of typical A&E viewer appeared in the *Christian Science Monitor* story.

72 The quote for the Louis Harris poll appeared in 'Lost Leisure Time Could Reshape Arts/Entertainment Industries', press release on *Americans and the Arts V*.

73 Paul Kagan data on ED VCRs, from interview with Tom Adams of Paul Kagan Associates, New York City, 16 March 1989.

73 *Billboard*'s comments, from interview with Israel Horowitz, classical music division, 27 March 1989.

73 J&R Music World's statement, from interview with J&R spokesperson, 30 March 1989.

73 Paul Kagan data on cassette rentals and Tom Adams quote from interview with Tom Adams of Paul Kagan Associates, New York City, 16 March 1989 and 13 September 1989.

73 Information on Kultur Video, from various sources, including 'Kultur Video Selected as One of America's 500 Fastest Growing Companies by *Inc.* Magazine', press release, 8 December 1988; interview with Dennis Headlund, president and founder of Kultur, 20 March 1989; and interview with Johanna Kelly of Kultur, 16 March 1989.

74 Companies using opera in commercials as well as Gerry Miller's quote is from 'Ads Hit High Notes', *USA Today*, 5 January 1989.

74 Miller's re-evaluation of baseball advertising appears in a special report, 'Sports Marketing', *Advertising Age* (13 March 1989).

74 The story of pro athletes' endorsements as well as Leigh Steinberg's quote from the 17 August 1987, issue of *Advertising Age*, p. 32.

74 Rawleigh Warner was quoted in 'Art, for the Sake of Business', the *New York Times*, 10 October 1985.

75 Total number of contributions from various sources to the arts, culture, and humanities is from *Giving USA, The Annual Report on Philanthropy for the Year 1987*, copyright 1988 American Association of Fund-Raising Counsel Trust for Philanthropy.

75 Figures on corporate support and sponsor list of National Gallery

shows are from an interview and information received from
Anne Diamonstein of the National Gallery of Arts, 3 April 1989.
76　Judith Jedlicka is quoted in 'Performers' Group Wins Broader
Support', *Wall Street Journal*, 15 January 1987.

3. THE EMERGENCE OF FREE-MARKET SOCIALISM

81–3 The Mikhail Gorbachev comments are from 'Soviet Farm
Reform', the *Financial Times*, 14 October 1988.

84　The Pavel Bunich quote is from a conversation with the authors in
July 1988.

84　The Vadim Zagladin quote is from a conversation with the
authors in November 1986.

85　The Aleksandr Gelman quote is from a conversation with the
authors in July 1988.

85　The authors met with Vladislav Starkov in July 1988.

85　The Aleksandr Gelman quote is from a conversation with the
authors in July 1988.

87　The Fyodor Burlatsky quotes are from conversations with the
authors in November 1986 and October 1988 and from 'Soviets
Now Hail China', the *Wall Street Journal*, 18 September 1987.

89　The mayor of Shenyang quote is from 'Comparing Two Communist Paths', the *New York Times*, 6 September 1987.

89–90 The Dimitri Lisovolik quote is from a conversation with the
authors in July 1988.

90–1 The Mikhail Gorbachev quotes are from 'Soviet Legislators
Adopt Gorbachev's Reform Plan', the Washington *Post*, 2
December 1988.

93　The Peter Lorincze quotes are from 'Hungary must Press On', the
Wall Street Journal, 3 July 1987.

94　The Istvan Foldesi quote is from 'Poland, Now Hungary?' *International Herald Tribune*, 7 September 1989.

94　The Leslie Colitt quote is from 'Listening to the Voice of
Hungary', the *Financial Times*, 28 April 1989.

95　The Ivan Lipovecz quote is from the Washington *Post*, 16
February 1987.

95　The Imre Pozsgay quote is from the *New York Times*, 3 December
1987.

96–7 Communications Ministry official quote and Zdislaw Zniniewicz
quote from 'Satellite Dishes Give Poles', the Washington *Post*, 16
February 1987.

97　The quote about Lech Walesa reported in 'A Burnt-Out Light
Bulb', the *New York Times Magazine*, 30 July 1989.

98   The Lech Walesa quote from 'Polish Parliament OKs Government', the *Rocky Mountain News*, 13 September 1989.

98   Economic Minister outline quote from 'Solidarity Tells How it will Cure Poland', Washington *Post*, 12 September 1989.

99   The Bronislaw Geremek quote is from 'Developing a Ruler's Psychology', the *Financial Times*, 15 July 1989.

99   The Lech Walesa quote is from the *Financial Times*, 6 April 1989.

99   The quote about Gorbachev is from the *Economist*, 25 April 1987, p. 45.

100   The Stanislaw Lem quote is from the *Financial Times*, 14 October 1988.

100   The quote from the School of Planning theorist is from 'Hungary Leads in Reform', the Washington *Post*, 6 April 1987.

101   The Willy Brandt quote is from 'Socialists Revise Objections', the *Financial Times*, 3 June 1989.

4. GLOBAL LIFESTYLES AND CULTURAL NATIONALISM

102   Paloma Picasso is quoted in 'Around the World of Designers', Washington *Post*, 8 November 1987.

102   The Leif Johansson quote is from 'Electrolux Goes for Global Lifestyles', *Financial Times*, 28 March 1988, as is the description of Electrolux's product strategy.

103   Results of the Landor Associates survey and John Diefenbach quote from 'Coke, IBM Put Their Brands on the World', *USA Today*, 15 November 1988.

103–4 'Speak Mandarin' campaign, Welsh, Catalan, and Quebeçois language, and Soviet nationalism are described later in the chapter.

104   Edward Cody's Washington *Post* story entitled 'Rise in Islamic Fundamentalism' which describes Islamic scarf ban, appeared 4 April 1989.

105   Figures on Japanese tourists in the United States, from the Japan National Tourist Organization, New York City.

105   US air travel today and in 2000 from the Federal Aviation Administration, US Department of Transportation. Global airline travellers, from the International Air Transport Association, Washington, DC. Worldwide air travel in 2000, from the International Civil Aviation Organization, Montreal, Canada.

106   Figure on Italian imports to the United States and number of French cheeses, from *Europe* June 1986, p. 16.

106   Gurume chicken from 'Melting Pot: Kosher Burritos', *Wall Street Journal*, 10 March 1987.

107   The quote from Terrence Conway and the description of Handy Company from *Insight* (13 July 1987), p. 44, and interview with spokesperson of the John T. Handy Company, 10 February 1989.

107   Description of Chili's and Barry Ritman's quote were from 'Kosher Tex-Mex food', Houston *Chronicle*, 30 December 1986.

107   Percentage increases in all restaurants as well as in Asian, Mexican, and Italian restaurants, from *American Demographics* (July 1987), p. 29.

107–8   All McDonald's information, from company publications, including *1988 Annual Report McDonald's Corporation*, 'McDonald's Reports 95th Consecutive Quarter of Record Operating Results', news release, 26 January 1989, and *McDonald's Corporation 1986 Financial Highlights*; interviews with Anne Tolle, McDonald's media relations associate, 13 February 1989, 12 June 1989, and 31 July 1989, and these print sources: *Economist*, 16 April 1988, p. 58; *Time*, 13 April 1987, p. 58.

108   Description of Beijing's Kentucky Fried Chicken, from 'A Kentucky Colonel in the Heart of Beijing', San Jose *Mercury-News*, 13 November 1987 and interview with Richard Detwiler Director of Public Affairs, Kentucky Fried Chicken, 9 February 1989.

108   Increases in US fast food in Japan between 1974 and 1984 and Shin Ohkawara quote, from 'Tokyo Takeout', *Wall Street Journal*, 3 March 1987.

108   US franchise outlets in Japan today, from *Franchising in the Economy 1986–1988*, International Trade Administration, US Department of Commerce, February 1988.

108   Kentucky Fried Chicken in Japan and worldwide, from interview with Richard Detwiler of Kentucky Fried Chicken, 9 February 1989.

108   Japanese wine imports, from *Trendscape* (Spring 1987), p. 73.

108   Kozozushi Honbu, McDonald's in 1986, and Daiei sales figures, from 'Fast Food on Every Corner', Miami *Herald*, 22 November 1987.

108   McDonald's current sales from *Forbes* (17 October 1988), p. 64.

108   7-Elevens in Japan, from *1988 Corporate Profile*, Southland Corp.

108   Kazutaka Kato is quoted in 'Fast Food on Every Corner', Miami *Herald*, 22 November 1987.

109   The sellout of American Studies review on cuisine is noted in 'French Swallow Their Words', Los Angeles *Times*, 22 December 1986.

109   Elaine Bourbeillon is quoted in 'US Food a Paris Rage', San Diego *Union*, 4 June 1987, which also describes the General Store.

110   Laurie Mallet is quoted in 'Around the World of Designers', Washington *Post*, 8 November 1987.

110   Description of *Elle* magazine and the number of international editions and new editions being discussed, from interviews with

Didi Guerin, president, Hachette Publications, New York, 2 August 1989; and Abbe Murray, *Elle* International, 31 July 1989. Circulation, from 'Wooing the Wealthy Reader', the *New York Times*, 14 October 1987.

110   Description of Harrods' catalogue from 'Can't Go to Harrods Sale?' *USA Today*, 14 July 1986, and interview with a Harrods spokesperson, 10 February 1989. Overseas sales and description of produce section, from 'Harrods is Shopping Centre for the Whole World', Denver *Post*, 2 August 1987.

110–11   Milan's *Paninari* are described in 'Latest Chic Look Borrows Americana from Italians', Miami *Herald*, 31 May 1987.

111   Chinese fashion, described in various sources, including 'Chinese Fashion Blossoms', *Christian Science Monitor*, 23 July 1987, and 'Dust-Defying Fashion Latest Blooming Trend', Baltimore *Sun*, 22 April 1987. Pierre Cardin in China, described in *Forbes*, 2 May 1988, p. 90.

111   Research and Design Centre and Pierre Berge actions, from 'Notes de la Mode', Washington *Post*, 23 July 1989; 'Chinese Fashion Blossoms', *Christian Science Monitor*, 23 July 1987.

111   An account of Saint Laurent show in USSR is published in 'Capitalist Chic Comes to Communist Bloc', Philadelphia *Inquirer*, 3 December 1986.

111–12   Information on Benetton, from various sources, including interview with Jeremy Weithas, media contact, Benetton's Service Corporation, New York, 14 February 1989, and these print sources: 'The Benetton Group, What Is Benetton?', press release; *Europe* January–February 1989, p. 20; 'Benetton Is Accused of Dubious Tactics', *Wall Street Journal*, 24 October 1988; *Business Week*, 14 March, 1988, p. 78; *New Yorker*, 10 November 1986, p. 53.

112   Description of Esprit customer, from *Esprit Corporate Book*, reported in *Newsweek*, 12 November 1984.

112   Numbers of Esprit stores, percentage of sales outside the United States, and description of headquarters, from interviews with Lisa DeNeffe, Esprit, 7 February 1989, and 20 July 1989.

112   Esprit does not release sales figures; estimate of Esprit sales from *Forbes* (21 March 1988).

112   Doug Tompkins is quoted in *Inside* magazine, published in Japan. Quote verified by Esprit.

113   That Laura Ashley is a favourite of Prime Minister Thatcher is reported in *Working Woman*, August 1986, p. 53.

113   History and numbers of Laura Ashley shops, from various sources, including interview with Sarah Callander of Laura Ashley North America, 24 March 1989; *Working Woman*, August 1986, p. 53; *Forbes*, 2 December 1985; and *Newsweek*, 17 September 1984.

113   Habitat/Conran's description from various sources, including interviews with Pat Grabel, Conran's press office, New York, 16 February 1989, and 2 March 1989; 'History of Conran's', news release; 'Pauline Dora, President', news release; *Working Woman* (August 1986), p. 53; and *Metropolitan Home* (December 1984), p. 71.

113–14 IKEA description and numbers, from various sources, including interview with Lynn Till, assistant to the president, IKEA North America, 9 June 1989; interview with spokesperson, 20 July 1989; *IKEA USA Facts*, 1989; *IKEA Facts 88/89*, September 1988; *Time*, 27 July 1987; and 'With Big Selection and Low Prices', *Wall Street Journal*, 17 June 1986.

114   Chanel electronic pricing, from interview with Chanel spokesperson, October 1988.

115   French and American films released in 1986, from 'France', *International Film Guide 1987*, p. 155.

115   First three months of 1988 French film market share, described in 'Dateline Hollywood', Washington *Post*, 1 July 1988.

115   French pop chart January 1987, from 'French Sing Blues over Their Songs', Los Angeles *Times*, 24 January 1987.

115   Li Delun's quote is from *World Press Review*, January 1986, p. 56.

115   Descriptions of dance and disco in China are from 'Young, Old Are Rockin' in China', Los Angeles *Times*, 7 May 1988.

116   Descriptions of Studebaker's is from 'US Gets Toyotas, Japan Gets Studebaker's', Houston *Chronicle*, 13 October 1986.

116   Disneyland in Japan and Toshio Kagami's quote are from *Business Week*, 9 March 1987, p. 69.

116   EuroDisneyland is described in various sources, including *Business Week*, 9 March 1987, p. 69, and 'World's Fourth Magic Kingdom Planned for Outskirts of Paris', Atlanta *Journal*, 27 July 1987.

116   The *Economist*'s 170-country circulation is from the *Economist*, 25 July 1987.

116   The figures on the percentage of TV imported from the United States are extremely conservative as our figures are more than four years old, *World Press Review*, October 1985, p. 34.

117   US television shows around the world, from following sources: *Dallas*, reported in *The Harper's Index Book* (New York: Holt, 1987.) New Zealand, from *Atlantic*, September 1986, p. 14; South Africa, from interview with a spokesperson for Listener Programmes in South Africa, 21 February 1989; China, from 'Peking Duck, New Market for an Old Bird', Philadelphia *Inquirer*, 27 October 1986; *Sesame Street* from interview with Mary Sue Holland, Children's Television Workshop, New York City, 10 February 1989.

117   The *Independent Television News*, from interview with spokesperson, the *Independent Television News*, Washington, DC, 22

February 1989, and 'English-Language TV News Now Reaching 14 Nations', Atlanta *Journal*, 3 February 1987.

117   Super Channel and Sky Television, from Super Channel, London; and the *Economist* (22 October 1988), p. 20.

117–18   Scope of CNN is from interview with CNN spokesperson, 24 May 1989.

118   Polish television options, described in 'Poland Enters Satellite Age', Philadelphia *Inquirer*, 21 September 1986, and 'Eastern Europe Picks Up BBC', *Financial Times*, 12 January 1988.

118   USSR TV in Israel is from 'Coming Attractions', Los Angeles *Times*, 21 July 1987.

118   Raphael Roncagliolo's quote, description of Ocobamba, Peru, and Carlos Romera's quote are from 'TV Opens Up Remote Villager's World', Washington *Post*, 10 March 1988.

118   *Dallas*'s popularity with Tuareg is described by Robert McCrum, William Cran, and Robert MacNeil in *The Story of English* (New York: Viking, 1986).

118   Number of potential viewers in India are from Indian Embassy, Washington, DC. Televisions and viewers in China from the Chinese Embassy Press Office, 21 February 1989.

118   The *World Press Review* report in the December 1986 issue, p. 27.

119   Richard Pawelko's quote appeared in 'Eyeing a Continental Audience', Boston *Globe*, 23 November 1986.

119   Georgie Anne Geyer's column appeared in the Washington *Times*, 27 February 1989.

119–20   Numbers who speak English as a second language and with some knowledge of English, cited in *US News & World Report*, 18 February 1985, p. 49.

120   English's official or semi-official status in sixty countries and English speakers by 2000, from *International Management*, February 1988, p. 59.

120   English as most taught language from Kurt Muller, National Council on Foreign Languages and International Studies, February 1988.

120   Numbers of Chinese English students and countries where English is a second language or widely studied are from *US News & World Report*, 18 February 1985, p. 49.

120   English study in various countries, reported in sources listed below: Hong Kong, France, and Japan, from *US News & World Report*, 18 February 1985, p. 49; USSR, Norway, Holland, and Portugal, from *International Management*, February 1988, p.59; Sweden, from the Embassy of Sweden; and Denmark, from the Embassy of Denmark.

120   English schools in Tokyo from 'Japanese Are Striving for International Flair', Dallas *Morning News*, 4 October 1987.

120   Information on Berlitz from various sources, including interview

with (and printed matter from) Patricia Sze, director of marketing, Berlitz Language Centres, 16 February 1989.

121   Werner Siems, chief of editorial services, US Coast Guard, Washington, DC, quote from interview, 17 August 1987.

121   English-language information in computers is from McCrum, Cran, and MacNeil, op. cit., p. 20.

121   Number of computers worldwide is from interview with Lloyd Cohen of International Data Corporation, 25 May 1989.

121   English telephone conversations, from *Harper's Index Book* op. cit., p. 43.

121   Mail, telexes, and cables data, from McCrum, Cran, and MacNeil, op. cit., p. 20.

121   Computer instructions and software, from *International Management*, February 1988, p. 59.

121   English scientific papers from *Newsweek*, 15 November 1982, p. 99.

121   Number of technical and scientific periodicals in English, from McCrum, Cran, and MacNeil, op. cit., p. 20.

121–2   Sources for use of English at multi-national corporations is as follows: Datsun and Nissan, Aramco and Chase Manhattan, from McCrum, Cran, and MacNeil, op. cit., p. 41; Mitsui and Company and Toyota, from *US News & World Report*, 18 February 1985, p. 49; Iveco, Philips, and Cap Gemini Sogeti SA, from *International Management*, February 1988, p. 59.

122   English at École des Hautes Études Commerciales from 'One of France's "Grand Écoles" Tries English', Houston *Chronicle*, 2 June 1986.

122   English in international organizations from McCrum, Cran, and MacNeil, op. cit., pp. 42–43. Number of languages in India and Gandhi's English address, reported in McCrum, Cran, and MacNeil, op. cit., pages 39 and 20 percentage who speak Hindi from *The Futurist*, July–August 1986, p. 9; English at European Free Trade Association, from the *Economist*, 18 July 1987, p. 18.

122–3   English in Africa, from *US News & World Report*, 18 February 1985, p. 49; 'Languages of the World', *Encyclopaedia Britannica*, 1987; World Council of Churches, Olympics, and Miss Universe, from McCrum, Cran, and MacNeil, op. cit., p. 20.

123   Numbers of US students studying foreign language, from 'Foreign Language Study on Rise', Los Angeles *Times*, 17 January 1988.

123   William Cipolla's quote is from 'It's Not Just "English Spoken Here"', *International Herald Tribune*, 8 August 1988.

123   Data on Spanish-language study is from the Modern Language Association, reported in *US News & World Report* cited above, p. 114.

124 American English at the Smithsonian is described in 'Learning to Sling the Slang', Boston *Globe*, 8 August 1986.

124 Akira Nambara is quoted in 'Japanese Are Striving for International Flair', Dallas *Morning News*, 4 October 1987.

124–5 Quebec, Catalonia, and Wales, discussed in greater detail in the chapter's remaining pages.

125 English restrictions in the Philippines, Malaysia and Sudan, from interviews with Dr Peter Lowenberg, professor, Georgetown University School of Languages and Linguistics, 9 November 1987, and Dr Dick Tucker, president, Centre for Applied Linguistics, 9 November 1987.

125 English limits in more than a dozen countries, from *Newsweek*, 15 November 1982, p. 99.

126 Moorhead Kennedy's *The Ayatollah in the Cathedral* is published by Hill and Wang (New York, 1986). Remarks cited from on pp. 54–55.

126 Resurgence of traditional Japanese culture from the *Economist*, 19 March 1988, p. 26.

127 Percentage speaking Welsh at end of nineteenth century, 1930s, and in 1983, from Jan Morris, *The Matter of Wales*, (London: Oxford University Press, 1984), pp. 240, 244.

127 Sources for examples of Welsh revival as follows: Modified Ulpans and the play school movement, from Bud B. Khleif, *Language, Ethnicity, and Education in Wales* (New York: Mouton Publishers, 1980), pp. 66–67. League of Youth is from Khleif, op. cit., p. 65, and interview with Stephen George, Education Services Division, Welsh Office, Cardiff, Wales, 21 March 1989. Radio, newspapers, and television, from the British Information Line, New York, New York.

127 Emlyn Davies is quoted in 'Eyeing a Continental Audience', Boston *Globe*, 23 November 1986.

127 Commute to Welsh schools is cited in Khleif, op. cit., p. 43.

127 Numbers of schools using Welsh or teaching no Welsh from interview with Jeff Penn, Education Services Division, Welsh Office, Cardiff, Wales, 20 March 1989.

127–8 Description of the Eisteddfod and Junior Eisteddfod and quote appear on pp. 64–65 of Khleif, op. cit., pp. 64–65.

128 This quote appears in Morris, op. cit., p. 1.

128 Impacts of Quebec's language laws cited in following sources: brain drain and French investment, from *US News & World Report* (18 February 1985), p. 45; loss of English newspapers and Sun Life's move, reported in 'Quebec and Montreal: Two Languages Add to Their Rivalry', *Christian Science Monitor*, 31 May 1985; French university enrolments, from *Daedalus* (Fall 1988), p. 265.

129 Violations of language laws, cited from 'Quebec's Bilingual

Battle Is No Mere War of Words', Los Angeles *Times*, 10 April 1988.

129 Catalan's percentage of Spanish economy, from Myrtha Casanova, Grupo Mega de Estudios de Tendencias y Prospectiva, SA, 21 February 1989.

130 Joan Brossa is quoted in *National Geographic* (January 1984), p. 95.

130–1 Examples of the Catalan renaissance are drawn mainly from interview Myrtha Casanova identified above, 21 February 1989. Additional information on book publishing from *Publishers Weekly*, 14 September 1984, p. 106. Gatherings, dances and quote from Jordi Pujol, from 'Catalonia: A Benign Bid for Change', Los Angeles *Times*, 26 April 1986.

131 Description of Speak Mandarin campaign and Prime Minister Lee Kwan Yew's concerns are reported in 'In the Global Village, Seeking an Exit', the *New York Times*, 5 November 1988.

131 Soviet nationalism, described in various sources, including 'Resurgent Nationalism', Washington *Post*, 9 August 1987, and *Christian Century* (25 January 1989), p. 81.

132 Language laws in Estonia and other USSR republics, reported in various sources, including 'Estonia Votes to Make Its Own Language Official', the *New York Times*, 19 January 1989, and 'Moldavian Language Proposals', Washington *Post*, 1 January 1989.

132 'Soviet republic replaces Russian', *Financial Times*, 1 September 1989; 'Latvians To Seek A "Special Status"', the *New York Times*, 1 September 1989.

132–3 Walter Truett Anderson writes in in *Utne Reader*, November 1988, p. 97.

5. THE PRIVATIZATION OF THE WELFARE STATE

134 The quote about Margaret Thatcher is from Peter Jenkins, *Mrs Thatcher's Revolution: The Ending of the Socialist Era* (London: Jonathan Cape, 1987).

135 The Madsen Pirie quote is from 'Governments Put Themselves out of Business', the *Christian Science Monitor*, 26 May 1987.

135–6 The John Biffen and Prime Minister Thatcher's quotes are from 'All Thatcherites Now', *Financial Times*, 6 October 1987.

137 The Neil Kinnock quote is from 'Kinnock Fights Copycat-Party Image', the *New York Times*, 30 September 1987.

137 The Clive Wolman quote is from the *Financial Times*, 31 March 1987.

138 The Sir John Egan quote is from 'Privatization: irreversible', the *Financial Times*, 25 March 1987.

140   The Corazon Aquino quote is from the *New York Times*, 24 May 1989.

141   The prime minister of Portugal (Anibal Cavaco Silva) quote is from 'Pragmatic Privatization', the *Financial Times*, 7 September 1987.

141   The Ruud Lubbers quotes are from an interview on the 'Monday Page', in the *Financial Times*, 15 December 1986.

142   The Turgut Ozal quote is from 'Turkey to Start Long Promised Programme,' the *Wall Street Journal*, 25 August 1987.

142   The Pierre Fortier quote is from 'Quebec's Drive to Sell off State Firms', the *Wall Street Journal*, 9 April 1987.

143–4   The Koffi Djondo quote is from 'In Africa, a Rush to Privatization', the *New York Times*, 30 July 1987.

144–8   The Peter Ferrara quotes are from 'Social Security and Private Options', the Washington *Times*, 1 July 1987.

146–7   The Stefano Draghi and Massino Pini quotes are from 'Italy's Communists', the *New York Times*, 21 June 1987.

148–9   The Bengt Westerberg and the Daniel Tarshys quotes are from 'Swedish Opposition Leader', the *Christian Science Monitor*, 10 September 1987.

149   The Abel Aganbegyan quote is from a conversation with the authors in May 1988.

151   AFDC figures, from the Department of Health and Human Services.

151   Charles Murray's *Losing Ground*, was published by Basic Books New York, 1984. The statistics cited appeared on pp. 8, 14.

152–3   Description of Massachusetts workfare programme, from interviews with Sharon Gillis of Massachusetts, Education and Training, 8 and 16 June 1989.

152   The Michael Dukakis quote appeared in 'Don't Punish Welfare Recipients; Hire Them', a *USA Today* interview with Michael Dukakis, 15 August 1985.

153   The Barry Schiller quote is from 'Workfare Not Such a Sweeping Success', *Wall Street Journal*, 14 May 1986.

153   The Charles Atkins quote is from 'Welfare Revised', *Wall Street Journal*, 23 July 1986.

153–4   Programme descriptions from the following interviews: Michigan, from Bob Harris, Director of Communications, 28 and 29 June 1989, and 24 July 1989; Oklahoma, from Verne Belknap, Administrative Officer, 20 June 1989; Illinois, from Dan Pitman, Information Officer, 9 June 1989.

154   The William Raspberry column, 'Workfare Works', appeared in the Washington *Post*, 17 December 1986.

154   The Ilene Margolin quote is from 'Albany Prepares 2 New Job Plans', the *New York Times*, 1 December 1985.

154–5 The Lawrence M. Mead quote is from 'The Value of Workfare', the *New York Times*, 12 November 1985.

155 Mitchell I. Ginsberg and Michael Dowling are quoted in 'Workfare in New York', the *New York Times*, 24 October 1985.

155 The Mario Cuomo quote appeared in 'Cuomo Wants to Go Beyond Workfare', the *New York Times*, 26 January 1986.

6. THE RISE OF THE PACIFIC RIM

Note: US Department of Commerce is abbreviated as Commerce Dept. The US Department of Commerce publication *Foreign Economic Trends and Their Implications for the United States*, is abbreviated as *Foreign Economic Trends* and name of country is appended. *Business America* is a publication of the US Department of Commerce.

158 Estimated percentage of world population for Asia and Europe, from *Europe* (May 1986), p. 30.

158 Size and growth of Pacific market, from World Trade Commission, Sacramento, California, 6 April 1989.

158 John Hay's quote appeared in *Facts on the Pacific Rim*, Office of Economic Research, California Department of Commerce, May 1987.

159 More Koreans than Britons in schools of higher education, from the *Economist* (20 June 1987), p. 9.

159 Pacific Rim's fastest growth rate, from *Department of State Bulletin* (June 1987), p. 80.

159 The *Economist* quote appeared in the 18 July 1987, issue, p. 3.

159–60 Only one Japanese bank in top ten, ten years ago, reported in the *Economist* (30 July 1988), p. 13; ranking of Japanese banks today from *American Banker* 24 July 1989.

160 Pacific Rim's GNP thirty years ago and by 2160, from 'World Economic Power Is Shifting', *Financial Times*, 30 June 1988.

160 Tiger export figures 1975 to 1988, from 'World Economic Power Is Shifting', *Financial Times*, 30 June 1988. Tiger's share of electronic exports, from 'A Push Towards Global Status', in same issue.

160 Taiwan's export-related jobs, from 'Taiwan Beginning to Make Trade with America', Dallas *Morning News*, 24 August 1987. Per cent of Singapore goods exported, from 'Singapore', *Economist* (22 November 1986). Foreign exchange reserves, reported in the *Economist* (30 July 1988), p. 13.

160 US exports (1988) to South Korea, France, Taiwan, Italy, and Sweden, from country desks, Commerce Dept.

160 Per capita 1986 sales in 'Move Now Toward a Pacific Free-Trade Area', *Christian Science Monitor*, 18 November 1987.

160   US trade in 1960, from *Highlights of US Export and Import Trade*, Bureau of the Census, Commerce Dept., FT 990, August 1967. Pacific trade exceeding Atlantic in 1983, from *Department of State Bulletin* (April 1989), p. 33. Trade in 1988 from *US Export and Import Fact Sheets* (December 1988), Commerce Dept., Trade Reference Room.

160   China trade with Taiwan, from 'Taiwan's Entrepreneurs Quietly Moving', *Wall Street Journal*, 6 May 1988; Taiwan desk, Commerce Dept.

161   Fall fashion show quote, from 'The Japanese Vanguard', Washington *Post*, 21 March 1987. Story on spring shows appeared 16 October 1987.

161   Japanese designers and Kawakubo's holdings, described in 'Very Much in the Western Style', *Financial Times*, 7 December 1988.

161   Quotes by Bernard Portelli and Jay Specter, from *Insight* (3 November 1986), p. 9.

161   Richard Bliath is quoted in the *Economist* (26 January 1985), p. 87.

162   Estimate of Japanese art buying, from 'Foreign Culture Squeezes Out Domestic Artists', *Financial Times*, 15 July 1987.

162–3   New Japanese artists' show and quote, from Alexandra Munroe 'Made in Japan', Los Angeles *Times*, 19 March 1989.

162   Singapore's Empress Palace from *Passport* newsletter, August 1989, p. 1.

162   Hong Kong arts scene, described in 'Home of a Vibrant Arts Scene', *Financial Times*, 18 June 1987. Academy of the Performing Arts described in 'Hong Kong School Breaks Down Cultural Barriers', Los Angeles *Times*, 19 March 1989.

162   Cinema attendance, reported in *Variety* (1–7 February 1989), p. 81. Films and prizes from *Beijing Review* (6–12 March 1989), p. VII.

162–3   Eddie Lau quote, reported by Joel Kotkin and Yoriko Kishimoto in *Inc.* (January 1987), p. 23.

163   Peter Sellars is quoted in 'A Look into the Future', Los Angeles *Times*, 19 March 1989.

163   Growth rates from *The World Bank Atlas 1988*; Taiwan, from Taiwan desk, Commerce Dept.

164   Hong Kong, Greece, and Portugal GDPs from country desks, Commerce Dept.

164   The *Wall Street Journal*'s report 'Riding the Golden Dragon', 25 September 1988 also describes Hong Kong's futures market and stock exchange.

164   Hong Kong as China's first trading partner, from 'A Restored Entrepot', *Financial Times*, 23 June 1988.

164   Hong Kong's position in foreign investment and projects, from 'Wealth in the Chinese Hinterland', *Financial Times*, 25 June 1988.

164 China–Hong Kong relationship in investment and trade, from the *Economist* (27 August 1988), p. 63.

164 Diplomat's quote, from 'Hong Kong Sees China Gold', Boston *Globe*, 13 December 1987.

165 Hong Kong industries, investment, and employment in Guangdong, from 'Wealth in the Hinterland', *Financial Times*, 23 June 1988.

165 T. W. Wong's quote appeared in 'Hong Kong's special charms', San Diego *Union*, 28 June 1987.

165 Per Capita GNP for 1965, from the *Economist* (20 June 1987); for 1988, from *Foreign Economic Trends, Korea* (June 1989). South Korea, Denmark Austrian economies from country desks, Commerce Department.

165 South Korea's exports, from Korean Economic Institute. Percentage to the United States, from Office of Pacific Basin, Commerce Dept.

165 Increases in industrial production from the *Economist* (20 June 1987), p. 9. Increases in exports from *Business Week* (5 September 1988), p. 44.

165 Korean Development Institute projection, from *Trendscape* (Summer-Fall 1987), p. 50.

165–6 Fairness of income distribution, cited in *Business Week* (5 September 1988), p. 44.

166 *Tokyo Business Today* quote, from March 1988 issue, p. 18.

166 Automobile figures: South Korea in top five by 2000, from 'International', Miami *Herald Tribune*, 1 November 1987; ranking of automakers, from Motor Vehicle Manufacturers Association, Washington, DC; autos produced and exported, from 'South Korea', *Economist* (21 May 1988); 1993 goals, reported in *Business Week* (5 September 1988), p. 44.

166 Private R&D funds, from 'South Korea', the *Economist*, 21 May 1988. Semi-conductor investment, from *Business Week* (5 September 1988), p. 44.

166 Electronics production and exports, from *Foreign Economic Trends, Korea* (October 1988).

166 Institute of Electronics Technology prediction, from 'Low Labour Costs Give an Edge', Boston *Globe*, 16 February 1986.

166 One-third high-tech exports, from 'S. Korea Sees Future in High-Tech', San Diego *Union*, 22 December 1986.

167 Kim Young Soo quote, from 'Technology Is Our Survival', San Jose *Mercury-News*, 13 December 1987.

167 Hsieh Shih-hui's prediction is reported in *Trendscape* (Summer–Autumn 1987), p. 67.

167 Wages and productivity gains for 1986, reported in *Tokyo Business Today* (March 1988), p. 18; average hours and wage increases, from *Fortune* (15 August 1988), p. 75.

167 GNP spent on defence by South Korea and the United States, from *Fortune* (15 August 1988), p. 75; by Japan, from Embassy of Japan, Washington, DC.

167 Ji Byung-Moon's quote appeared in *Business Week* (5 September 1988), p. 44.

167 Growth rate in Singapore, from the General Analysis and Policy Division of the United Nations.

167 Singapore's savings rate, from *The Economic Survey of Singapore*, 1988, p. 8, provided by Singapore Economic Development Board, Washington, DC.

167 Singapore's 1978 per capita income, from *Fortune* (March 28, 1988), p. 126; 1988 income from the Singapore Economic Development Board.

167 Per capita 1988 GNP, from *Economic Trends Report, Singapore* (June 1988), Commerce Dept.

168 Gary Fowler quote, from 'Singapore's Business of Building Homes for Business', *Christian Science Monitor*, 13 October 1987.

168 Peng Yuan Hwang quote, in *World Press Review* (June 1985), p. 82.

168 The number of US multi-national companies in Singapore, from Office of Pacific Basin, Commerce Dept.

168 Apple Computer in Singapore, from *Fortune* (28 March 1988), p. 126. Disc drives imported to US from 'Asian Nation's Economy', *Christian Science Monitor*, 25 August 1989.

168 The quote by Eddie Foo and description of Singatronics are reported by Joel Kotkin and Yoriko Kishimoto in *Inc.* (January 1987), p. 23.

168 Vincent Yip is quoted in *High Technology* (November 1986), p. 33.

169 Per capita GDP, from *Foreign Economic Trends, Taiwan* (March 1989). Per capita GDP of Greece and Portugal, from country desks, Commerce Dept.

169 Trade figures from 1988: Taiwan, from *Foreign Economic Trends, Taiwan* (March 1989); South Korea, Sweden, from country desks Commerce Dept.

169 Taiwan's 1981 trade surplus, from 'Taiwan', *Economist* (5 March 1988); in 1988, from *Foreign Economic Trends, Taiwan* (March 1989).

169 Taiwan's foreign exchange reserves, from 'Taiwan', *Economist* (5 March 1988); Japan's, from *Foreign Economic Trends, Japan* (October 1988).

169 Taiwan trade with mainland, from *Economist* (23 April 1988), p. 38.

169 Decline of agriculture from 'Taiwan', *Economist* (5 March 1988).

169 Taiwan investment in the United States, reported in 'Taiwanese Tentacles', *Christian Science Monitor*, 9 March 1988.

169 Factories in Taiwan, from Coordination Council For North American Affairs, Washington, DC.

170 Jiao Zhou Road market, from 'Farmers Reap Rewards', *Philadelphia Inquirer*, 21 September 1986.

170 GNP growth rate in recent years, from China desk, Commerce Department. GNP growth from 1978 to 1988, from China desk, Foreign Demographics, Bureau of the Census, Commerce Department.

170 Exports in 1986, from *FET, People Republic of China* (August 1988); in 1988, from China desk, Commerce Department. China as US trade partner, from *Business America* (10 April 1989), p. 30.

170 Figures on businesses engaged in free enterprise, employing more than eight people, and jobs in the private sector, from *Far Eastern Economic Review* (24 August 1989), p. 24.

170 Factory owner incomes, from *Business Week* (11 April 1988), p. 70.

170 Inflation in 1989, from the *Economist* (19 September 1989). Tourism earnings, reported in 'Beijing's Economic Ills', the *Wall Street Journal*, 3 August 1989.

171 Beijing University freshman class, from *Asiaweek* (8 September 1989), p. 28.

171 Guangdong exports and investment in 1987, from *Business Week* (11 April 1988), p. 70; and 'Guangdong: The "Golden Goose"', *Washington Post*, 17 November 1988.

172 Wealth in Guangdong, from various sources, including 'Guangdong: The "Golden Goose"', *Washington Post*, 17 November 1988; *Business Week* (10 October 1988) p. 54; the *Economist* (10 December 1988). Thailand and Turkey, from country desks, Commerce Dept.

172 Figure on incomes exceeding more than 10,000 yuan a year, from 'Chinese Farms', *The Christian Science Monitor*, 6 August 1987.

172 Shishi and Xiamen, described in 'Dispatches From a Chinese Frontier', the *New York Times*, 15 August 1989; 'On China's Bustling Coast', the *New York Times*, 6 August 1989.

172 *Washington Post* article 'Guangdong: The "Golden Goose",' appeared 17 November 1988.

172 Shift from farming to industry, reported in 'Chinese Leaders', *The Christian Science Monitor*, 8 September 1987. Farmers in China, from 'Family Farms', *San Jose Mercury News*, 12 December 1987. Increase in rural income, from 'Chinese Farms', *Christian Science Monitor*, 6 August 1987; and 'China Surges Ahead', *Chicago Tribune*, 27 November 1988. Poverty in China, reported in 'Gansu Province', *Washington Post*, 18 November 1988.

173 Chen Yizi quote, from 'China Dismisses Culture Minister', *International Herald Tribune*, 5 September 1989.

173 Richard Nixon's comments, from 'Don't Shut the Door', the *Sunday Times* (London), 25 June 1989.

173   Japanese businesses returned, from 'Japan moving to normalize China ties', *Japan Economic Journal*, 26 August 1989.

173   Anna Chennault, from *Asiaweek* (8 September 1989), p. 30.

174   The report is *Discriminate Deterrence*, Report of the Commission On Long-Term Strategy, January 1988. China's growth rate in recent years, from China desk, Commerce Department.

174-5   Deng Xiaoping remarks, from the *Economist* (13 August 1988), p. 62.

175   The Malaysia section is based largely on the survey 'Malaysia', which appeared in the *Financial Times*, 28 September 1989; *Far Eastern Economic Review* (24 August 1989), p. 54; and *Asiaweek* (8 September 1989), p. 65.

175   Thailand's growth rate and comparison, from the General Analysis and Policy. Division of the United Nations.

176   The *Asian Wall Street Journal* article is cited in 'Thailand's Economy Shifting', *Christian Science Monitor*, 24 June 1988.

176   Export earnings from commodities, in 'Treading the Right Path', *Financial Times*, 2 December 1987; from manufactured goods in 1985 in 'Industry over Agriculture', *Financial Times*, 30 June 1987. Export increase in 1988, from *Business America* (10 April 1989), p. 33. Growth in manufactured exports, from 'A Fifth "Tiger"', *Seattle Times*, 13 November 1988.

176   Tourism, reported in *Foreign Economic Trends, Thailand* (December 1988).

176   Percentage of farmers, from 'Thailand's Economy Shifting', *Christian Science Monitor*, 24 June 1988.

176   Urban versus rural population, from 'Thailand', *Economist* (31 October 1987).

176   Per capita 1988 GNP, from *Business America* (10 April 1989), p. 33.

176   The quotes from Makoto Ikeda and Damri Darakananda and description of Saha-Union, from *Fortune* (28 March 1988), p. 126.

176   Thailand as a developed country in ten years, reported in the *Economist* (25 June 1988), p. 39.

176-7   Factories and investment, from *Business America* (10 April 1989), p. 33.

177   Edward Chen's prediction appears in 'Thailand's Economy Shifting', *Christian Science Monitor*, 24 June 1988.

177   The *Economist*'s 'Thailand', appears in the 31 October 1987, issue.

177   The Sathirakul quote appears in the *Economist* (25 June 1988), p. 39.

177   Richard Holbrooke writes in *Newsweek* (17 October 1988), p. 42.

178   Investment in Australia, from Embassy of Australia.

178   Asian-American college grads, from Joel Kotkin and Yoriko Kishimato, *The Third Century: America's Resurgence in the Asian Era* (New York: Crown, 1988), reported in *Business Week* (26 September 1988), p. 16.

178　Asian-American population, from Racial Statistics, Bureau of the Census, Commerce Dept.

178　Incomes by nationality, from a US Civil Rights Commission study, reported in the Washington *Post*, 16 July 1988.

179　Students in school beyond legal age, from *Europe* (December 1986), p. 41, and *Economist* (30 April 1988), p. 22.

179　Percentage of science degrees from *Europe* (December 1986), p. 41.

179　Japanese students and *juku*, from various sources, including 'Japan and USA Trade School Secrets', *USA Today*, 21 January 1986; *Trendscape* (Winter 1986), p. 36; and 'Experts Say US Could Learn from Japan', San Diego *Union*, 19 August 1987.

179　The Julia Ericksen quote appeared in *Time* (23 January 1989), p. 57, which describes Japanese purchase of US colleges.

179　Percentage of Koreans in university, from 'South Korea', *Economist* (21 May 1988). Percentages by nationality who stay in secondary school, from 'Creativity Replaces Learning', *Financial Times*, 30 June 1988.

179　Koreans and Britons in higher education, from the *Economist* (20 June 1987), p. 9.

179　Half are students or grads, from 'South Korea', *Economist* (20 February 1988).

179　Comment by Ms Pak from 'Hyundai vs Honda', *Christian Science Monitor*, 16 March 1987.

179–80　The Daewoo recruitment need from *Business Week* (5 September 1988), p. 44.

180　Applied science grads, from 'South Korea', the *Economist* (21 May 1988). Engineers per capita, from a study by McKinsey & Company, reported in *Newsweek* (22 February 1988), p. 42.

180　Institute publication, as well as source for corporate universities, is *Korea's Economy* (December 1988), p. 16.

180　Percentages that attend college in countries listed (except Korea and Taiwan), from *Europe* (December 1986), p. 41; Korea, from *Korea's Economy* (May 1988), p. 20; Taiwan, from 'Creativity Replaces Learning', *Financial Times*, 30 June 1988.

180　Taiwanese stay in school, from 'Creativity Replaces Learning', *Financial Times*, 30 June 1988. University accommodations, in *High Technology* (November 1986), p. 24. Study abroad, from 'Taiwan', *Economist*, 5 March 1988. Students sent to the United States, from *Inc.* (September 1988), p. 71.

180　Chinese students who return home, from the *Economist* (26 November 1988), p. 36.

181　Mount Edgecumbe's language and Pacific Rim programmes and governor's goal, described in 'Specifically Pacific Lessons', *Christian Science Monitor*, 21 March 1988.

181　Washington's trade jobs, from 'The Toshiba Case Is a Symbol',

Seattle *Times*, 28 February 1988. John Anderson quote, from 'Gardner Forms Alliance', Seattle *Times*, 23 September 1987.

181   Bank of the Orient, from interview with bank official, 5 May 1989, and 'California Bank Opens Full-Service Branch in China', Orlando *Sentinel*, 19 August 1987.

182   Size and ranking of California's economy, from *The Facts*, a publication of the state's Department of Commerce, 1988. Prediction for 2000, from a California Department of Commerce advertisement in the *Economist* (26 March 1988). California's GSP, from *California Republic*, a publication of the state's Department of Commerce, 1988. Growth rate, computed from California Department of Finance and *California Republic*, loc. cit. figures.

182   California's high-tech companies, from the *Economist* advertisement cited immediately above; biotech firms, from a California Department of Commerce advertisement in *Technology Review* (May–June 1988).

182   Scientists and engineers, from *California Republic*, loc. cit.

182   Japanese interests in California, from *Newsweek* (22 February 1988), p. 42. It is also source for deposits in Los Angeles and New York City.

182   S&Ls in California, from Office of Policy and Economic Research, Federal Home Loan Bank Board, Washington, DC.

182   California port trade and Pacific percentage, from California Economic Development Corporation, Sacramento, California.

182   California trade with Japan, from World Trade Commission, Sacramento, California.

182   Foreign investment through California, from *California Republic*, loc. cit.

183   Percentages of trade through California ports, from *California Business* (November 1988), p. 26. Other California and New York port information from the California Association of Port Authorities and the New York Port Department.

183   Populations and projections for 2000, from the Bureau of Economic Analysis, Commerce Dept.

183   Norman Pfeiffer quote, from 'Museum Mania', Los Angeles *Times*, 23 May 1986.

183   Ronald Chase quote, from 'Art and Money Go South', the *New York Times*, 16 October 1988.

183   Description of work force, professions, economy, and trade jobs, from '"Laid-Back" LA', Seattle *Times*, 14 August 1988.

184   James Miscoll's quote and success of southern ports appeared in 'Art and Money Go South', the *New York Times*, 16 October 1988.

184   Tom Brown writes in '"Laid-Back" LA', Seattle *Times*, 14 August 1988.

184   Description of Asian neighbourhoods and restaurant figures, from 'Capital of the Rim', Seattle *Times*, 14 August 1988.

184 California's population in 2000, from *California Republic*, loc. cit.

185 The Carol Jones quote, from *Business Week* (21 July 1986), p. 95.

185 Description of Seattle's garment business, from interview with Ed Backholm, Seattle Pacific Industries, 3 May 1989; *Business Week* (21 July 1986), p. 95; and 'The World's Love Affair with Jeans', Seattle *Times*, 29 November 1987.

185 John Haley quote, from 'Top Programme vs Bottom Line', Seattle *Times*, 13 November 1988.

186 The John Ni quote, Taiwan's ban on Japanese cars, and K Y Lee comment, from *Fortune* (5 December 1988), p. 177.

186 Buy American policy in Taiwan, from Taiwan desk officer, Commerce Dept.

186 Singapore exports from US-owned firms, reported in *Fortune* (28 March 1988), p. 126.

187 New consumers by 2000 in Europe and Pacific countries, computed with figures from *World Population Profile: 1987*, WP-87, Bureau of the Census, Commerce Dept., December 1987.

187 US investment in Europe versus Japan, from a Booz Allen & Hamilton Inc., study, reported in 'Foreign Firms Thrive in Japan', *Wall Street Journal*, 29 September 1987.

187 Population projections for Europe and Asia, derived from *World Population Profile: 1987*, loc. cit.

187 The Reymond Voutier quote appeared in 'Asian Trade Centre', San Jose *Mercury-News*, 29 August 1988.

187 Hyundai store description, from *Business Week* (5 September 1988), p. 44.

187 Japan's 1988 GNP growth rate, from Embassy of Japan.

187 US 1988 export increases, reported in *Business America* (10 April 1989), p. 29.

188 Foreign wines in Japan, from *Business Week* (15 August 1988), p. 57; and 'Japan Soars Along with Yen', *International Herald Tribune*, 28 November 1988.

188 Orders for US Census Bureau study, described in 'America's Asian Destiny', Washington *Post*, 3 July 1988. China's imports from Japan and the US reported by the Chinese Embassy.

188 Trading companies in Japan, US products sold there, and Maureen Smith quote, from *Nation's Business* (November 1988), p. 85.

188–9 Schick and Imatron information, from *Nation's Business* (November 1988), p. 85. Additional Imatron data, from company.

188 Coca-Cola and Polaroid market shares, reported in *US News & World Report* (15 December 1988), p. 93.

189 Japanese tourists, in 'Banff Is Learning Japanese', Seattle *Times*, 17 November 1987.

189 Decrease in US exports to Europe and increase to Japan

(1980–1986), from 'America's Asian Destiny', by Joel Kotkin and Yoriko Kishimoto Washington *Post*, 3 July 1988. Increase in sales after 1986 from country desks Commerce Dept.

189 US 1988 exports to Japan, West Germany ($14.3 billion), France ($10.1 billion), and Italy ($6.86 billion), from country desks, Commerce Dept.

189 US agricultural sales, from 'US Farm Sales to Japan', *Asian Wall Street Journal*, 27 March 1989.

190 Kenichi Ohmae's calculations are reported in *Financial World* (23 February 1989), p. 28.

190 Rise of US exports to Tigers from the *Economist* (30 July 1988), p. 14.

190 US–Taiwan trade, from various sources, including *US Trade with Key East Asian and Pacific Countries 1986*, *Feb 1988*, Fact Sheet, and *1987*, *1989*, Fact Sheet, Office of Pacific Basin, Commerce Depts; *Fortune* (5 December 1988), p. 177; Motor Vehicle Manufacturers Association, Washington, DC; and Taiwan desk, Commerce Dept.

190 US trade with South Korea, from the *Economist* (30 July 1988), p. 13, and the Commerce Dept fact sheets listed directly above.

190 US export increases, reported in *Business America* (10 April 1989), p. 30.

190 The survey is *JETRO's 1988 Survey of Japanese-Affiliated Manufacturing Plants in the United States*, Japanese External Trade Organization, New York, December 1988.

190–1 Taiwanese ventures in United States, from *Business Week* (11 January, 1988), p. 56.

191 Americans in Japanese companies and Japanese in US companies, from advertising section prepared in cooperation with the Japan Chamber of Commerce, 'The US and Japan', *US News & World Report* (26 December 1988–2 January 1989).

191 Prediction of new American jobs created by Japanese, reported in *Newsweek* (2 February 1987), p. 42.

191 US states with offices in Japan, as of May 1989, from the National Governors Association, Washington, DC.

191 US municipal bonds underwritten by Japanese banks, from 'Japan Pulls More Strings', Seattle *Times*, 14 May 1987.

191 Japan's investment in US companies, reported in 'US Had a Plan to Compete', *International Herald Tribune*, 29 November 1988.

191 Robert Ingersoll quote, from *Business Week* (11 July 1988), p. 64.

191 Chairs endowed research spending by Japanese companies, Patricia Steinhoff quote and honorary doctorates from *Business Week* (11 July 1988), p. 64.

191–2 The Japan Centre for International Exchange is in New York City. University of Arizona at Tucson, from interview with Dr Dallas, Head of Radiology Research Division, 5 October 1989.

Georgia Institute of Technology, from interview with Dr Tudor Thomas, Principle Research Scientist, 5 October 1989.

192   Paragraph on Japan's influence in the Pacific, based on data from *Europe* (May 1986), p. 30; 'World Economic Power Is Shifting', *Financial Times*, 30 June 1988; 'Japan Goes Past US in Aid', *Christian Science Monitor*, 13 January 1988; 'Once Shunned, Japan is Again a Giant', Washington *Post*, 14 October 1988; and *Business Week* (10 April 1989), p. 32.

192   Japanese investment in Asia Pacific, from 'World Economic Power Is Shifting', *Financial Times*, 30 June 1988. Sony's decentralized production, from *Fortune* (28 March 1988), p. 6.

192   Investment in Thailand, from various sources, including 'Once Shunned, Japan Is Again a Giant', Washington *Post*, 14 October 1988; 'Asia Aims for More Self-Reliance', *International Herald Tribune*, 26 September 1988; and *Fortune* (28 March 1988), p. 6.

192   *Business Week* quote appeared in the 10 April 1989, issue, p. 42.

192   Foreign students in Japan today from the Japanese Embassy; and in 2000, from *Trendscape* (Spring 1987), p. 6.

192   Students in United States from China and Hong Kong, and in California alone, from Institute of International Education, New York City. Percentage of students in United States from East Asia, in *Department of State Bulletin* (April 1989), p. 33. Number of Japanese in US high schools (1988), from *Foreign Affairs* (Spring 1989), p. 3.

193   The *Economist* quote appeared in the 30 July 1988, issue, p. 13.

7. 1990s: DECADE OF WOMEN IN LEADERSHIP

195   Increase of 200 per cent in women workers, from *American Demographics*, September 1986, p. 25.

195   Percentages of working: men and women, from *Monthly Labour Review*, March 1988, p. 6.

195   *Working Woman* circulation numbers, from 'Editor's Notes', September 1988 issue.

195   Women starting businesses at twice rate of men from US Small Business Administration. Women-owned businesses in foreign countries from the *Economist*, 14 March 1987, p. 61.

197   John Kotter is quoted in *Nation's Business*, October 1988, p. 67.

197   Russell Palmer's quote appears in *Fortune*, 24 October 1988, p. 66.

198   Figures on college-educated women in 1965 from *American Demographics*, September 1986, p. 27. Today's figures from *Current Population Survey*, unpublished data, Bureau of Labour Statistics, US Department of Labour.

198 Peter Drucker quote, from interview, 27 June 1989.

198 Data on education of work force, from *Monthly Labour Review* (January 1988), p. 3.

198–9 Drucker quote, from interview, 27 June 1989.

199 Mark Sussman quote and loyalty survey, 'The Demise of Corporate Loyalties', cited in New York *Newsday*, 28 September 1987.

199 *Success* magazine survey, from June 1987 issue, pp. 49–53.

199 'Better leadership', cited in telephone survey by Corporate Issues Monitor, from 'The Demise of Corporate Loyalties', loc. cit.

199–200 Michael Maccoby's *Why Work?*, *The Gamesman* (1977), and *The Leader* (1981), all published by Simon & Schuster.

201 T. Stephen Long quote, from *Nation's Business* (March 1988), p. 23.

202 Percentages of women physicians, lawyers, architects and computer scientists from various *Current Population Surveys*, Bureau of Labour Statistics, US Department of Labour.

202 Women in finance from 'ABA Data Shows Women Continue Gains', American Bankers Association press release, 28 August 1989. Percentages of women accountants from various *Current Population Surveys*, loc. cit.

202 Women in manufacturing from various current *Population Surveys*, loc. cit.

202 Percentages of women at Procter & Gamble, Arthur Andersen, from *Fortune* (3 August 1987), p. 78. At Gannett from 'Companies Breaking Glass Ceiling', the Washington *Post*, 8 March 1988.

203 The Heidrick & Struggles survey is *Corporate Woman*, 1986.

203 Percentages of women earning MBAs from *Degrees and other Formal Awards Confired*, National Centre for Educations Statistics, US Department of Education, various years, 1987 figures from preliminary data.

203 Percentages of women physicians and lawyers from *Current Populations Survey*, loc. cit.

203 Women law and medical school graduates from *Degrees and Other Formal Awards Confired*, loc. cit.

204 Apple Computer percentages and quotes from Jennings, Swersky, and Laurie, from *Fortune* (3 August 1987), p. 78.

204–5 NAWBO figures from NAWBO press release, 26 July 1988.

205 Lou Harris-Steelcase poll cited is *The Office Environment Index 1988*, detailed findings, p. 11.

205 Jan Carlzon's *Moments of Truth* is published by Ballinger Publishing Co. (New York: 1987). SAS financial data from 'SAS's Nice Guy', *Wall Street Journal*, 2 March 1989.

205 Everett Suters, 'Show and Tell', *Inc.* (April 1987), p. 111.

206 Terry Armstrong is quoted in 'Coaching the Corporation', Orlando *Sentinel*, 25 October 1987.

206   Domino's Pizza, and Jeff De Graff quote from 'When Are Employees Not Employees?', *Wall Street Journal*, 9 November 1988.

206   Averitt Express, and Garry Sasser quote from 'The 21st Century Executive', *US News & World Report* (19 March 1988), p. 51.

206   Information on Motorola's training initiative, from *Assessment of Immediate Training Needs of America's Workforce*, testimony before the Senate Subcommittee on Investments, Jobs, and Prices of the Joint Economics Committee, 12 March 1988, and from *Fortune* (8 June 1987), p. 87.

207   Data on Metal Forming & Coining, from 'Companies Education Investment Pays', *Wall Street Journal*, 26 October 1987.

207   Robert Wright quote, from *Nation's Business* (March 1988), p. 19.

207   J. William Grimes quote, from *Success* (June 1988), p. 37.

207   Michael Cooper comments from *Inc.* (November 1987), p. 23.

208   Mike Shore is quoted in 'IBM Sets Flexible Work Rules', Washington *Post*, 19 October 1988.

208   Estimates of new job creation and decrease in labour supply, from various *Current Populations Surveys*, loc. cit.

208   Estimates on early retirees and non-working mothers who might rejoin labour force, from *Across the Board* (January–February 1989), p. 25.

208–9 Quote from Art Strohmer, from 'Wooing Workers in the 90s', the *New York Times*, 20 July 1988.

209   Percentage of working women in childbearing years compiled from statistics in *Employment and Earnings*, US Department of Labour, 1989.

209   Increase in companies providing day care, number of on-site facilities, and information about Dominion Bankshares Corporation and Nyloncraft, reported in 'It May Be the Benefit of the 90s', *USA Today*, 21 September 1988.

209   The Survey of Employer-Provided Child Care Benefits was reported in *Monthly Labour Review* (September 1988), p. 42.

210   Public schools as day-care providers and Bill Ewing quote, from *US News & World Report* (5 December 1988), p. 73.

210   One-third of adults involved in eldercare and 1500 adult centres, from *US News & World Report* (12 September 1988), p. 73.

210   Percentage of female care-givers from a survey by the American Association of Retired Persons reported in 'Caring for Your Parents', *Money*, October 1989, p. 136.

210   The Trans-America survey was reported in 'The Sandwiched', Los Angeles *Times*, 15 May 1988.

210–11 Figures on adult day-care centres and people cared for from *US News & World Report*, 12 September 1988. Number of corporate-sponsored centres from a National Council on the Ageing figure cited in 'Caring for Your Parents', *Money*, October 1989, p. 136.

211 Stride Rite information from interview with company spokesperson, 28 September 1989.

211 Mike Shore quote, from 'IBM Sets Flexible Work Rules', Washington *Post*, 19 October 1988.

211 Catalyst study from *Across the Board* (July–August 1988), p. 34.

211 Colgate-Palmolive and Aetna leave policies are cited in 'Labour Letter', *Wall Street Journal*, 19 July 1988.

211–12 Merck policy, from *Work & Family Life Support Activities*, Merck & Company, August 1988.

212 Diane Dalinsky and J. Douglas Phillips, quoted in 'Wooing Workers in the 90s', the *New York Times*, 20 July 1988.

212 Part-time work force in countries listed and US estimates in *Business Week* (28 November 1988), p. 20.

212 Job-sharing in *US News & World Report* (14 November 1988), p. 74.

212–13 Lechmere's new approach to part-time work from *Fortune* (13 February 1989), p. 62.

213 The Korn/Ferry University of California study is cited in *Working Women* (October 1986), p. 107.

213 Regina Herzlinger writes in 'Dancing on the Glass Ceiling', *Wall Street Journal*, 17 February 1988.

214 Jan Carlzon's international plans are discussed in *Business Week* (17 October 1988), p. 31.

214 Thomas Horton, quoted in the 'Swedish Management Revolution', *Christian Science Monitor*, 7 February 1989.

214–15 The Body Shop is described in *Continental Profile* (September, 1988), p. 28 and *New Age Journal*, May–June 1989, p. 52.

215 Middlesex Truck, from interview with Brian Maloney, CEO, 31 July 1989, and *Business Age* (July–August 1987), p. 42.

215–16 Abraham Krasnoff's business, described in *US News & World Report* (7 March 1988), p. 52.

216 General Electric and Motorola examples, cited in *Fortune* (13 February 1989), p. 54, as is the McKinsey & Company model.

217 Charles Exley is quoted in *High Technology* (May 1988), pp. 46–49.

217 Labour force participation rates for Japanese women from Embassy of numbers in management, cited in 'Many Working Women in Japan', the *New York Times*, 4 December 1988.

8. THE AGE OF BIOLOGY

222 The Senator Gore quote is from 'The Ethics of Genetic Engineering', *Christian Science Monitor*, 25 September 1986.

223–4 The David Baltimore quotes are from 'Setting the Record Straight on Biotechnology', *Technological Review* (October 1986).

225–6 The Jesse Jaynes information and quotes are from 'Biotechnology—Perfect Tomatoes and Supercows', *Christian Science Monitor*, 1 June 1988.

226 William Hiatt and Alan Bennett are quoted in 'Science vs the Mushy Tomato', Los Angeles *Times*, 19 August 1988.

227 The Richard Lester quote is from 'Agriculture Biotechnology', the *New York Times*, 8 November 1987.

229 The Richard Bock quote is from 'A Real Gas of a Gene Could Put the Bite on Any Bad Apples', *Wall Street Journal*, 1 September 1988.

229 The Tom St John quote is from 'Playing God in Your Basement', Washington *Post*, 31 January 1988.

230 The Steen Willasden quote is from 'Better Farm Animals Duplicated by Cloning', the *New York Times*, 17 February 1988.

231 The Katherine Gordon quote is from the *New York Times*, 27 December 1988.

234 The Lynn Klotz quote is from 'Genetic Engineering' the Washington *Post*, 31 January 1988.

234 The Brian Seed quote is from 'Genetic Engineering', Washington *Post*, 31 January 1988.

235 The Philip Leder quote is from 'Gene Studies Emerging as Key Engine of Science', the *New York Times*, 6 September 1988.

237 The Kenneth Warren quote is from 'Biotechnology Will Trigger the Revolution', *Financial Times*, 13 April 1988.

238 The Lynn Klotz quote is from 'Genetic Engineering', Washington *Post*, 31 January 1988.

238 The Everett Rogers quote is from 'Genetic Engineering' the Washington *Post*, 31 January 1988.

238 The *Economist* quote is from 'Tomorrow's Animals', 15 August 1987.

239 The Robert Haynes quote is from 'Gene Studies Emerging as Key Engine of Science', the *New York Times*, 6 September 1988.

241 The Robert Jordan quote is from 'States Spurring Investment in Biotechnology', the *New York Times*, 20 February 1988.

241 The *Economist* quote is from 'The Genetic Alternative', 30 April 1988.

241 The Wataru Yamaya quote is from 'Japanese Now Target Another Field the US Leads: Biotechnology', *Wall Street Journal*, 17 December 1987.

241 The Akiyoshi Wada quote is from the *Wall Street Journal*, 12 December 1987.

243 The Neal First quote is from 'Better Farm Animals Duplicated by Cloning', the *New York Times*, 17 February 1988.

243 The Lyman Crittenden quote is from 'Value Added Animals:

What is on the Horizon', *Christian Science Monitor*, 2 June 1988.

243 The Jeremy Rifkin quote is from 'Jeremy Rifkin: Just Say No', the *New York Times Magazine* (16 October 1988).

243 The *Economist* quote is from 'Battling Biofundamentalists', 27 June 1987.

244 The *New York Times* quote is from 'Gene Studies Emerging as Key Engine of Science', 6 September 1988.

244 Philosophers employed by hospitals, the government, prisons and business, from the *Economist* (26 April 1986), p. 95.

245 The Institute for the Advancement of Philosophy for Children is associated with Montclair College, Montclair, New Jersey.

245 School districts requiring values education or character instruction, from Thomas Jefferson Research Centre, Pasadena, California.

245 Nathan Quinones quote from *Newsweek* (13 October 1986), p. 92.

245 Business ethics courses started during the 1970s, from the *Economist* (26 April 1986), p. 95.

245 Patrick McCarthy quote, from 'Gwinnett's Plan to Teach Morals', *Atlanta Journal*, 18 December 1986.

246 Council on Ethical and Judicial Conduct declaration and Harvard Survey, reported in 'Allowing the Terminally Ill to Die', *Washington Post*, 26 January 1988. States that allow living wills, from the Society for the Right to Die, New York City.

246 David Larson and Brenda Winner quotes, from *Newsweek* (28 December 1987), p. 62.

246 Figure on children born to surrogate mothers, and states and surrogacy, from The Foundation on Economic Trends, Washington, DC.

247 Justice Wilentz's comments, reported in 'Surrogate Deals for Mothers', the *New York Times*, 4 February 1988.

9. RELIGIOUS REVIVAL OF THE THIRD MILLENNIUM

248 Mormon membership and the Charismatic movement are discussed later in the chapter.

249 Reconstructivist Jews are described in 'Reconstructionist Jews Turn to the Supernatural', the *New York Times*, 9 February 1989.

249 Youth for Christ in *Christianity Today* (11 November 1988), p. 42.

250 Harvey Cox interviewed in *Publishers Weekly* (7 October 1988), p. 96.

250 Norman Cohn, *The Pursuit of the Millennium*, rev. exp. ed. (New York: Oxford University Press, 1970).

250–1 The occurrence of the millennium concept in various religions is from Hillel Schwartz, 'Millennarianism', *The Encyclopedia of Religion* (New York: Macmillan, 1987).

251–2 Martin Marty's remarks appeared in *US News & World Report* (29 December 1986–5 January 1987), p. 43.

252 *The Power of Myth* was on the *New York Times* best-seller list for forty-seven weeks; *The Hero with a Thousand Faces* for ten weeks.

252 The discussion on the church and feminism is based largely on 'Feminism and the Churches', *Newsweek* (13 February 1989), p. 58.

252–3 Membership figures cited are based on an interview with Constant H. Jacquet, Jr, of the National Council of Churches of Christ in the United States, 6 January 1988, and the *Yearbook of American & Canadian Churches 1988*, (Nashville: Abingdon Press, 1988).

253 The *Official Catholic Directory* numbers were reported in 'Good, Bad News in Catholicism Numbers', Washington *Post*, 16 July 1988.

253 Bishop Richard Wilke is quoted in 'Protestant Denominations Seek Fervor, Flash', Detroit *Free Press*, 21 May 1986.

253 Congregation growth is from an interview with Constant H. Jacquet, Jr, 28 June 1989.

253 Geographic distribution of church and synagogue goers is reported in the *Yearbook of American & Canadian Churches 1988*, loc. cit.

254 Sources of surveys and polls cited on religion and spirituality as follows: The 1987 Gallup poll is *Religion in America*, April 1987, Report No. 259; 69 per cent and 49 per cent of baby boomers are from a survey by the Centre for the Vietnam Generation described in 'Theme for the 90s: A Rebirth of Faith', the *New York Times*, 31 December 1988; the *USA Today* poll appears in 'We Search for "Spiritual Well-being"', *USA Today*, 3 September 1987.

254 The 1988 Gallup poll *The Unchurched American . . . 10 Years Later* was published by the Princeton Religion Research Centre.

254 George Gallup is quoted in 'Fewer Adults Go to Church, Poll Finds', Washington *Post*, 16 July 1988.

254 Description of Congress 88 is from various sources, including 'Fewer Adults Go to Church', Washington *Post*, 16 July 1988, and 'Poll Finds Believes on Rise', Chicago *Tribune*, 5 August 1988.

255 Estimate of new religious groups formed between 1987 and 1989, from interview with Dr J. Gordon Melton, February 19, 1988.

255 Followers of Islam from 'Islam: At the Heart', *USA Today*, 31 August 1989.

255 *The Encyclopedia of American Religions Second Supplement* (Detroit: Gale Research Co., 1979).

255   Japanese Buddhist sects and the number of Hindu temples are from *Christianity Today* (19 February 1988), p. 15.

255   The *Rocky Mountain News* article 'From Mecca to the West' appeared 26 February 1989.

256   Diane Eck is quoted in 'From Wichita to the World, a Vision', the *New York Times*, 2 November 1988.

256   Il Sik Sam Choe quoted in *Christianity Today* (3 March 1989), p. 56.

256–7 The study by the Centre for Social and Religious Research, directed by Dr David Roozen, is described in 'More Attend Church from "Baby Boom" Age', *Daily Telegraph* (London), 22 November 1986.

257   The Jewish renaissance in the San Francisco area from 'On West Coast, a Newly Vital Judaism', the *New York Times*, 18 May 1988.

257   The religious education percentage is from the 1988 Gallup poll *The Unchurched American . . . 10 Years Later*, loc. cit.

257   Americans who describe themselves as 'born-again', from *Religion in America*, loc. cit.

257   Southern Baptist membership, from the Southern Baptist Convention in Nashville, Tennessee.

257   Evangelical church gains, reported in *America* (27 September 1986), p. 142. Evangelical percentage gains and mainline losses, are from *US News & World Report* (19 December 1988), p. 53.

257   Jehovah's Witnesses, Seventh-day Adventists, and Assemblies of God membership numbers are from the *Yearbook of American & Canadian Churches 1988*, loc. cit.

257   The number of Pentecostals globally is from David Barrett, *World Christian Encyclopedia*, reported in *Christianity Today* (16 October 1987), p. 16. The numbers of Church of God in Christ and Assemblies of God Pentecostals appear in the same article. The number of Charismatics globally is from David Barrett, in *Christianity Today* (4 September 1987), p. 44.

257   Mormon membership in 1940 is from the *Yearbook of American & Canadian Churches 1988*, loc. cit. Other numbers and projections, except 1987 membership increase, are from 'Mormon Church Grows', Miami *Herald*, 6 March 1987. The 1987 membership increase was reported in 'Mormon Membership Rises', Washington *Post*, 16 April 1988.

258   Bold New Growth Mississippi is described in 'Mississippi Baptists', Jackson, Mississippi, *Clarion-Ledger*, 3 October 1987.

258   The *America* article appeared in the 11 April 1987, issue, p. 297.

258   The *Humanist* article from the January–February 1986 issue, p. 11.

258–9 Audience numbers: Swaggart, from 'Swaggart Calls Himself "Holy Ghost Preacher"', Houston *Chronicle*, 17 August 1987; PTL, from *Business Week* (1 January 1988), p. 32; Falwell, from *Christianity Today* (18 March 1988), p. 36; Schuller, from interview with a Crystal Cathedral spokesperson.

259 The 1987 Gallup Poll is *Religion in America*, loc. cit.

259 Arbitron ratings in *Christianity Today* (3 February 1989), p. 32.

259 Percentage of New Agers in the United States is from *US News & World Report* (9 February 1987), p. 69. Maryland Poll is reported in 'Poll of New Age Beliefs', Washington *Post*, 3 January 1988.

260 The Northwest Foundation and Ken Eyer quote from 'The 1980s Low-Dogma Approach', Seattle *Times*/Seattle *Post-Intelligencer*, 18 January 1987.

260 Channels listed on this page are described in following sources: Pittman, in 'The Great Leap of Consciousness', St Petersburg *Times*, 1 January 1988; Pursel and Knight, from various sources, including *US News & World Report* (9 February 1987), p. 67, and *Christianity Today* (18 September 1987), p. 22.

260 Estimate of channels and quote, from interviews with Dr J. Gordon Melton, 10 February 1988 and 2 August 1989.

260 Estimate of channels in Los Angeles comes from an article in the 18 September 1987, issue of *Christianity Today*, p. 22.

261 Ralph White is quoted in *Time* (7 December 1987), p. 62.

261 New Age ministries are described in 'The Great Leap of Consciousness', St Petersburg *Times*, 1 January 1988, and Rainbow Reflection Centre is in 'Through "Channels" New Agers Are Now Turning into the Past', Miami *Herald*, 31 August 1987.

261 The Open Centre is described, and Walter Beebe is quoted, in 'A Spirited Movement', *USA Today*, 4 June 1987.

262 Description of the debate and Elizabeth Burrows quote are from 'New Age vs Orthodox Christianity', Seattle *Times*/Seattle *Post-Intelligencer*, 23 January 1987.

262 Most recent Unity membership number and Eiffler quote, from interview with Edward Eiffler, 9 February 1988.

262 Puget Sound chapter membership, described in 'The Coming of a New Age', Seattle *Times*, 18 November 1987.

262 Description of national Unity Church, from interviews with Unity spokespeople, 11 February 1988, and 27 March 1989.

262 Avery Fisher Hall's use as a Unity Church sanctuary is described in *Forbes* (1 June 1987), p. 156.

263 Ruth Montgomery, *Strangers Among Us* (New York: Ballantine, 1970), pp. 219–226.

263 Hal Lindsey, *The Late Great Planet Earth*, (Grand Rapids, Michigan: Zondervan Publishing House, 1970). This quote appears in the January 1971 edition, p. 168.

264 Hippolytus' prediction is recounted in Bernard McGinn, *Visions of the End, Apocalyptic Traditions in the Middle Ages* (New York: Columbia University Press, 1979), pp. 22, 23, 51.

264 Sources for the dates when the millennium has been predicted are Cohn, op. cit. (1260, 1420 and 1533); 'Seventh-Day Adven-

tist', *The Encyclopedia of Religion* (1843, 1844, 1845, and 1847); and the *Dictionary of Religion* article on Charles Taze Russell (1914).

264 Abbot of Fleury's writings from McGinn, op. cit., pp. 89–90.

264–66 The description of events around the year 1000, the new Roman Empire and its founder's vision are based on Oscar Halecki, *The Millennium of Europe* (South Bend, Ind: University of Notre Dame Press, 1963). The direct quote is from p. 128.

266 Christianity in the Soviet Union is written about in *Christianity Today* (2 September 1988), p. 42, (16 September 1988), p. 17, and (19 February 1988), p. 56, and in 'Moscow Marks Christian Millennium', *Washington Post*, 6 June 1988.

266 The *American Demographics* article appeared in August 1988, p. 28.

267 Numbers of Charismatic Catholics, from the National Charismatic Renewal Centre, South Bend, Indiana.

267 *Miracle in Darien* was written by Bob Slosser, a member of St Paul's Congregation in Darien, Connecticut and published by Logos International, in Plainfield, New Jersey.

267 Description of Truro Episcopal Church, interview with Dan Derrick, administrator, Truro Episcopal Church, 27 March 1989.

267 Description of Faith Alive, interview with Roberta Gibbs, administrative director, Faith Alive, 10 February 1988.

268 Reverend Ben Armstrong is quoted in 'Interfaith TV Channel', Louisville, Kentucky, *Courier-Journal*, 30 January 1987.

268 Mother Mary Angelica is quoted in 'Mother Knows Best', Philadelphia *Inquirer*, 19 May 1987, which also describes EWTN. Additional information from interview with Dee Park, EWTN, 22 March 1989.

268–9 Jack Sims is quoted in *American Demographics* (August 1988), p. 28, which also describes his philosophy and is the source for the *American Demographics* quote.

269 Willow Creek Community Church is described in and Bill Hybels is quoted in *Time* (March 6, 1989), p. 60.

269–70 Norman Whan is written about in 'Churches Turn to Telemarketing', *Washington Post*, 13 February 1988. Additional information from interviews with Norman Whan on 3 April 1989, and 3 August 1989 and 8 September 1989.

269–70 Dr Wagner's comments and quote are from the same *Washington Post* article.

270 Jack Sims is quoted in *American Demographics* (August 1988), p. 28.

270 The Christian Booksellers Association numbers are from interview with Robert Brenner, director of member services, 29 March 1989, and 'Christian Booksellers Face New Challenges', *Rocky Mountain News*, 9 July 1989.

271 Sacred Melody Centre is described in the August 1988 issue of *American Demographics*, p. 28.

271   Sales of Hanna-Barbera videos, from *Success* (April 1989), p. 80.

271   Edward Thomas and Bill Marr are quoted in 'Churches in Demand and Supply', Orlando *Sentinel*, 28 December 1986, which also describes the building boom.

271   First Baptist Church of Christ of Orlando in Calvary Assembly are described in 'Church of the Future a Reality Now', Orlando *Sentinel*, 13 April 1987.

271   Jay Ogilvy of the Esalen Institute estimate of New Agers in the September 1988 issue of *American Demographics*, p. 34.

272   *New Age Journal* readers' profile from advertisement in *New Age Marketing opportunities* described in note p. 266. John Garrett quote, and numbers from the National Opinion Research Council of the University of Chicago are found in *American Demographics* (September 1988), p. 34.

272   *New Age Journal* description is from the magazine's February 1988 issue, p. 50 and circulation figures from interview with Joseph Kottler, advertising director, 27 March 1989.

272   The *National New Age Yellow Pages* was published by Highgate House, Publishers, Fullerton, California, in 1988. It was described in 'How to Find a Psychic', the *New York Times*, 9 October 1988.

272   *New Age Marketing opportunities* (Sedona, Arizona: First Editions, 1988).

273   New Age books at Bodhi Tree, from interview with spokesperson, 24 March 1989.

273   Bantam Books is described in *US News & World Report* (9 February 1987), p. 68.

273   The New Age Publishing and Retailing Alliance and the number of New Age bookstores, from interview with Marilyn McGuire, executive director of New Age Publishing and Retailing Alliance, 27 March 1989.

273   Ingram Book Company titles and sales are described in 'As New Age Books Prosper', *Wall Street Journal*, 10 March 1988.

273   Sales figures of New Age titles, records, audio and videotapes are from *ADWEEK Special Report* (1 August 1988), p. M.R.C.4.

273   The section on 'A New Age for Corporations?' is based on *Newsweek* (4 May 1987), p. 38; 'Spiritual Concepts Drawing a Different Breed of Adherent', the *New York Times*, 6 December 1986; and an interview with Michael Ray, 24 May 1989.

274   Harvey Cox is quoted in *Publishers Weekly* (7 October 1988), p. 96.

274   The discussion of the 'Ideal of Progress' is based largely on its treatment in I F Clarke, *The Pattern of Expectation 1644–2001*, (New York: Basic Books, Inc., 1979).

274   Daniel Bell is quoted in 'A Political Philosopher Ruminates on

Society and Its Contradictions', the *New York Times*, 7 February 1989.

274–5   Dystopic films and literature, described in Clarke, op. cit.

10. TRIUMPH OF THE INDIVIDUAL

278   The BDO Seidman study, export figures, small businesses exporting examples, and the Export Now programme are described in 'Export Davids Sling Some Shots at Trade Gap Goliath', *Wall Street Journal*, 8 March 1989.

280   Figures on Americans who voted for President in 1988, 1984, and 1968, from *Voting and Registration in the Election of November 1988 (Advance Report)*, Current Population Reports, Series P-20, No. 435, February 1989. Bureau of the Census, US Department of Commerce.

280   Burdett Loomis's book (New York: Basic Books, 1988) was reviewed in the *Wall Street Journal*, 26 January 1989.

281   The George Gilder quotes are from *An American Vision* (Washington, DC: Cato Institute, 1989), pp. 349, 354.

282   The Bill McCue quote appears in 'Fax Lowers the Cost of Business', *Rocky Mountain News*, 21 February 1989.

282   Figures on fax machines and documents, from various sources, including 'Fax Machine', *USA Today*, 2 June 1989.

283   John P. Eberhard describes what he calls 'The Eight Great', in 'Building the City of Tomorrow', Washington *Post*, 26 June 1988.

284   Jack Lessinger's comments, migration quote, and Penturbia description, from *Snow Country* (February 1989), p. 68, and *Mother Earth News* (March–April 1988), p. 68. Professor Lessinger in the author of *Regions of Opportunity* (New York: Times Books, 1986).

284   The Thomas Miller quote and Centre for Future Research projections are from *American Demographics* (December 1988), p. 31.

285   City population projections in 2000 and 1950 figures, from *Estimates and Projections of Urban, Rural and City Populations, 1950–2025; 1982 Assessment* (New York: United Nations, 1985). New York City will be the largest consolidated metropolitan area, but Los Angeles will be the largest metropolitan area, as cited in the Pacific Rim chapter.

CONCLUSION

289   The T. George Harris quote appears in the February 1987 issue of *Fitness in Business*, p. 141.

Index

Index

Gorbachev, Mikhail
elected president, 90
and environmental issues, 21, 290
and Pacific Rim, 177
reforms, 19, 77, 80–5, 86, 87, 88, 89, 91–2, 99–100
war denounced by, 20
and world economy, 22, 78
mentioned, 266
Gordon, David, 34
Gordon, Katherine, 231
Gore, Albert, Jr, 222
Great Britain
arts, 53, 63, 67
economy, 11, 28
and European Community, 45, 49–50
investment in US, 27–8
museums, 61
politics, 11
privatization, 134–9, 140
religion, 249–50, 254
tax reform, 17
Greece, 51
Greenspan, Alan, 18
Grimes, J. William, 207
Group of Seven, 21–2
growth, no limit to, 14–15
Guangdong, 165, 171–2

Habitat, 113
Halecki, Oscar, 266
Haley, John, 185
Harris, T. George, 289
Harrison, Bennett, 32
Harrods, 110
Hawke, Bob, 79
Hay, John, 158
Haynes, Dr Robert, 239
Herzlinger, Regina, 213
Hiatt, William, 226
Hindus, Hinduism, 256
Holbrooke, Richard, 177
holism, 261
Holy Roman Empire, 265
Hong Kong, 80, 120, 159, 162, 162–3, 163, 163–5
Hoos, Janos, 93
Horton, Thomas R., 214
Hoving, Thomas, 60
human beings, 6–7, 54
genetic engineering, 235–7
rights, 133
Hungary, 92–5
Huxley, Aldous, 274, 280–1
Hybels, Bill, 269

IKEA, 113–14
Ikeda, Makoto, 176
Illinois, 154
India, 118
individual, importance of, 79, 276–87
Indonesia, 19, 163
inflation, 18
information economy/society, 38–40, 79, 198, 217, 219
Ingersoll, Robert S., 191
inheritance, 36
insurance, against unemployment, 145–6
interest rates, 18
Iran, 125, 126
Irish Republic, 50
Islam, Muslims, 104, 125–6, 249, 251, 255
Isozaki, Arata, 67, 162
Italy, 45, 47, 48, 146–7

Jacquet, Constant H., Jr, 253
Japan
American cultural exports to, 116
American franchises in, 108
art and design, 161–2
biotechnology, 240, 241
economy, 13, 18, 29–30, 159, 163, 166, 167, 182, 187–93
education, 179
English language studied, 120
and European Community, 44
immigration policy, 31
investment in US, 27–8, 29, 182
museums, 61, 161
religion, 249
tax reform, 17
women, 217, 218
Jaynes, Jesse, 225–6
JEC, 32, 34
Jedlicka, Judith A., 65, 76
Jehovah's Witnesses, 251, 257
Jennings, Professor Eugene, 203
Jews, Judaism, 248, 257
job-sharing, 212
Johansson, Leif, 102
Jones, Carol, 185
Jordan, Robert B., 241

Kagami, Toshio, 116
Kaku, Ryuzaburo, 44
Karube, Isao, 220
Kennedy, Moorhead, 126
Kennedy, Paul, 23
Kennedy Centre, 67
Kentucky Fried Chicken, 108
Kenya, 143
Khleif, Bud, 128

John Adair
Effective Leadership £5.99

The fully revised and updated guide to developing leadership skills

Some people are born leaders, some people become leaders, and some have leadership thrust upon them. The art of good leadership is highly prized, and demands a keen ability to appraise, understand and inspire both colleagues and subordinates.

In *Effective Management*, now wholly revised and updated, John Adair, Britain's foremost expert on leadership training, shows how every manager can learn to lead. He draws up numerous examples of leadership in action – commercial, historical and military – all pinpointing the essential requirements.

Effective Leadership is carefully structured to ensure a steady, easily acquired insight into leadership skills, helping you to:

★ understand leadership – what you have to be, know and do

★ develop leadership abilities – defining the task, planning, briefing, controlling, setting an example

★ grow as a leader – making certain your organization encourages leaders to emerge

With *Effective Leadership*, John Adair has provided an invigorating book that reflects his vivid experiences as a worker, researcher and teacher, making it the ideal passport to the development of leadership.

All Pan books are available at your local bookshop or newsagent, or can be ordered direct from the publisher. Indicate the number of copies required and fill in the form below.

Send to: **CS Department, Pan Books Ltd., P.O. Box 40,
                 Basingstoke, Hants.   RG21 2YT.**

or phone: 0256 469551 (Ansaphone), quoting title, author
                 and Credit Card number.

Please enclose a remittance* to the value of the cover price plus: 60p for the first book plus 30p per copy for each additional book ordered to a maximum charge of £2.40 to cover postage and packing.

*Payment may be made in sterling by UK personal cheque, postal order, sterling draft or international money order, made payable to Pan Books Ltd.

Alternatively by Barclaycard/Access:

Card No.

Signature:

Applicable only in the UK and Republic of Ireland.

While every effort is made to keep prices low, it is sometimes necessary to increase prices at short notice. Pan Books reserve the right to show on covers and charge new retail prices which may differ from those advertised in the text or elsewhere.

NAME AND ADDRESS IN BLOCK LETTERS PLEASE:

....

Name————————————————————————

Address————————————————————————

————————————————————————————

————————————————————————————

————————————————————————————

3/87